101 Ways to Promote
Your Web Site

Other Titles of Interest from Maximum Press

Top e-business Books

- *Social Media for Business*
- *3G Marketing on the Internet*
- *Protecting Your Great Ideas for FREE*
- *101 Internet Businesses You Can Start From Home*
  and many more...

For more information go to *maxpress.com*
or email us at *info@maxpress.com*

101 Ways to Promote Your Web Site

Eighth Edition

Filled with Proven Internet Marketing Tips, Tools, Techniques, and Resources to Increase Your Web Site Traffic

Susan Sweeney

MAXIMUM PRESS
605 Silverthorn Road
Gulf Breeze, FL 32561
(850) 934-0819
maxpress.com

Publisher: Jim Hoskins

Production Manager: Jacquie Wallace

Cover Designer: Lauren Smith

Copyeditor: Ellen Falk

Proofreader: Jacquie Wallace

Indexer: BIM Indexing & Proofreading Services

Printer: P. A. Hutchison

Library of Congress Cataloging-in-Publication Data

Sweeney, Susan, 1956-

101 ways to promote your web site : filled with proven Internet marketing tips, tools, techniques, and resources to increase your web site traffic / Susan Sweeney. -- 8th ed.

   p. cm.

ISBN 978-1-931644-78-5

1. Internet marketing. 2. Web sites--Marketing. I. Title. II. Title: One hundred one ways to promote your web site. III. Title: One hundred and one ways to promote your web site.

HF5415.1265.S93 2011

658.8'72--dc22

2010028433

Acknowledgments

I am truly blessed. This book—all of my books, my business, and my success so far—would not have been possible without so many people who have contributed and made a difference to me in so many ways.

Many thanks to social media marketer extraordinaire, Kara Sweeney (who just happens to be my daughter), for all the help with this edition of *101 Ways to Promote Your Web Site*. This book was definitely a team effort.

Thanks to my great team at Verb Interactive (*http://www.verbinteractive. com*): Ed Dorey and Andy MacLellan who have been with me since their university days, and our whole team of Internet marketing experts.

Thanks to my Indaba team and great friends, Lea and Sharon, for our many great meetings of minds and souls and the progress we have made on our spiritual and business journeys—what a difference you've made in my life.

Thanks to Colleen Francis for our regular brainstorming calls that always leave me invigorated and ready to conquer the world. Also for the amount I get done the day prior to those calls in anticipation.

Thanks to my Canadian Association of Professional Speakers family, my National Speakers Association family, and my International Federation of Professional Speakers family, and to all the incredible people I have had the pleasure to listen to and learn from over the years. Never have I met a more sharing, giving, and thoughtful group of people. I am truly blessed to have found you. Thanks, Cathleen Filmore, for introducing me to this fabulous business of professional speaking.

Thanks to the many businesses and organizations and amazing people around the world that I have the pleasure and honor of working with. You keep me on my toes, keep things exciting, and continually help me grow.

The Internet is a fascinating and vast publicly accessible resource from which we can learn a great deal. I'd like to thank all those people who share their information so freely on the Web.

Many thanks to my large network of experts I know I can always call on to get the latest scoop on what's really happening.

Thanks to Jim Hoskins and Gina Cooke at Maximum Press. This is our eighteenth book together. It's always a pleasure to work with you. One of these days we're going to have to meet face to face!

Special thanks to my absolutely wonderful husband, Miles, who makes all things possible. I wouldn't be able to do what I do if not for you. Also thanks to our three amazing children—Kaitlyn, Kara, and Andrew—for their love, encouragement, and support. Love you more than the last number!

Special thanks to my mom and dad, Olga and Leonard Dooley, for always being there and for instilling in me the confidence to know that I can do anything I set my mind to. It's amazing what can be done when you "know you can."

Disclaimer

The purchase of computer software or hardware is an important and costly business decision. While the author and publisher of this book have made reasonable efforts to ensure the accuracy and timeliness of the information contained herein, the author and publisher assume no liability with respect to loss or damage caused or alleged to be caused by reliance on any information contained herein and disclaim any and all warranties, expressed or implied, as to the accuracy or reliability of said information.

This book is not intended to replace the manufacturer's product documentation or personnel in determining the specifications and capabilities of the products mentioned in this book. The manufacturer's product documentation should always be consulted, as the specifications and capabilities of computer hardware and software products are subject to frequent modification. The reader is solely responsible for the choice of computer hardware and software. All configurations and applications of computer hardware and software should be reviewed with the manufacturer's representatives prior to choosing or using any computer hardware and software.

Trademarks

The words contained in this text which are believed to be trademarked, service marked, or otherwise to hold proprietary rights have been designated as such by use of initial capitalization. No attempt has been made to designate as trademarked or service marked any personal computer words or terms in which proprietary rights might exist. Inclusion, exclusion, or definition of a word or term is not intended to affect, or to express judgment upon, the validity of legal status of any proprietary right which may be claimed for a specific word or term.

Your "Members Only" Web Site

The online world changes every day. That's why there is a companion Web site associated with this book. On this site you will find the latest news, expanded information, and other resources of interest.

To get into the Web site, go to *promote.maxpress.com*. You will be asked for a password. Type in:

sat

and you will then be granted access.

Visit the site often and enjoy the updates and resources with our compliments—and thanks again for buying the book. We ask that you not share the user ID and password for this site with anyone else.

Susan Sweeney's Internet Marketing Mail List

You are also invited to join Susan Sweeney's Internet Marketing Bi-weekly Internet Marketing Tips, Tools, Techniques, and Resources Newsletter at *http:// promote.maxpress.com*.

Table of Contents

Chapter 3:
Web Site Elements That Keep 'Em Coming Back   36

Chapter 4:
Permission Marketing   50

Chapter 11:
Consumer-Generated Media   108

Chapter 12:
Establishing Your Private Mailing List   117

Chapter 13:
Developing a Dynamite Links Strategy   140

Chapter 14:
Winning Awards, Cool Sites, and More   156

Chapter 15:
Online Advertising   163

Chapter 16:
Maximizing Media Relations   180

Chapter 17:
Increasing Traffic through Online Publications   193

Chapter 18:
Marketing through Blogs   206

Chapter 19:
Social Media
214

Chapter 20:
Facebook
222

Chapter 21:
LinkedIn
236

Chapter 26:
Interactive Mapping   275

Chapter 27:
The Power of Partnering   285

Chapter 28:
Web Traffic Analysis   289

1

Planning Your Web Site

There are millions of Web sites, selling millions of products on the Internet everyday, and they are all competing for viewers; many of them are competing for the same viewers you are! How do you get the results you're looking for? When asked if they are marketing on the Internet, many people and organizations say, "Yes, we have a Web site." However, having a Web site and marketing on the Internet are two very different things. Yes, usually you need a Web site to market on the Internet. However, a Web site is simply a collection of documents, images, and other electronic files that are publicly accessible across the Internet. Your site needs to be designed to meet your online objectives and should be developed with your target market in mind. Internet marketing encompasses all the steps you take to reach your target market online, attract visitors to your Web site, encourage them to buy your products or services, and make them want to come back for more.

Having a Web site is great, but it is meaningless if nobody knows about it. Just as having a brilliantly designed product brochure does you little good if it sits in your sales manager's desk drawer, a Web site does you little good if your target market isn't visiting it. It is the goal of this book to help you take your Web site out of the desk drawer, into the spotlight, and into the hands of your target market. You will learn how to formulate an Internet marketing strategy in keeping with your objectives, your products or services, and your target market. This chapter provides you with an overview of this book and introduces the importance of:

- Defining your online objectives

- Defining your target markets and developing your Web site and online marketing strategy with them in mind

- Developing the Internet marketing strategy that is appropriate for your product or service.

The Fundamentals—Objectives, Target Markets, and Products and Services

Things have changed dramatically over the past several years in terms of Web site design and development methodology. Back in the old days—a couple of years ago in Internet years—it was quite acceptable, and the norm, for an organization to pack up all of its brochures, ads, direct-mail pieces, news releases, and other marketing materials in a box, drop it off at the Web developer's office, and after a short conversation, ask when they might expect the Web site to be "done." The Web developer would then take the marketing materials and digitize some, scan some, and do some HTML programming to develop the site. By going through this process, organizations ended up with a Web site that looked just like their brochure—hence the term "brochureware." Brochureware is no longer acceptable on the Web if you want to be successful. Sites that are successful today are ones that are constantly being updated, providing a reason for visitors to visit on a regular basis. The site is just one element in the company's online presence along with their blog, Facebook page, YouTube channel, and accounts in other social media applications. Your Web site and all online presence applications should be designed around:

- Objectives of the organization

- Needs, wants, and expectations of your target markets

- Products and services that are being offered.

Everything related to Internet marketing revolves around these three things—objectives, target markets, and products or services. It is critically important to define these things appropriately and discuss them with your Web developer. It is your responsibility, not your Web developer's, to define these things. You know (or should know) what your objectives are more clearly than your Web developer does. If you don't articulate these objectives and discuss them with your Web developer, it is impossible for him or her to build a site to achieve your objectives!

You know your target markets better than your Web developer does. You know what your visitors want, what they base their buying decisions on, and what their expectations are. You need to provide this information so that your Web developer can build a Web site that meets the needs, wants, and expectations of your target market.

Let's spend the remainder of the chapter on these fundamentals—objectives, target markets, and products and services—so you can be better prepared for the planning process for your Web site.

Common Objectives

Before you even start to create your Web site, you must clearly define your online objectives. What is the purpose of your site? Brainstorm with people from all parts of your organization, from the frontline clerks, to marketing and sales personnel, to customer support, to order fulfillment and administration.

Generate a comprehensive list of primary and secondary objectives. If you're going to build this Web site, you might as well build it to achieve all of your online objectives. If you don't brainstorm with your stakeholders, document the objectives, and discuss these objectives with your Web developer, it will be impossible for the Web developer to build you a Web site that addresses all of your objectives.

Every element of your site should relate back to your objectives. When you decide to update, add, or change any elements on your Web site, examine how these changes relate to the primary and secondary objectives you have identified. If there is not a clear match between your objectives and your intended changes, you might want to reconsider the changes. It's amazing how many Web sites have been developed without adequate planning or without ensuring that the Web site ties in with the corporate objectives.

Some of the most common primary objectives include:

- Advertising your product or service

- Selling your product or service

- Providing customer service and support

- Providing product or corporate information

- Creating and establishing brand identity and brand awareness or company identity and awareness.

Other Objectives to Consider Up Front

Although setting your primary objectives is vital, it is just as important to identify your secondary objectives. By setting appropriate secondary objectives, you will be more prepared to achieve all of your online goals. Many companies identify only primary objectives for their Web site and completely neglect secondary objectives that can help them succeed online. Following are some common secondary objectives to consider:

- Your site should be designed to be search engine friendly. (See Chapter 2 for more information on designing your site for high search engine ranking.)

- Your site should promote your blog and other social media accounts, and vice versa. (See Chapters 18–24 on doing business through these accounts.)

- Your site should be designed to encourage repeat traffic. Chapter 3 describes many of these repeat-traffic generators in much more detail.

- Your site should have viral marketing elements that encourage visitors to recommend your products or services to others. These are discussed in detail in Chapter 5.

- Your site should incorporate permission marketing, where visitors are encouraged to give you permission to send them email, newsletters, and e-specials on a regular basis. Chapter 4 has examples of ways to encourage visitors to request to be added to your email list, and Chapter 12 provides all the details on staying in touch with those who give you that permission.

- Your site should be designed to encourage customer loyalty.

- Your site should incorporate stickiness and interactive elements, encouraging visitors to stay a while and visit many areas of the site.

A Final Word on Objectives

Setting your Web site's objectives before you begin building your site is essential so that you can convey to your Web developer what you want your Web site to achieve. You obviously will have a number of different objectives for your site, but many of these objectives can work together to make your Web site complete.

Whatever your objectives might be, you must carefully consider how best to incorporate elements in your Web site and your Internet marketing strategy to help you achieve them. Successful marketing on the Web is not a simple undertaking. Before you begin to brainstorm over the objectives of your Web site, be certain you have read and studied all the information that is pertinent to the market you are attempting to enter. Read everything you can find, and examine the findings of industry experts.

Your Web site objectives form a critical element in your Web site design and development, as you will see in the next section.

Target Markets

It is important to define every one of your target markets. If you're going to build this Web site, you might as well build it for all of your target markets. For each and every one of your target markets, you need to determine:

- Their needs

- Their wants

- Their expectations.

For each and every one of your target markets, you should also try to determine an appropriate "WOW" factor. What can you provide for them on your Web site that will WOW them? Your objective should be to exceed the target market's expectations.

Your main target market might be your potential customer, but other target markets might include existing customers, or the media, or those who influence the buying decision for your potential customers.

When you look at—really look at—potential customers versus existing customers, you realize that what these two groups want and need from your

Web site is probably different. Someone who is an existing customer knows your company. Learning about your products, services, business practices, and the like, is not a priority for this person. A potential customer needs to know about these things before giving you his or her business. "Customer" is such a huge target market; it needs to be broken down into segments. If you were a hotel, for example, your customer target market might be broken down further into:

- Business travelers

- Vacation travelers

- Family travelers

- Meeting planners

- Handicapped travelers

- Tour operators

- Golfers

- Outdoor adventure enthusiasts

- Eco-tourists.

You get the idea. You need to segment your customer target market and then, for each segment, you need to do an analysis of needs, wants, and expectations.

Products and Services

It is important to define the products and services you want to promote online. Sometimes the products and services you offer offline in your physical store are the same as in your online store, but quite often there are differences.

Business owners that have a bricks-and-mortar location sometimes assume that their online storefront is an extension of their offline storefront and that they will provide exactly the same products and services online as offline. In some cases, fewer products are offered online than in the physical store. This is often the case if you are test marketing, but also if some of the products you sell in your physical location are not appropriate for online sales because of competitive pricing or shipping logistics.

In other cases, your online store might offer more products or services than the bricks-and-mortar location. For example, your offline bookstore might not offer shipping or gift wrapping. If your online bookstore does not offer these services, you will lose a lot of business to your online competition. When a site's product offerings include items that are appropriate for gift giving, it is essential to also offer wrapping, customized cards, shipping to multiple addresses, and shipping options. The consumer is "king" and is very demanding. You have to meet and beat your consumers' expectations online to garner market share. People shopping for gifts online are looking for convenience, and the site that provides the greatest convenience and the greatest products at the lowest prices will be the winner.

You will want to look at how to get a "greater share of wallet" with every online sale. Are there opportunities for you to up-sell? Is there an opportunity to show purchasers things like "Customers who bought this product also bought . . ." to encourage additional sales. Once customers add a product to their shopping cart and click "Continue Shopping," what landing page are you sending them to?

The Fundamentals

Once you have clearly defined your online objectives, your target markets, and the products or services you want to promote online, you are ready to move to the next phase of planning your Web site—doing your competitive analysis.

Using Competitor Sites to Your Advantage

You have to realize that your online competition is different from your offline competition. Online, you are competing with all organizations that have an online presence and sell the same types of products and services you do. When doing your competitive analysis online, you want to select the "best of breed"—those fantastic Web sites of the organizations selling the same products and services you do—no matter where they are physically located.

One of your Web site's objectives is to always meet and beat the competition in terms of search engine rankings and Web site content. To do so, you must understand exactly what it is your competition is doing. Take the time to research competitors and compare them on an element-by-element basis.

There are a number of ways you can identify your competition online. You can find them by conducting searches with the appropriate keywords, seeing which competing Web sites rank highly in the major search engines and directories. Similarly, there are many other online resources you can use to research your competition, including industry-specific Web portals and directories.

Once you have gathered a list of competing Web sites, analyze them element by element to determine which Web elements your competitors include on their sites and how their sites compare to one another. You want to look at what types of content they are providing to your target market. Other components you should analyze include the visual appeal of your competitors' sites, content, ease of navigation, search engine friendliness, interactivity, and Web site stickiness, or what they do to keep people coming back to their site. You will also want to look at the competition's total online presence: Do they have a Facebook page? Twitter account? YouTube channel? Blog? How are they growing their fans, followers, and friends in their social media accounts? This information can provide you with details on what you need to incorporate into your site and your social media accounts to meet and beat the competition.

When we do a competitive analysis for clients, we reverse-engineer (or dissect) the competing Web site from a number of different perspectives. Generally, you will choose five or six of the absolute best competing Web sites. Then you start to build a database using Excel or a table in Word.

Start with the first competing Web site, and from your review, start to add database elements to the first column. Note any types of content, target markets defined, repeat-traffic techniques used, viral marketing techniques used, search engine friendliness features used, download time for different types of Internet connections, cross-platform compatibility, cross-browser compatibility, and innovative elements. When you have dissected the first competing Web site and have noted appropriate database elements for comparative purposes, move on to the second competing Web site. Go through the same process, adding those elements that are new or different from what you already have in your database. Continue building the first column of your database by continuing through all the sites you want to include in your competitive analysis.

The next step is to develop a column for each of the sites you want to include in the competitive analysis. Then add two more columns—one for your existing Web site, to see how your site stacks against the competition, and the second for future planning purposes.

The next step is to go back and compare each site against the criteria for column 1, noting appropriate comments. For content information, you want to note whether the particular site has the same specific content, and how well it was presented. For download speeds, note specific minutes and seconds for each type of connection. For each repeat-traffic generator, you may choose to include details, or just yes/no. Continue with this process until you have completed the database, including your own existing site.

By this time, you should have a good feel for users' experiences when they visit your competitors' sites. Now you are ready to see how your site stacks up against the competition. The next column should have your Web site. Compare your site against all the criteria in column 1. Now you can see in black and white how your site compares to your competition.

Now you are ready to do your planning. In the last column of your database, review each of the elements in the first column, review your notes in your competitive analysis, and, where appropriate, complete the last column by categorizing each of the elements as one of the following:

- A—Need to have; essential, critical element; can't live without

- B—Nice to have if it doesn't cost too much

- C—Don't need; don't want at any price.

Remember that users usually visit at least three Web sites before they make their buying decision. When they have visited a number of sites that have certain elements incorporated, such as a virtual tour, that element becomes the norm or an expectation. If your site does not have that virtual tour (or whatever that certain element is), they may feel as if you are not keeping up with industry standards, that you are not meeting their expectations. The bar is constantly being raised. Once a person sees something on three or four of your competitors' sites, it becomes an expectation. The Internet has helped create very demanding consumers with very high expectations.

Having completed identification of your objectives, target markets, products and services, and now your competitive analysis, you are ready to develop your storyboard, plan, or blueprint for your site.

Storyboarding Your Web Site

Before you start construction on your Web site, there are many steps to be taken. First you must have the storyboard, or the blueprint of your site, developed. In Web development, the majority of the time should be spent in the planning stage—integrate your objectives, your target market information, the findings

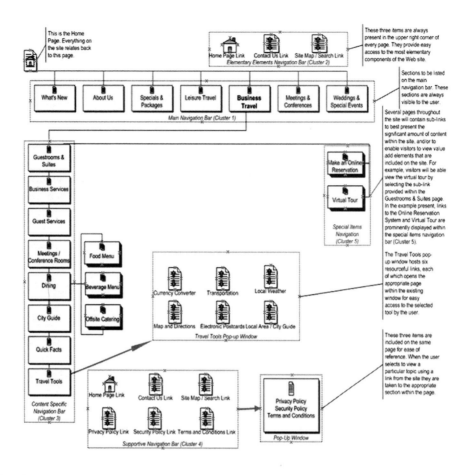

Figure 1.1.   Storyboard for a hotel.

of the competitive analysis, and your own ideas, as well as those of others. This is done through the process of storyboarding.

The storyboard is the foundation of your Web site. Consider it the plan or blueprint of your site. It should show you, on paper, the first draft of the content and layout of your site. It gives you the chance to review the layout and make changes before development begins.

The storyboard can be created with a software program like Microsoft Visio, with sheets of paper, or with any other mechanism. (See Figure1.1 for an example of a storyboard we developed for one of our hotel clients.) Quite often when we begin storyboarding a project for a client, we'll start with yellow sticky notes on a wall. Very low tech, but it works! It is very easy to get a visual of the navigation structure and easy to fill in the content pages (one per sticky note) in the appropriate places. It is also very easy to edit—simply move a sticky from one section to another, or add another sticky note for a new page.

Detailed Web Site Planning

In the previous section of this chapter you learned how to develop your storyboard. Now you need to develop the specific content, text, and graphics for each page of your site.

The first draft of the text for each page should be developed by you. You know your target market better than anyone—you know what makes them buy, you know what they want, and you know the buzz words for your industry far better than your Web developer.

Once the first draft of the text is done, you want to have this text reviewed and edited by an online copywriter. Your online copywriter can be a person from your own organization, someone from a Web development organization, or an outsourced third party. Online copywriters often have a background in PR or advertising, and they know how to get the message across in as few words as possible. Online copywriters know how to grab your readers' attention and get them to do what you want them to do. Internet users don't want to read pages and pages of text—they want to get what they're looking for quickly. Online copywriters know that the text should be short, to the point, and written so it can easily be scanned.

Always review what the online copywriter has done. You want to make sure that the substance of your text has stayed the same and only the form has been changed.

After you have reviewed and approved the online copywriter's work, you want to have the content reviewed and edited by an Internet marketer. Again, the Internet marketer can be a person from your own organization, someone from a Web development organization, or an outsourced third party. Be sure that the Internet marketer you choose has expertise in search engine optimization, repeat-traffic generators, social media marketing, viral and permission marketing, as well as the latest trends in online marketing, such as mobile marketing and interactive mapping.

The Internet marketer will review and edit the text and graphics, making sure that the keywords are used in the appropriate places for high search engine ranking. The keyword assigned to a particular page should be used appropriately in the page title, the text throughout the page, the meta-tags for keyword and description, the headers, the Alt tags, and the comments tags. There is a real science to this, so be sure to choose your Internet marketer carefully. You'll learn more about designing your site to be search engine friendly in Chapter 2.

The Internet marketer should also ensure that you have used the appropriate repeat-traffic generators (see Chapter 3), appropriate permission marketing techniques (see Chapter 4), and appropriate viral marketing techniques (see Chapter 5). Again, you need to review and approve the changes to make sure your message is still presented appropriately for your target market.

Once you are satisfied with the Internet marketer's work, the next step is graphic design. The graphic designer will develop the "look and feel" for your site—the navigation bar, the background, and the separator bars. The graphic designer knows that your online and offline corporate identity should be consistent. Again, you will review and approve the graphic design. This is critically important as you don't get a second chance to make a first impression, and your Web visitor is just a click away from your competition if they are not wowed in the first three to five seconds.

Once all this is done, and everything has been reviewed and approved, you are ready for the programming to start.

Internet Resources for Chapter 1

I have developed a great library of online resources for you to check out regarding planning your Web site. This library is available on my Web site, *http://www.SusanSweeney.com,* in the Resources section, where you can find additional tips, tools, techniques, and resources.

I have also developed courses on many of the topics covered in this book. These courses are available on two of my Web sites, *http://www.SusanSweeney. com* and *http://www.eLearningU.com* (which contains other instructors' courses as well). These courses are delivered immediately over the Internet, so you can start whenever is convenient for you.

2

Designing Your Site to Be Search Engine Friendly

When Internet users are looking for a particular product, service, subject, or information pertaining to an area of interest to them, how do they do it? The most common research tool used is the search engine—85 percent of people doing research online use search engines to find what they are looking for.

Because search engines can bring significant volumes of traffic to your site, you must understand how the major search engines work and how the design of your site can influence the indexing of your site by the search engines. You must also know about the elements that are included in the search engines' algorithms, or formulas, that are outside your Web site and what you can do to ensure that you earn maximum points for those things you can influence. Social media, for example, is significantly influencing search engine ranking.

When people conduct Internet searches, they rarely go beyond the first page of results. If you want to be noticed, ideally you want to appear on the top half of the front page of search results. Before you submit to the search engines, you have to be sure your site has been designed to be search engine friendly. In this chapter, we cover:

- The methodology to make your site search engine friendly

- How the search engines rank sites

- The key elements of Web site design to accommodate search engines

- The all-important content

- The importance of keywords in all aspects of your Web site

- The elements that are in the search engine algorithms or formulas that are outside your Web site

- The importance of link popularity and link relevancy to your search engine placement.

Understanding Search Engines and How They Rank Sites

For this section we are talking about **organic listings** rather than pay-per-click or sponsored listings. Those are discussed in Chapter 8.

Organic listings are the search results that are displayed to the left of the page and below the sponsored listings. Organic listings are free listings and are gained by how your site is ranked based on a unique formula, or algorithm, for each search engine. Pay-per-click or sponsored listings, on the other hand, are listings that are paid for and gained through a bidding process. Sponsored listings are always displayed at the top of the results and down the right-hand side of the page. Ranking high in the pay-to-play search engines is discussed more in Chapter 9.

Organic listing

A free listing of a site in the search results ranked by the search engine's ranking formula or algorithm.

See Figure 2.1 for a visual explanation of organic and pay-per-click positioning on the search engine results page.

Search engines use programs or intelligent agents, called **bots,** to actually search the Internet for pages that they index using specific parameters as they read the content. The bot reads the information on every page of your site and then follows the links. For example, Google's spiders continually crawl the Web looking for sites to index and, of course, index sites upon their submission. Google is obviously very important in the search engine community, so be sure your site is easily accessible to its spider.

Bots

Programs used by search engines to search the Internet for pages to index.

Each search engine has its own unique ranking criteria and its own unique algorithm, or formula, giving different weighting to each of the criteria in its formula. For the search engines that you have decided to focus on, you have to learn as much as you can about their ranking criteria and relative weighting. See Figure 2.2 for a breakdown of how the search engines score sites. The site with the highest score appears at the top of the results, and the rest appear in descending order of their score.

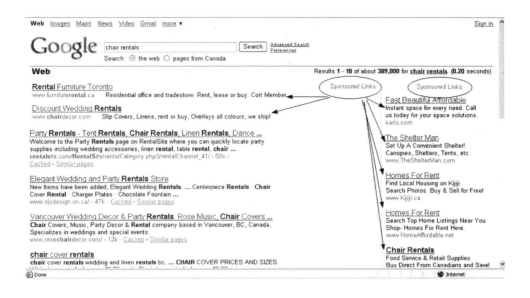

Figure 2.1. Pay-per-click or sponsored listings appear at the top of the search results and along the right hand side of the page, whereas organic listings appear on the left hand side of the page and under the sponsored listings.

To maximize your score, you need to address all three areas. You need to make sure your site is optimized for keyword phrases. (That is what this chapter is all about.) You need to maximize your link popularity and link relevancy points; we talk more about this later in this chapter as well as in Chapter 13 on links. You need to scoop up the miscellaneous points; some of these are easy and some you don't have much control over. We cover these points more in this chapter, too.

The search engines are all fighting for market share. The more market share a search engine has, the more valuable the company is. To gain market share, a search engine has to provide better results than its competition. It is for this reason that the search engines are changing and improving their formulas on an ongoing basis. You have to keep up with changes in these formulas, tweak your site accordingly, and resubmit when necessary.

The search engines have different algorithms or formulas for their ranking. They have different weighting for the various elements within their formula. They change their formulas over time and they change their ranking over time. Social media has had an impact on search engine ranking, and we are seeing changes in the search engine formulas to make sure that the appropriate weight is attached to those elements and manipulation of search engine ranking is kept at a minimum. Sound complicated? Let's get started.

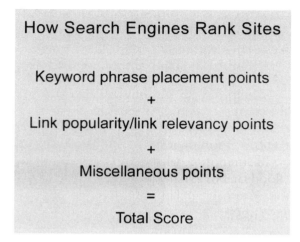

Figure 2.2. Formula for how search engines rank Web sites.

Methodology to Maximize Your Site's Search Ranking

There are a number of steps we'll take to maximize your search engine ranking:

1. Decide which search engines are critical for your success. Learn as much as you can about their ranking criteria and the weighting given to each criterion in their algorithm.

2. Determine the keyword phrases you are going to focus on in your search engine optimization. You are looking for those keyword phrases that your target market is using in the search engines to find what you have to offer when they don't know that your particular company exists.

3. Assign those keywords to specific pages throughout your site.

4. Populate the pages with the assigned keywords in the appropriate places given the ranking criteria for your targeted search engines.

5. Have a link strategy and start the implementation.

6. Make sure you have done what you can to maximize your miscellaneous points.

7. Get yourself on Google Maps if you can. Notice that the maps appear in the search results before the organic listings!

8. Manually submit your site to the major search engines.

The remainder of this chapter walks you step-by-step through this process.

Step 1. Decide Which Search Engines Are Important

To start this process, you want to decide which search engines you are going to be concerned about when taking steps necessary to rank high in their search results.

You want to select a number of the most popular search engines for your concentration. You also want to be indexed in topic-specific search engines for your industry. You can find the most popular search engines by doing your research online through sites such as Search Engine Watch *(http://www. searchenginewatch.com)*. You can keep up with what's happening with search engine market share by Googling "search engine market share report" and reviewing the latest reports.

As it stands at the time of this writing (Figure 2.3), the major players in the search engine industry are:

- Google Sites—63.7 percent

- Yahoo! Sites—18.3 percent

- Microsoft Sites—12.1 percent

- Ask Network—3.6 percent

- AOL Network—2.4 percent.

Step 2. Learn the Search Engine Ranking Criteria

Things have changed quite a bit from the early days. Elements that used to have significant weighting may now have very little weight. You have to remember that it is the highest total score you are looking for, so even if an element has

comScore Core Search Report* May 2010 vs. April 2010 Total U.S. – Home/Work/University Locations Source: comScore qSearch			
Core Search Entity	Share of Searches (%)		
	Apr-10	May-10	Point Change May-10 vs. Apr-10
Total Core Search	100.0%	100.0%	N/A
Google Sites	64.4%	63.7%	-0.7
Yahoo! Sites	17.7%	18.3%	0.6
Microsoft Sites	11.8%	12.1%	0.3
Ask Network	3.7%	3.6%	-0.1
AOL LLC Network	2.4%	2.3%	-0.1

Figure 2.3. comScore Core Search Report on search engine market share.

reduced weighting, if the element has any points at all you want to incorporate that element to maximize your total score. Sometimes the top sites are within a small number of points of each other.

It is not as daunting as it might sound, because the major search engines tend to look at similar information but weight the relevancy for particular items differently in their algorithms. That having been said, here are the most important areas on a Web page that you must address when performing organic search engine optimization:

- Title tags (page titles)

- Keyword meta-tags

- Description meta-tags

- Alt tags

- Hypertext links (e.g., anchor text)

- Domain names and file names

- Body text (beginning, middle, and end of page copy)

- Headers

- Between the "NOFRAMES" tag of framed Web sites.

Page titles and text-based page content are the most important of the noted placement areas. Keyword meta-tags are not as critical as they once were, but they are still applicable for some engines. Remember—it is the absolute highest score you are looking for; if there are any points available, you want to design your site to take advantage of them.

Step 3. Determine Your Most Important Keyword Phrases

Keyword phrases (hereafter referred to as keywords) are the terms and phrases that your target market uses when searching the major search engines and directories for the products and services you sell. Your keywords are used in everything you do and are the key determining factor in how you rank in the search results among many of the major search engines.

A critical step in natural search engine optimization is to select the right keywords for your business, products, or services (including descriptive words), and your target market. Understand whom you are targeting and build your search engine optimization efforts around your audience.

You need to choose keyword phrases that are going to bring sustainable targeted traffic consisting of potential customers—not just visitors; you are looking for targeted traffic. What you may think is the perfect keyword phrase may not be used at all by your target market in their search queries, which is why it is so critical to research and validate your keywords.

Ideally, each page of your Web site is going to focus on a different set of keywords that are specific to the content at hand. If you were to focus on the same set of keywords on every page, then you would hit only one small portion of your market potential because you are only going to hit those same keywords over and over again—it is self-defeating.

First, you want to gather a master list of all possible keyword phrases. How do you create your master keyword list? Here are four solid techniques for generating a list of potential keyword phrases:

1. Brainstorm, survey, and review promotional material.

2. Review competing and industry-leading Web sites.

3. Assess your Web site traffic logs.

4. Use keyword suggestion and evaluation tools.

As you work your way through the list of techniques, you want to cycle back to some of the techniques because you will come across search terms that can expand the scope of your original efforts and open the door to new, more targeted phrases that you might have missed the first time around.

Brainstorming, Surveying, and Reviewing Promotional Material

Try to think as your target market would if they were to do a search for information on a topic contained within your site. Do not just think about what people would do to find your site, but what they would do if they didn't know your business existed and were looking for the types of products and services you sell.

Your current corporate materials, brochures, and other marketing collateral can be a valuable source of keyword phrases. Begin by indiscriminately highlighting any words that people might search for if looking for products or services your company has to offer.

Review Competing and Industry-Leading Web Sites

Check out your online competition. The term *competition* is referenced quite loosely in that industry leaders with whom you may not directly compete are also included here. Look at the sites for which you have a record and look for sites in the major search engines using some of the keyword phrases you have gathered so far.

You want to see what sites are in the top ten positions and understand them. By reviewing top-ranking Web sites, you can look for themes and patterns in the sites that give you a good indication of what they are going after and how they are doing it. You can then turn around and apply this newfound knowledge to your own Web site.

When reviewing competing Web sites, you should look at the same general areas you would optimize on your own Web site.

By searching for your most important keywords and observing what the top-ranking sites are using with respect to their page content, title tags, description meta-tags, keyword meta-tags, and so on, you can formulate a good plan of attack. Remember that if you don't appear in the first two or three pages of search results, it is unlikely that prospective visitors will access your site through the search engine.

To check your competition's title and meta-tags in Microsoft Internet Explorer, you simply go to their site, then click "View" on your menu bar, and select "Source" from the drop-down menu. This brings up the source code for that page.

Assess Your Web Site Traffic Logs

Your Web site traffic logs can be a source of pertinent keyword information. You can view your traffic logs to see what search terms and search engines people are using to locate your Web site and to help you fine-tune future search engine optimization efforts.

If you are not sure whether you have access to a Web site traffic analysis program, check with your current Web site host to see if they provide one to you. If not, there are plenty of tools available to you. (See Chapter 28, "Web Traffic Analysis," for helpful information.)

Keyword Suggestion and Evaluation Tools

There are a number of services available that can help you with selecting the most appropriate keywords for your site. These services base their suggestions on results from actual search queries. Google provides a great keyword tool *(https://adwords.google.com/select/KeywordToolExternal)* to assist with keyword selection. Wordtracker (*http://www.wordtracker.com*) is another example of such a service.

Keyword research tools can help meet your current needs, whether you're looking for a place to start, are plum out of ideas, or simply feel like you're missing something. See the Resources section of my Web site at *http://www. SusanSweeney.com* for a list of keyword research tools.

Fine-Tuning Your Keyword Phrases

Now that you have your master keyword list, probably with a few hundred keyword phrases, you have to drill down and figure out which keywords you are going to target for each page of your Web site that you want to optimize. Keep in mind that each page you optimize should lean toward a different set of keywords. Why? What good is buying 100 lottery tickets for the next drawing if they all have the same number? It is the same idea here.

Your efforts should focus around those keyword phrases that bring in a fair volume of traffic and that are highly targeted. The return on investment for such keywords will be much higher. When reviewing your keyword list, you need to consider:

- Which keywords are vital to your objectives

- Which keywords are popular enough to generate reasonable, sustainable traffic

- Which keywords do not have so much competition that it would be counterproductive considering the time and effort necessary to target them.

You can begin editing the list by deleting words that either are too generic (for example, *business*) or are not appropriate for keyword purposes. Review each word and ask yourself, "Would people search using this word if they were looking for the products and services available through my Web site?"

For each page that you are optimizing, take a copy of the comprehensive master list and delete words that are not appropriate for that particular page. Reprioritize the remaining keywords based on the content of the page you are indexing. Now take the keyword phrase you have assigned to this page and put it at the top of the list. This is the keyword list for that particular page. Repeat this procedure for every page you are optimizing. This is also a great procedure when you are developing the keyword meta-tag for each page of your site.

What I just covered is a very basic approach to organizing keywords. If you are up to the challenge, you can take it further by adding weights and multipliers to your keyword list to further refine it.

Here are some additional tips to keep in mind when refining your keywords master list:

- Plural and singular keywords—Google matches exactly what the user searches for, so it is important to use both where possible.

- Using the names of your competitors—Never include a competitor's name in your keywords. Because several search engines read only a small amount of content for keywords, you lose valuable page real estate to irrelevant keywords when you use your competitor's name.

- Common misspellings of words—There are many words that people misspell on a frequent basis. The question here is, do you include those misspelled keywords in your site or not? My stance is "no." Although people use them in their searches, it hurts your credibility in that you come off as a company incapable of correctly spelling its own products and services. There are exceptions to every rule. Canadian sites often have U.S. customers as their target market and U.S. sites often have Canadian customers as their target market. There are a number of words that are spelled differently by these countries—theatre in Canada is theater in the United States, centre in Canada is center in the United States, colour in Canada is color in the United States, for example. If you are caught with one of your important keywords spelled differently by your target market, you might want to optimize a page of your site to accommodate this. Perhaps you might offer a page that is designed for "Our Canadian Friends" or for "Our American Friends."

- Filter and stop words—Filter words are words that search engines simply ignore during searches. Stop words are extremely common words that search engines use as triggers to stop grabbing content on a given page, such as "and," "a," and "the." Some search engines view stop words and filter words as the same thing, but you need to remember only one thing: search engines bypass these words to save time, as these words are not considered to add any value to the search. It is best to try to avoid using stop words where possible in your keyword phrases.

- Modifiers—A modifier is a keyword you add to your primary keyword phrase to give it a boost. Who simply searches for a hotel at random? It doesn't make sense. You look for a hotel in combination with a destination. In this case, the destination is the modifier.

- Multiple-word keyword phrases—Two- or three-keyword phrases perform better than single keywords.

Step 4. Assign Specific Keywords to Specific Pages

The next step is to allocate specific keywords to specific pages of your site for search engine optimization. You then populate each page in the appropriate places with the assigned keyword. You do this because you want to ensure that no matter which keyword or keyword phrase your target market decides to search on, one of the pages on your site is likely to rank in the first couple of pages of search results.

To assign specific keyword phrases to specific pages, we're going back to grade 2. Remember when the teacher gave you a page with words down one side and definitions down the other? Well, we're going to do something similar. Take a piece of paper and write down the pages you are going to optimize on the right side of the page. Then take the same number of important keyword phrases and write those down on the left side of the page. Now try to match the keyword phrase to the page where there is an opportunity to get the keyword phrase into the content of the page you are going to optimize.

Step 5. Populate Each Page with the Assigned Keyword

When you have allocated your keywords to the various pages on your site, you will populate or include the keyword phrases assigned in the appropriate places for that particular page. Let's take a closer look at all those appropriate places.

Title Tags—Use Descriptive Page Titles

It is extremely important that all Web pages have titles. Title tags are viewed as one of the most important elements of search engine optimization when it comes to keyword placement. Each of the pages on your Web site should have a different title, as each page is focusing on a different keyword phrase for optimization purposes.

The title is inserted between the title tags in the header of an HTML document. <HEAD> indicates the beginning of the header, and the ending of the header is marked by </HEAD>. A simplified version might look like:

- <HTML>

- <HEAD>

- <TITLE>Document Title Here</TITLE>

- <META-NAME="keywords"   CONTENT="keyword1,   keyword2, keyword3">

- <META-NAME="description"   CONTENT="200-character   site description goes here">

- <META-NAME="robots" CONTENT="index, follow">

- <!—Comments tag, repeat description here>

- </HEAD>

Title tag information identifies and describes your pages. Most Web browsers display a document's title in the top line of the screen. When users print a page from your Web site, the title usually appears at the top of the page at the left. When someone bookmarks your site or adds it to their "Favorites," the title appears as the description in his or her bookmark file. These are all reasons that it is important that a page's title reflect an accurate description of the page. More importantly, the title tag is typically what the target market sees in search results in some of the major search engines. In Figure 2.4 you can see that a typical search result consists of the title tag as the link to the Web site, a brief description of the Web site, and the URL.

Every page of your Web site should have a unique title tag, and each title tag should accurately describe the page content. Your target market should be able to read the title tag and understand what the page they are about to view contains.

Figure 2.4. A typical search result consisting of the title tag as the link to the Web site, a brief description of the Web site, and the URL.

Keep your title tags brief—in the realm of five to ten words. The longer your title tag is, the more diluted your keywords become and the more likely your title tag is to be truncated by a search engine. Google displays a maximum of 66 characters. Yahoo! Search, on the other hand, permits up to 120 characters for a title tag.

The shorter and more accurate the title tag is, the higher the keyword density and relevancy for that title tag. Try to keep your use of a keyword phrase to a single instance if possible, unless the title tag truly warrants duplication. In the case of a hotel, the word *hotel* might appear twice in a title—once for the hotel's proper company name and once in a descriptive term such as a targeted geographic area.

Keywords Meta-Tag

Although in recent years fewer points have been allocated to content in the keywords meta-tags, it is important to keep your eyes on the total score—if there are any points at all allocated to this element, you want them all. As we've already mentioned, the site with the highest total score appears at the top of the search results, so you are going after every point you can get.

The keywords meta-tag, <META-NAME="keywords" CONTENT="..."> tells search engines under which keywords to index your site. When a user types one of the words you listed here, you are telling the search engine that your site should be displayed in the results. A space or comma can be used to separate the words. Do not repeat the keyword frequently; rather, repeat the keyword about five times in different phrases. Be wary of keyword dilution by using too many different terms in this tag. You should create a unique keywords tag for each page of your site that lists the appropriate keywords for that particular page.

Description Meta-Tag

<META-NAME="description" CONTENT="..."> should be included on every page of your Web site. The description meta-tag is used to supply an accurate overview of the page to which it is attached. The description meta-tags can influence the description in the search engines that support them.

It is best to keep the description meta-tag to somewhere between 200 to 250 characters in total. Be sure to use the same keywords applied elsewhere on the page being optimized in the description meta-tag for consistency and relevancy.

It helps to include a call to action encouraging the target market to visit your Web site or take some other action, as this description is often what users see in the search results as a description for your site.

Alt Tags

Some search engines use the information within Alt tags when forming a description and determining the ranking for your site. Alt tags are used to display a description of the graphic they are associated with if the graphic cannot be displayed. Alt tags appear after an image tag and contain a phrase that is associated with the image.

Ensure that your Alt tags contain the keywords assigned to the particular page wherever you can. This gives your page a better chance of being ranked higher in the search engines. For example:

<image src="images/logo.gif" height="50" width ="50" alt="Best Western Hotel Orlando">

You do not want your Alt tags to look something like "company logo" because this does not include any keywords. Be sure you apply proper Alt tags to all images on your site to achieve best results. Keep in mind that users who browse with graphics disabled must be able to navigate your site, and proper use of Alt tags assists them in doing so.

Hypertext Links

A hypertext link consists of the description of a link placed between anchor tags. Here is an example of an absolute link, where the link includes the total path to where the document can be found:

<a href="http://www.DomainName.com/HotelOrlando">. This is the anchor text for the sample link </A>.

The text inside a hyperlink, or anchor text, is important for search engine optimization. The major search engines have points available for including the keyword phrase being searched on in the text around the link pointing to your Web site.

If links on other Web sites pointing to your Web site include the same string of keywords, your site's relevancy gets a boost. When you encourage other Web sites to link to yours, or when you provide links to your Web site through your blog, posts to others' blogs, or in your social media posts and tags, make sure you get the keyword phrase you have assigned to that particular page in the text around the link. Similarly, when you submit your Web site to directories and other link sources, provide the comparable link or title text.

Domain Name and File Names

Use of keywords within your domain name and file names can help with search engine positioning.

It does not take much effort to give your images and file names meaningful names—names that include the keyword phrase you have assigned to that page—so take the time to do it. For example, instead of a car dealership, say Chrysler, using *http://www.chrysler.com/page1.html* for a page that is focusing on their trucks, it would be much better to use *http://www.chrysler.com/trucks*.

Body Text—Header Tags and Page Copy

The body text of a Web page consists of all the visible text between the body and </body> tag, such as headings and the page copy encased in paragraphs. Along with page titles, body text is the next important area on which to focus your search engine optimization efforts. Body text is where you want to spend the bulk of your time.

Headings—Header Tags</H1>

Use your HTML header tags effectively to indicate the subject and content of a particular page. Most people use them only as a method of creating large fonts. Some search engines, including Google, use the content included within the header text in their relevancy scoring. The H1 tag is the most important, followed by H2. Include your most important keywords in your header tags. If you can, work a couple of H2 tags into your page and get the keyword phrase you've assigned to that page within the header tag. Some developers use a larger font instead of H1 and H2 tags; the search engines give the points only if the keyword phrase is between the <H1> tag and the </H1> tag.

Page Copy

You want to ensure that the keyword you have assigned to a specific page appears as close to the beginning of that page as possible, and certainly within the first 200 characters. The higher up on a page, the greater the keyword prominence. Search engines tend to lend more weight to page content above the fold. The fold is where your browser window ends and where vertical scrolling begins, if necessary.

The assigned keyword should appear at the beginning of the text on the page, in the middle, and again at the end. You want to build a theme on your page, and to do so you have to spread your keywords throughout the page, not just focus on the first paragraph.

Always have a descriptive paragraph at the top of your Web page that describes what can be found on the page for your target market and for the major search engines. Search engines use this as their source for a site description and keywords on your site. Be sure to use the most important keywords first, preferably within the first two or three sentences. This is enormously important. Make sure that the keywords you use flow naturally within the content of the opening paragraph and relate to the content and purpose of your site. You don't want the search engines to think you're trying to cram in words where they don't fit.

Keyword density is the number of times a keyword, or keyword phrase, is used on a Web page, divided by the total number of words on that particular page. Your keyword density should be between 3 percent and 8 percent. If your keyword density is below 3 percent, it is not there often enough to count. If your keyword density is above 8 percent, it may appear as if you are attempting to manipulate the search engines.

The search engines can't read text embedded in your graphics for content. Very often I see a site that has the company name used only in a graphic logo. If someone were to do a search on the company name, they may not earn enough points to score on the first page of results.

As a final note, before you submit your site, be sure the content on the page you are submitting is complete. Some of the major search engines will ignore your submission if you have an "under construction" or similar sign on your page.

Spamming

Search engines want to provide the most accurate and complete search results they can to their target market. After all, this is what drives all aspects of their business model. If people have no faith in a search engine, the traffic dries up and the sponsored listing fees as well as other advertising fees cease to exist.

In the olden days, Internet marketers used various techniques to trick the search engines into positioning their sites higher in search results. These tricks do not work with the search engines today, and if it is discovered that you are trying to dupe the search engines, some may not list you at all. Search engines are programmed to detect some of these techniques, and you will be penalized in some way if you are discovered. A few of the search engine tricks that used to work—BUT THEY DO NOT WORK TODAY, SO DON'T USE THEM—pertaining to Web site design are included below. I include them so you can go back to look at your site to see if they have been used on your site, and if they have, this is probably the reason you are having difficulty with search engine placement.

- *Repeating keywords*—Some Web sites repeat the same keywords over and over again, by hiding them in the visible HTML, in invisible layers such as the <NOFRAMES> tag, and in meta-tags. Repeating keywords over and over again by displaying them at the bottom of your document after a number of line breaks counts as well! For example:

  <META-NAME="keywords"CONTENT="cabins, cabins, cabins, cabins, rental cabins, cabins, cabins, forest cabins, lakeside cabins, cabins, cabins, cabins, cabins">

- *Keyword stacking*—It is quite obvious when a site is using this ill-fated technique. Its not-so-obvious cousin is called keyword stuffing, which is when you exercise the same stacking techniques on aspects of the Web site that should not be optimized, such as spacer images. A spacer image is used by Web developers for just that—properly spacing items on a page. It is not good practice to include descriptive text in an Alt tag for a spacer image.

- *Jamming keywords*—If you are displaying keywords on your Web pages using a very small font, then you are jamming keywords. Why would you even do this unless you were specifically trying to manipulate search results? Don't do it. This spam technique is called "tiny text."

- *Hidden text and links*—Avoid inserting hidden text and links in your Web site for the purpose of getting in more keywords. For example, you can hide keywords in your HTML document by making the text color the same as the background color. Another example is inserting keywords in areas not visible to the end user, such as the hidden layers in style sheets.

- *Misleading title changes*—Making frequent and regular title changes so that the bots think your site is a new site and list you again and again is misleading. In the case of directories, you could change the name of your site just by adding a space, an exclamation mark (!), or "A" as the first character so that you come up first in alphabetical lists.

- *Page swapping*—This practice involves showing one page to a search engine, but a different one to the end user. Quite often you find people hijack content from a top-ranking site, insert it on their page to achieve a top ranking, then replace that page with a completely different page when a desired ranking is achieved.

- *Content duplication*—Say you have one Web page and it is ranking pretty well. You decide it would be nice to improve your ranking, but hey, it would be good to keep your current position too. You decide to duplicate your page, fine-tune a few things, and call it something different. You then submit that page to the search engine. Your ranking improved and now you have two listings. Not bad! Why not do it again? And so on and so forth. If you are caught duplicating Web pages, you will be penalized. Search engines want to provide unique content, not the same page over and over again.

- *Domain spam (mirrored sites)*—Closely related to content duplication, this is when an entire Web site is replicated (or slightly modified) and placed at a different URL. This is usually done to dominate search positions and to boost link popularity, but in the end all it does is hurt you when you get caught. You will be banned for practicing this technique.

- *Refresh meta-tag*—Have you ever visited a site and then been automatically transported to another page within the site? This is the result of a **refresh meta-tag**. This tag is an HTML document that is designed to automatically replace itself with another HTML document

> **Refresh meta-tag**
>
> *A tag used to automatically reload or load a new page.*

after a certain specified period of time, as defined by the document author—it's like automatic page swapping. Do not abuse this tag. Additionally, don't use a redirect unless it is absolutely necessary. A permanent redirect (HTTP 301) can be used to tell the search engines that the page they are looking for has a new home; this tells them to go there to index it.

   If you do use a refresh meta-tag to redirect users, then it is suggested that you set a delay of at least 15 seconds and provide a link on the new page back to the page they were taken from. Some businesses use refresh meta-tags to redirect users from a page that is obsolete or is no longer there. Refresh meta-tags also may be used to give an automated slideshow or force a sequence of events as part of a design element.

- *Cloaking*—This technique is similar to page swapping and using the refresh meta-tag in that the intent is to serve search engines one page while the end user is served another. Don't do it.

- *Doorway pages*—Also known as gateway pages and bridge pages, doorway pages are pages that lead to your site but are not considered part of your site. Doorway pages lead to your Web site but are tuned to the specific requirements of the search engines. By having different doorway pages with different names (e.g., indexy.html for Yahoo! or indexg.html for Google) for each search engine, you can optimize pages for individual engines.

  Unfortunately, because of the need to be ranked high in search engine results and the enormous competition among sites that are trying to get such high listings, doorway pages have increasingly become more popular. Each search engine is different and has different elements in its ranking criteria. You can see the appeal of doorway pages because this allows you to tailor a page specifically for each search engine and thus achieve optimal results.

  Search engines frown upon the use of doorway pages because the intent is obvious—to manipulate rankings in one site's favor with no regard for quality content. Do not use them.

- *Cyber-squatting*—This term refers to stealing traffic from legitimate Web sites. If someone were to operate a Web site called "Gooogle.com" with the extra "o" or "Yahhoo" with an extra "h," that would be considered cyber-squatting. Domain squatting is when a company acquires the familiar domain of another company, either because the domain expired or the original company no longer exists. The new company then uses the familiar domain to promote completely unrelated content. Google, in particular, frowns on cyber-squatting.

- *Links farms*—These are irrelevant linking schemes to boost rankings based on achieving better link popularity. Having thousands of irrelevant links pointing to your Web site does more damage than good. The search engines are on to this technique and they don't like sites that try to manipulate placement. For best results, only pursue links that relate to your Web site and are of interest to your target market.

How do you know if you are spamming a search engine? If the technique you are employing on your Web site does not offer value to your end user and is done solely for the intention of boosting your search engine rankings, then you are probably guilty of spam.

Search engines post guidelines for what they consider acceptable practices. It is advised that you read each search engine's policy to ensure that you conform to their guidelines. Following is Google's policy (*http://www.google.com/webmasters/guidelines.html*) on quality.

Quality Guidelines—Basic Principles

- Make pages for users, not for search engines. Don't deceive your users or present different content to search engines than you display to users.

- Avoid tricks intended to improve search engine rankings. A good rule of thumb is whether you'd feel comfortable explaining what you've done to a Web site that competes with you. Another useful test is to ask, "Does this help my users? Would I do this if search engines didn't exist?"

- Don't participate in link schemes designed to increase your site's ranking or PageRank. In particular, avoid links to Web spammers or "bad neighborhoods" on the Web, as your own ranking may be affected adversely by those links.

Step 6. Link Strategy

Most of the search engines are giving heavy weighting to link popularity and link relevancy—that is, the number of links to your site from other sites, blogs, social media, rating and review sites, and other places on the Internet. The search engines are getting very sophisticated in the weighting of link popularity, with the search engines giving extra points for link relevancy—that is, how high the site with the link to your site would rank for the same keyword. Other points are awarded based on the keywords in the text around the link pointing to your Web site. For strategies on generating significant links to your site, see Chapter 13.

Step 7. Miscellaneous Points

The search engines also have a number of miscellaneous items in their formula. Some of these you have control over and others you don't. These miscellaneous points include things like:

- The age of your domain. The longer you have been around and the more established you are, the more points you get.

- How long you have bought your domain into the future. If you have secured your domain for the next 10 years, the search engine knows you're planning to be around. They like this—more points.

- Clean code. The search engines like it when you don't have programming errors. Check your site with NetMechanic's HTML Toolbox to see if you have problems with your site.

- Frequency of updates. Search engines like sites that update frequently. They don't like to send their users to stale sites. More updates, more points.

- Traffic and time users spend on your page. The search engines feel that if you have significant traffic and the users spend time on your site, it must be a valuable resource. They like their users to feel that they have been provided with a valuable resource—more points.

Step 8. Get Yourself on the Maps

All the major search engines show the same sequence of results. At the top of the page are sponsored listings, next is the map, and then the organic listing. If you have a bricks-and-mortar operation, get yourself on the map! How do you do this? Search in Google ("How do I get on Google Maps?" The URL is way too long for me to provide here ☺), follow the links, fill in the form. Repeat for Yahoo! and Bing. It's free.

Step 9. Manually Submit Your Site to the Search Engines

Search engine submissions need to be handled manually rather than by an automated application. Google and Yahoo! Search both require you to type in your Web address as well as a code that is embedded in a graphic on the submission form page. The text that is embedded on that page is dynamically generated, meaning that it is different for each visitor. Submission software would be unable to read the text embedded in the graphic and, therefore, would be unable to input the required code into the submission form.

To add your site to:

- Google, go to *http://www.google.com/addurl*

- Yahoo!, go to *http://siteexplorer.search.yahoo.com/submit*

- Bing, go to *http://www.bing.com/webmaster/SubmitSitePage.aspx.*

Internet Resources for Chapter 2

I have developed a great library of online resources for you to check out regarding search engine friendliness. This library is available on my Web site, *http://www.SusanSweeney.com,* in the Resources section, where you can find additional tips, tools, techniques, and resources.

I have also developed courses on many of the topics covered in this book. These courses are available on two of my Web sites, *http://www.SusanSweeney. com* and *http://www.eLearningU.com* (which contains other instructors' courses as well). These courses are delivered immediately over the Internet, so you can start whenever is convenient for you.

3

Web Site Elements That Keep 'Em Coming Back

There are many little things that will spice up your Web site to "keep 'em coming back." Learn the tips, tools, and techniques to get visitors to return to your site again and again. In this chapter, we cover:

- Why repeat traffic is important

- Attractive Web site content

- Feeds from your blogs and social media

- Contests, coupons, discounts, specials, and other repeat-traffic generators

- Blogs, podcasts, and RSS feeds

- Ensuring that you are bookmarked.

Rationale for Encouraging Repeat Visits

Just as you would want customers to visit your business frequently, so too online you want present and potential customers to visit often. The more often people visit your site, the more likely they are to purchase something. You want to ensure that the techniques you use to get repeat traffic are appropriate for your target market. For example, if you were having a contest on your site targeted toward children, you would not want to give away a bread-maker as the prize. That would be fine, however, if your target market was families or homemakers. You want to offer something of interest to the market you are targeting. If your target market is gardeners, then a free half-hour landscaping session or free flower bulbs might work.

I am a big proponent of leveraging everything you do for maximum marketing results. Almost every repeat-traffic generator provides an opportunity for permission marketing and also for viral marketing. Make sure you review the repeat-traffic generators you use on your site and incorporate the appropriate permission and viral marketing elements.

The more often a person visits your site:

- The more your brand is reinforced

- The more your target market feels a part of your community (and people do business with people they know and trust)

- The more likely they are to give you permission to stay in touch

- The more likely they are to tell others about you, your products, and your services

- The more likely you will be first in mind when they decide to buy.

Use Feeds for Repeat Visits

There are a number of **widgets** that enable you to add your most recent tweets or blog posts to your Web site. This provides fresh content on a regular basis to your site and a reason for your followers to visit. By doing this and providing a "Follow Me on Twitter" link close by, you will also grow your Twitter followers. There are several widgets and tools for this in the Resources section of my Web site (*http://www.SusanSweeney.com*).

Widgets

Widgets are small applications that provide functionality and content online.

Free Stuff—Everyone Loves It

Offering free things is a great way to increase traffic—everybody likes a freebie. If you provide something for free that is valuable to your target market, you are sure to have a steady stream of repeat traffic. When you have freebies or giveaways on your site, your pages can also be listed and linked from the many sites on the Internet that list places where people can receive free stuff. To find these listings of free stuff, simply go to a search engine and do a search on "Free Stuff Index" or "Free Stuff Links." You will be amazed at how many people are giving things away online.

You don't have to give something away to everyone. You could simply have a drawing every week. You could then ask entrants if they would like you to notify them of the winner, which again gives you permission to email them.

To get people into your restaurant, you could offer a coupon for a free dessert with purchase of an entrée. To get a number of people to visit your mechanic shop, you might have a buy-three-oil-changes, get-one-free coupon. You might also have a free gift upon joining for a fitness facility or a gym.

You should change your freebie often and let your site visitors know how often you do this. Something like "We change our free offer every single week! Keep checking back" or "Click here to be notified by email when we update" also works well.

Freebies make great Facebook posts and Twitter tweets. Remember: . . . leverage, leverage, leverage.

Freebies provide ideal viral marketing opportunities as well. Have a "Tell a friend about this site" button near the freebie so site visitors can quickly and easily tell their friends.

Everyone Wants the Best Price—Coupons and Discounts

Offer coupons and discount vouchers that can be printed from your site. By partnering with noncompeting businesses, and by offering their coupons to your visitors, you can get people to come back to your site again and again. For example, if you are a fitness facility, partner with a health food supplier and offer their coupons to your visitors. You can change the coupon daily or weekly to encourage repeat visits. People will come back to your site again and again if they know they can find good deals there. You can ask people if they want to be notified by email when you update the coupons on your Web site. This, once again, gives you the opportunity to present them with new information about your business. Offering coupons is a great idea if you have a physical location as well as a Web site. These can be your loss leaders to get customers to come into your business.

You can develop a coupon banner ad that links to your site, where the coupon can be printed. The banner ads should be placed on sites frequented by your target market. You can trade coupons with noncompeting sites that target the same market you do; your coupon on their site links to your site, and their coupon on your site links to their site.

By offering coupons from your Web site, you also cut down your overhead cost because people are printing the coupons on their own printers, thus not using your paper. Remember that you should have terms and conditions on the coupons that are available for printing. For example, you should have an expiration date. Someone could print a coupon, then visit your operation in a year and try to use it. You should try to have the expiration date close to the release of the coupon. This will create some urgency, enticing the visitor to use the coupon more quickly and then come back for more coupons.

We are seeing an increase in the number of coupon-related sites that are appearing on the Internet. CoolSavings.com (*http://www.coolsavings.com*) is an online coupon network where businesses can advertise and place coupons for their products and services, as seen in Figure 3.1. Sites like this are a good way to promote your business, for they receive a high amount of traffic. Another

Figure 3.1. CoolSavings.com offers coupons from businesses to people all over the USA.

benefit is that the traffic is already in a buying mood. CoolSavings.com has been a household name since it launched its national advertising campaign in the late 1990s. If you offer coupons from your site, it benefits you to be listed on these types of sites. If you are not aiming for a national appeal, you should search to find out if there are coupon networks in the geographic location that you are targeting. There are meta-indexes to sites with coupons or discounts from which you can be linked for greater exposure.

Coupons provide ideal social media and viral marketing opportunities—for example, "Send this coupon to a friend," tweet the link to the coupon, and make it a post on Facebook.

Specials, Promotions, and Packages

Everyone likes to get a deal. You might consider having a special promotions section on your Web site. You'll want to change your promotion fairly frequently and let your site visitors know: "We change our specials every week. Bookmark our site and keep checking back!"

You might employ permission marketing here as well: "We change our discount packages every week. Click here if you'd like to be notified when we update" or "Join our e-club and receive our e-zine, advance notice of deals, members-only e-specials, and other great stuff every week." If you send e-specials via email, make sure you give viewers a reason to visit your site and provide the appropriate hypertext links in the email.

Make it easy to have your site visitors tell their friends about your specials or vacation packages. Have a "Tell a friend about this special" or "Tell a friend about this package" or even a "Share This" button placed next to each one of your special promotions. You can leverage the viral marketing with an incentive: "Tell three friends about our special and be included in a drawing for (something appropriate for your target market)."

Again, look for other sites that are frequented by your target market when they are looking for related information to see if you can have your specials or packages promoted on their sites. Leverage by sending your specials, promotions, and packages as tweets or posts in your social media.

A Calendar of Events Keeps Visitors Informed

For certain types of businesses, a comprehensive, current calendar of events related to your business can encourage repeat visits. Your calendar should always be kept up to date and be of value to your readers. When someone is planning a trip to a particular destination, they are often interested in what's going on while they are there. Sometimes a great calendar of events can encourage a visitor to stay longer.

A calendar of events can encourage a lot of repeat traffic as long as the calendar is kept current and complete. Again, you can ask people if they'd like to be notified via email when you update your calendar of events.

If you have a great calendar of events, you can encourage others to use it by providing a link to it from their Web site. This offer works well because it is win-win—you are providing them with great content that is kept current and they are providing you with traffic.

If you don't have the time or inclination to develop your own calendar of events but one would be great content for your site, you might provide a link from your Web site to a calendar you consider top-notch. If you do this, make sure your link opens a new browser window rather than taking the visitor from your site to the referred site.

Luring Customers with Contests and Competitions

Contests and competitions are great traffic builders. Some sites hold regular contests on a weekly or monthly basis to generate repeat visitors. Holding contests is also a great way to find out about your target market by requesting information on the entry form (Figure 3.2).

Having a contest with your product or service as the prize or part of the prize is great, as all contest entrants are telling you that they are a potential customer. They wouldn't enter the contest if they didn't want the prize.

You can simply request that people fill out an electronic ballot to enter the contest. If you want to find out something about the people entering, ask them to answer an appropriate question or two. If you want to do some market research, again, ask a question or two. Make it easy and unobtrusive. The more fields they have to fill out, the fewer people will enter your contest. Be selective with the questions you ask.

If your product or service is appropriate for a prize or part of the prize for other people's contests, the benefits can be many:

- You can receive exposure for your business if the contest site has a significant number of visitors.

- A link from the contest site will give you targeted traffic.

Figure 3.2. Contests are a great way to encourage repeat traffic.

- The link will help your search engine positioning. (See Chapter 13 on links.)

You might have contestants answer three questions relating to your business on the entry form. Of course, to find the answers to the questions, the visitor has to visit a number of pages on your site, and the three questions are marketing related, sending the visitor to pages that may influence the sale or get them to take a desired action. A question like "What do you get when you join our e-club?" will take them to your e-club sign-up page to find that they get 15 percent off their next order when they join the e-club. Chances are they'll sign up while they are on the page.

You can have the contest be one where you get information about your target market. When contestants enter the contest, have them rank what influences their buying decision. The information you request can also provide you with demographic or psychographic information.

Allow site visitors to enter your contest often. It boggles my mind when I see contests that limit the number of times a visitor can enter. The objective of the contest is to get visitors back to your site on a regular basis! I'd suggest that to accomplish this objective it might be more appropriate to tell your Web site visitors to "Enter today! Enter often!" "Bookmark this site—The more times you enter, the more chances you have to win!"

You might consider changing the information on the contest Web page around the entry form on a regular basis. Create Web site stickiness by providing links to other areas of your site—perhaps to other repeat-traffic generators you are using on your site, such as your coupons or your e-specials.

Whatever type of contest you determine best meets your marketing objectives, be sure you encourage permission marketing ("Join our eClub to be notified when we have a new contest") and viral marketing ("Tell a friend about this great contest"). Tweet it out. Post it on your Facebook fan page. Leverage, leverage, leverage: "Tell five friends and receive five extra ballots for yourself."

Make your contest conditional: "Sign up to receive our weekly e-specials and be included in our drawing for (something of interest to your target market)."

Before you go ahead with holding any kind of contest, find out if any legal issues concern you. There may be restrictions that you are not aware of. (For instance, you might be required to purchase a legal permit to hold lotteries.) You should also remember to ask the entrants the email address where they want to be notified of the winner. This, again, grants you permission to email them to tell them who the winner is, and also to inform them of the new contest or specials that you might have on your site that month.

You want to promote your contest through your social media accounts, public and private mail list postings, group postings, your email signature file, press releases, and links from contest sites.

It always amazes me when I see an online contest where the winner is announced only on the Web site. What a missed opportunity! If your product or service is part of the prize, the people who entered the contest have identified themselves as potential customers. Don't let them get away! As much as contest owners might like to think that all the people who entered the contest are anxiously awaiting the date the contest ends and the winner is announced (perhaps they have even put a reminder in their scheduler) so that they can beat a path back to your site to see if they were the winner—it's not going to happen! To take full advantage of having the contest and achieving your objectives, you want to send an email to all contest participants notifying them of the winner and, in the same email, offering them the contest prize at a discount available only to the contest entrants for a limited time, or for the first 20 respondents. In the same email you also may want to tell them about your new contest and provide a link back to the new contest entry form.

Creating Useful Links from Your Site

Provide visitors with links to other sites similar to yours or a meta-index of links that would be of interest to your target market (Figure 3.3). If you are a supplier of skates and accessories and you cater to hockey players, you might

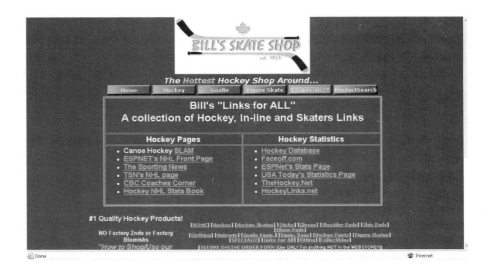

Figure 3.3.   Bill's Skate Shop provides useful links for hockey, in-line, and skater enthusiasts.

develop a list and links to all the hockey rinks in your area. If your target market is figure skaters, you might have a list and links to all the figure skating clubs in your area.

Do not put outbound links on your home page. Place them down a level or two after the visitors have seen all the information you want them to see before you provide the links away from your site.

Links can be incorporated in two ways. The first is where clicking the link loads the new page in the same browser window. (It replaces the content of your page with the content of the linked page.) The second and preferred method is to have the link open a new browser window. (Your page stays where it is and the content from the linked page opens up in the new browser window.) This is preferred because once visitors are finished with the new page, they can close the new browser window and your page is still there in the "old" browser window. Try exchanging links with others so you receive a link from their site to your site. As long as the links are of value to your visitors, people will come back to use your resource.

You might consider asking visitors if they are interested in being notified when you update your list of links or just make updates to your site in general. By offering this, if they choose to participate, you have the opportunity to send people an email message and remind them about your site while presenting them with new information about what might be going on with your site.

Providing a "Featured Tip" or "Tip of the Day/Week" to Encourage Repeat Visits

Have a section that offers cool tips that relate to your business, your products or services, or your target market, as in Figure 3.4. These tips can be from one sentence to one paragraph long. In the example shown in Figure 3.4, Cosy Homes provides a "Quick Tip of the Week." This tip is about watering your garden, but they change to a different subject every week. You can be guaranteed that homeowners will return to this site on a regular basis to read the quick tip of the week.

If visitors find your advice helpful, they will return repeatedly to see what interesting piece of information you have displayed that day. Ask your visitors

Figure 3.4. Cosy Homes provides a "Quick Tip of the Week." Tips of the day, week, or month can encourage repeat visitors.

if they would be interested in receiving the tip via email or if they would like to be notified when the tip has been updated so they can then visit your Web site. Encourage people to send the tip to a friend. You can also encourage others to use your tip on their Web site as long as they provide a link back to your site as the source. You can go a step further and syndicate your content, putting it up on appropriate sites to be accessed and made available by anyone looking for content for their newsletter, e-zines, or Web sites. You can also make it available to other sites by way of an RSS (really simple syndication) feed.

All of these techniques work equally well for a featured section on your site. What is featured will be different for different Web sites.

This technique has been used very effectively by a number of businesses—featured treatments by spas, featured destination of the week by travel agencies, gardening tip of the week by gardening sites, ski tip of the week by ski hills, golf tip of the week by golf courses, or fishing tip of the week for fishing camps. There are as many options for tips and featured sections as there are businesses.

MP3s/Podcasts/Videos

Many sites are incorporating downloadable audio content, videos, or podcasts (see Chapter 23 for more details on video and podcasting) and are adding new content on a regular basis to encourage repeat visitors.

This is becoming very popular because people like to download and listen to this type of content at their own convenience; they can do an hour of research or planning while working out, or sitting on the beach, or riding the subway, or traveling by air.

If you do plan to add video or podcasts on a regular basis, you will want to let visitors to your Web site know that you have new podcasts available every week, every two weeks, or every month, depending on how often you are prepared to develop these.

Leverage this repeat-traffic generator with permission marketing by asking them if they'd like to receive an email when you have new downloads available. Allow them to subscribe through RSS. Use the updates as fodder for your social media applications.

Once you have developed podcasts, you might want to make them available and downloadable through a number of the online podcast directories like Podcast.net (*http://www.podcast.net*) and syndication sites like TubeMogul (*http://www.tubemogul.com*).

Figure 3.5. When you see a "Bookmark this site now!" or "Bookmark us!" call to action, nine times out of ten you will at least consider it.

Ensuring That Your Site Gets Bookmarked

Encourage visitors to add your site to their Favorites or Bookmarks in their browser or to add it to the social bookmarks. To get them to add to their Favorites or Bookmarks, you would display the call to action: "Bookmark This Site!" (Figure 3.5.) at appropriate parts of your site. A call to action is often effective—it's amazing how often people do what they are told to do! Make sure the title of the page that has the "Bookmark this site!" clearly identifies your site and its contents in an enticing way, because the title is what appears in the bookmark file as a description. Whenever I see "Bookmark this site now!" I always consider it. Sometimes I do and sometimes I don't, but I always consider it. Often, when the call to action is not presented, I don't think about it and don't bookmark it. Then, days later when I want to go back there, I wish I had remembered to bookmark it.

Share This/Add This

Repeat-traffic generators are things that people want to tell others about. People like to spread the word about great deals, specials, promotions, coupons, and the like. Make it easy for them to do so with tools like ShareThis (*www.sharethis.com*) (Figure 3.6) or AddThis (*www.addthis.com*) (Figure 3.7). These tools are free widgets that make it easy for your visitors to quickly and easily spread the word through Facebook, Twitter, Digg, and a host of other services.

These tools also have amazing capabilities. AddThis has automatic translation into over 50 languages. It also automatically optimizes itself for each visitor to your site. If a user usually shares to Facebook, Digg, and Twitter, these will be the first ones presented. AddThis also provides analytics to show you the most popular content that visitors are sharing.

Social Bookmarking

Wikipedia defines *social bookmarking* as "a method for Internet users to share, organize, search, and manage bookmarks of Web resources. Unlike file sharing, the resources themselves aren't shared, merely bookmarks that reference them. Descriptions may be added to these bookmarks in the form of metadata, so that other users may understand the content of the resource without first needing to download it for themselves. In a social bookmarking system, users save links to Web pages that they want to remember and/or share. These bookmarks are usually public, and can be saved privately, shared only with specified people or groups, shared only inside certain networks, or another combination of public and private domains. The allowed people can usually view these bookmarks chronologically, by category or tags, or via a search engine." We discuss social bookmarking further in Chapter 13 on links.

Internet Resources for Chapter 3

I have developed a great library of online resources for you to check out regarding elements that keep people returning to your Web site. This library is available on my Web site, *http://www.SusanSweeney.com,* in the Resources section, where you can find additional tips, tools, techniques, and resources.

I have also developed courses on many of the topics covered in this book. These courses are available on two of my Web sites, *http://www.SusanSweeney.com* and *http://www.eLearningU.com* (which contains other instructors' courses as well). These courses are delivered immediately over the Internet, so you can start whenever is convenient for you.

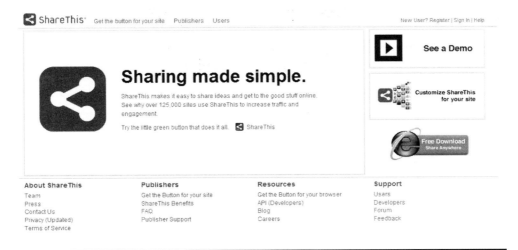

Figure 3.6. ShareThis makes it easy for visitors to share the repeat traffic generators on your site.

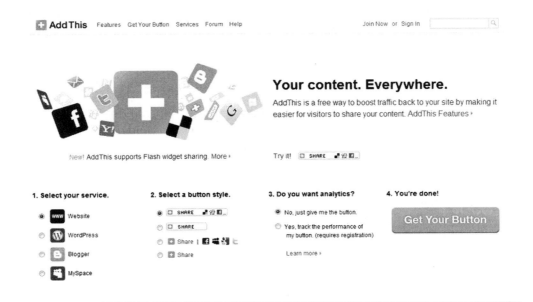

Figure 3.7. AddThis is another widget that makes it easy for visitors to share your site.

4

Permission Marketing

Permission marketing is an extremely important aspect of Internet marketing for any business. While legislation imposes restrictions on what you can and cannot send via email, permission marketing can be a valuable asset to any marketing campaign if it is used in the right way. This chapter provides details on what permission marketing is and how it can be incorporated into your site. Chapter 12 on private mail list marketing provides all the details on how it is sent, how to grow your database, and how to make sure your permission-based email is not treated as spam.

Permission Marketing Explained

Permission marketing boils down to asking your target market and Web site visitors for their permission to send them information on a regular basis. Many businesses compete for the attention of their target market on a daily basis, but it is very difficult to break through all of the advertising clutter the market is already receiving.

The key to a successful permission marketing campaign is to get your target market to willingly volunteer to participate. In order to get your target market do this, whatever it is you are proposing must be of value to them. Remember, before your target market agrees to participate in your permission marketing campaign; they will stop and ask themselves, "What's in it for me?" If they see no benefit in participating, then they will not participate—it's that simple.

Chapter 3 discusses many ways to encourage repeat visits to your Web site. Repeat-traffic generators provide great opportunities for permission marketing. A few examples include:

- "We update our packages every week! <u>Join our e-club</u> to be notified as soon as we update."

- "<u>Join our e-club</u> and receive our biweekly newsletter filled with coupons and information on new products and packages."

- "We constantly update our Calendar of Events. Keep checking back or <u>Join our e-club</u> if you'd like to be notified by email every time we update."

With legislation rapidly evolving, I expect that the next round will allow you to send only those things that people have specifically requested. That is, if someone has given you permission to send them your e-specials, you don't have their permission to send your newsletter or your last-minute discounts. It might be a good idea to consider integrating your permission marketing requests with an e-club.

If you have an e-club and encourage people to "Join our e-club to receive member-only packages, new coupon offers, advance notice of upcoming events, and other great specials available only to e-club members," you are essentially getting umbrella permission to send all types of marketing information.

Permission marketing is extremely effective because it's not intrusive. Your target market volunteered to receive your information because it is of interest to them. Because of this, your target market is expecting to receive your information and is more likely to take the time to view it and be receptive to it. When implemented correctly, permission marketing can be a valuable asset in acquiring new customers and maintaining relationships with existing ones.

Uses of Permission Marketing

Permission marketing is a great way to increase your online success. There are many ways in which you can integrate permission marketing with many other Internet marketing tools like repeat-traffic generators, customer loyalty programs, newsletters, surveys, contests, and so on. Chapter 3 covers many repeat-traffic and customer-loyalty-building tools that you can use on your Web site. Permission marketing is an excellent way to enhance and leverage the use of those tools—a few of which are covered in depth in this chapter.

Newsletters are one of the most popular resources for integrating permission marketing on many sites. With newsletters you can ask visitors if they would like to receive notification of new spa treatments, new investment opportunities, family getaways, updates to your site, industry news, and so on—whatever might be of interest to your target market. People who sign up to receive your newsletter do so because they have a clear interest in the information you have to offer. In your newsletter you can integrate strategic promotional opportunities to encourage readers to come back to your site or to take some other course of action.

If your newsletter is about recent happenings in the home-improvement industry, or new activities happening at your local library, then encourage readers to "follow this link" to see the updates or additional details. When they click on the link, take them to the particular page that has that specific content on your Web site.

A newsletter is a great way to keep in front of your target market and constantly remind them of your presence. Permission marketing opens the door for communication with your target market; this is an important step in building a long-lasting and profitable relationship with them.

Personalization

Make it easy, keep it simple! When asking permission to communicate with your target market, don't have them complete a long form where they have to provide all kinds of information. You want to make it as easy and as simple as possible for your target market to give you permission.

Have a simple form where they have to provide only their email address and their first name. It is important to get their first name so that you can personalize your communication. You want to personalize the text in the body of the message.

Most mail list software programs these days allow for easy personalization of all messages. You want to use a software program that manages all the permissions—the unsubscribes as well as the subscribes. See Chapter 12 on private mail list marketing for details.

Sell the Benefits

You need to sell the benefits of your e-club and the communication a visitor will receive when he or she becomes a member.

People are inundated with junk email on a regular basis and need to be "sold" on why they should subscribe to or join your communication list. As stated before, they need to know what's in it for them. "Join our weekly newsletter" just doesn't cut it. Something that states "Join our e-club to receive our members-only specials, coupons, and sweepstakes" will get you more subscribers. You have to know your target market well and know what is enticing enough to get their permission.

Cooperative Permission Marketing

Cooperative marketing is where you form an alliance with other sites that are trying to reach the same target market as you. Once you have found the appropriate sites, you come up with a way to do some win-win marketing together. For example, if you have a monthly newsletter, you can allow subscribers to sign up to receive your alliance partners' newsletters at the same time they sign up to receive yours. In return, your alliance partners do the same. This same technique can be used for many other repeat-traffic generators like coupons, e-specials, e-zines, etc. Get innovative!

Incentive-Based Permission Marketing

Increase the response to any permission marketing opportunity by offering an incentive. For example, "Join our eClub today and receive 15% off your next stay with us." This is exactly what Myer Hotels of Branson, Missouri has done, as you can see in Figure 4.1.

You can also try offering a free gift to new e-members or subscribers. It could be a discount on a purchase over $50, a free shampoo with a haircut, or extra reward points; just make sure it is of interest to your target market.

A Closing Comment on Permission Marketing

Permission marketing adds leverage to your online marketing campaigns. Once you are in front of your target market, you want to take every opportunity to stay there and continue to communicate with them time and time again. Permission marketing helps you achieve this, but it is a game of give and take. You give them a reason to give you permission to send them email—they give

Join Our e-Club & Save!

Join our e-Club today and receive 15% off your next stay with us!

Here are some benefits of e-Club membership:

- Priority notification of package specials
- Special discounts and benefits
- Notice of upcoming events
- Exclusive offers with printable coupons
- What's new in Branson, Missouri

And when you sign up today, you'll receive a coupon worth 15% off your next stay with us!

To receive Branson information, special hotel deals and values, please fill out the following information and click 'submit.' Once you click 'submit' a new page will appear. All you need to do is print that page and present it at check-in at any of our locations.

Fields marked with an asterisk (*) are required.

* First
Name

Figure 4.1. Myer Hotels provides a list of incentives to join their e-club.

you the permission you are looking for; you take their personal information and they take your valuable content via your newsletter. There is a trade-off and the cycle continues.

Over time, you will gain more knowledge about your target market, which will empower you to provide them with a better overall experience in dealing with your company through better targeted promotions and better fulfillment of customer needs. See the dynamic personalization coverage in Chapter 12.

To summarize, permission marketing can return a much higher response rate over intrusive advertising; it can increase sales, build your brand, and help develop relationships with your target market; all while being cost-effective.

See Chapter 12 for more tips, tools, techniques, and resources related to permission marketing.

Internet Resources for Chapter 4

I have developed a great library of online resources for you to check out regarding permission marketing. This library is available on my Web site, *http://www. SusanSweeney.com,* in the Resources section, where you can find additional tips, tools, techniques, and resources.

I have also developed courses on many of the topics covered in this book. These courses are available on two of my Web sites, *http://www.SusanSweeney. com* and *http://www.eLearningU.com* (which contains other instructors' courses as well). These courses are delivered immediately over the Internet, so you can start whenever is convenient for you.

5

Spreading the Word with Viral Marketing

Have you ever visited a Web site and found an article, a coupon, a special, or something else that impressed you so much that you immediately sent an email to your friends about it? If you have, you've already been bitten by the viral marketing bug! Viral marketing, which is often referred to as "word-of-mouse" marketing, is a low-cost, highly effective way to market your product or service using the Internet. Just like a flu virus in humans, viral marketing replicates and propagates itself online. Viral marketing enables you to capitalize on referrals from an unbiased third party—the consumer!

The power that peers and reference groups have over the purchasing decision is phenomenal. Similar to how a positive testimonial from a reliable source can add credibility to a product or service, the opinions of friends, business associates, and family can also help influence a consumer's purchasing decision. By implementing various viral marketing techniques on your Web site, you are provided with a dynamite opportunity to leverage the opinions of your Web site visitors.

There are many viral marketing opportunities provided by social media that will be covered in the various social media chapters.

In this chapter, we cover:

- How you can use viral marketing to increase traffic

- Word-of-mouth viral marketing

     – Pass-it-on viral marketing

     – Tell-a-friend scripts

- Various ways to leverage your viral marketing campaigns

- Incentives to encourage viral marketing.

Capitalizing on Viral Marketing Opportunities

Viral marketing can be one of your most powerful online marketing techniques, using the power of associations to spread the word. Today we see several common forms being used:

1. Word of mouth—such as "Tell a friend," "Send this coupon to a friend," or "Recommend this service package to a friend"

2. Pass it on—when we receive an e-zine, a newsletter, e-specials, or a funny or branded video and then forward it to friends

3. Product or service based—when a free tool or application is used online and that tool includes an embedded marketing message

4. "ShareThis" button (Figure 5.1) on your site.

Word of Mouth

You can use viral marketing techniques in a number of different ways throughout your Web site. By placing a "Tell a friend about this lawn care service" or "Share this product information with a friend" button on your site, you enable users to quickly and easily spread the word about your site and your products and services.

Visitors can click on the button, provide appropriate information in the "To" and "From" fields (including name and email address of both the recipient and the sender), and include a brief message. Although the message is personalized, you can include additional information, including details about the service, your product, the price, and a link directly to the page where the recipient can make a purchase. Because the message is personalized from a friend, the recipient will see the friend's name in the "From" field. Because it comes from

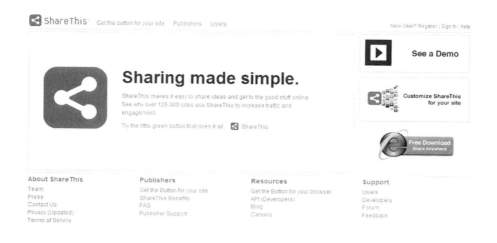

Figure 5.1.   The free ShareThis widget enables easy viral sharing of your site.

someone they know and trust, they are more apt to open the email and visit the site to find out more about the product than they would be if the email came from a traditional corporate email campaign.

In addition to the aforementioned techniques, there are many different ways you can implement viral marketing techniques on your Web site. If you have a newsletter on your site, you can add a "Tell a friend about this newsletter" button.

You can also incorporate a message in the body of your email newsletter encouraging readers to forward a copy to friends they think would benefit from the information included in the newsletter. You should also include information in the message on how to subscribe to the newsletter for those recipients who receive the newsletter from a friend. The recipients will then be able to send a copy of the newsletter to their friends, who will in turn be presented with the opportunity to subscribe and regularly receive the newsletter. The opportunities for viral marketing are endless.

Below the fold

Content of a Web page that is not seen by the visitor unless he or she scrolls down the page.

A good word-of-mouth viral marketing strategy enables a visitor to your site or a recipient of your email to share your site or email content with others with just one click of a button or link. The design and placement of that link or button is critical to the success of the campaign. Most people don't scroll **below the fold**.

You should look to every repeat-traffic generator you have on your site for viral marketing opportunities. Repeat-traffic generators like coupons, newsletters, e-specials, and contests all provide ideal opportunities for "Tell a friend" or "Send a copy to a friend" links and buttons. Once you have determined the viral marketing techniques you are going to use, you want to make it easy for the site visitor or email recipient to spread the word.

To be effective, you have to make it obvious what you want your visitors to do. Use a call to action to get them to do it. A button with "Send this coupon to a friend" or "Tell a friend about this e-special" works well. Don't assume that people will take the time to open their email program and send an email to a friend about your e-special or coupon or will include the URL to the page on your Web site just because you have a great offer—it doesn't happen! You have to make it easy.

Here are some tips to make your viral campaign effective:

- Have a fantastic button or graphic that grabs visitors' attention.

- Provide a call to action telling the visitors what you want them to do.

- Place the button in an appropriate place away from clutter.

- Have the button link to an easy-to-use "Tell a friend" script. The "Tell a friend" script accepts the name and email address(es) of the friend(s) and the name and email address of your site visitor who is sending the message to a friend. You need to provide a section for a message (Figure 5.2). You might provide clickable options for this, such as "Thought this might be of interest" or "Knew you'd be interested in this."

- Give clear instructions on how to participate; make it simple, intuitive, and easy.

- Offer an incentive to encourage visitors to do what you want them to do: "Tell a friend and be included in a drawing for (something of interest to the target market)."

- Leverage, leverage, leverage: "Tell five friends and be included in a drawing for (something of interest to the target market)."

- Avoid using attachments in the message you want spread. This will avoid any potential technical problems with opening the attachments as well as allay any fears related to viruses.

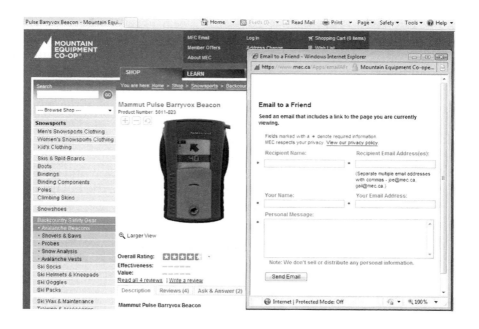

Figure 5.2. Mountain Equipment Co-Op uses "Email to a Friend" as one of its viral marketing techniques.

- Have your privacy policy posted. If the user is going to pass along a friend's email address, he or she wants to be assured that you will not abuse the contact information.

Viral marketing will only be successful if the content is good enough or valuable enough to be passed along.

Pass-It-On Viral Marketing

When we find a great resource, a funny video, or a cool **app**, we usually forward it to our colleagues or friends who we know will be interested in it. This old "they tell two friends and they in turn tell two friends" formula works very effectively online to enable you (with the right content) to reach a large segment of your target market.

For this type of viral marketing to be successful, you have to start with great content that recipients will want to share with others. It can take many forms:

- Apps

- Ebooks

- Fun videos

- Checklists

- Podcasts

- Articles.

> **App**
>
> *Application, often referred to as an app—A fun or useful software program.*

The pass-it-on viral marketing methodology works best using small files that can easily be spread around.

EBooks and iBrochures

Ebooks and iBrochures are very big these days. If you have great content, an ebook or iBrochure can do wonders to create great exposure for you, your site, and your products and services. Ensure that you have clear references to yourself and links to your Web site or social media accounts that provide a reason for people to click through. You might provide additional resources on your site or encourage people to visit for copies of other ebooks or iBrochures you have developed. Then market, market, market. Encourage e-zine and newsletter providers to send a copy to their subscribers, and promote it through your sig file, in newsgroups, and in publicly accessible mail lists.

Fun Videos

Nothing seems to spread faster on the Web than funny video clips. We've all seen the bear taking salmon from the fisherman. Sometimes these video clips are cartoons, seen one slide at a time with embedded audio, and other times they seem to be full-scale productions. Savvy marketers are developing very innovative videos that incorporate their brand, their destination, or their products, with the objective of having a winner that will be passed on many times.

Checklists

If you have a checklist that others might find useful, why not include links to your site in it and then provide it to your target market for use? For example, you might have a great checklist for retirement planning, meeting planning, wedding planning, or cruise planning. Think about your target market and what they might find useful. Always remember to encourage them to pass it on through viral marketing.

Podcasts, MP3s, or Audiozines

Today's technology enables you to very quickly and easily forward podcasts, sound bytes, MP3s, or audiozines. As long as the content is relevant, pertinent, and of value to your target market or people in the industry you serve, people will pass it on.

Articles

Writing articles that can be distributed as content for newsletters or e-zines is another form of viral marketing. Submit these articles to syndication sites so that they can be distributed to other sites to be used as Web site content. Just make sure that you have clearly stated that others are free to use your article as long as they include it in its entirety verbatim and include the Source box. The article should contain links to your site. The Source box should include information on you, your company, and your Web site.

You should track your viral marketing rate of infection. You want to know what is working and how fast it is working. You can always include a graphic in the article or ebook or digital game that is accessed from your site. Then you can use your Web traffic analysis to find information on the effectiveness of your pass-it-on viral marketing campaigns.

Internet Resources for Chapter 5

I have developed a great library of online resources for you to check out regarding viral marketing. This library is available on my Web site, *http://www. SusanSweeney.com,* in the Resources section, where you can find additional tips, tools, techniques, and resources.

I have also developed courses on many of the topics covered in this book. These courses are available on two of my Web sites, *http://www.SusanSweeney. com* and *http://www.eLearningU.com* (which contains other instructors' courses as well). These courses are delivered immediately over the Internet, so you can start whenever is convenient for you.

6

Great Content

Once Internet users have been drawn to your site using the key elements explained in this book, your next step is to keep them there and convert them from a visitor to a customer. You can achieve this by having a site with great content. A Web site with great content is one that not only meets, but exceeds the expectations of the Internet user.

If something is seen on the Internet three times, it then becomes an expectation. For example, if a consumer is searching the Internet for an all-inclusive golf vacation and three of the five sites they visit have a virtual tour of the golf course, club house, or resort rooms, the consumer suddenly expects to see a virtual tour on all golf resort sites. Any site that does not have a virtual tour will be seen as not keeping up with the latest trends.

By providing great content on your site, you will ensure a higher conversion rate among your Web site visitors and position yourself to be seen as a leader in your industry. Great content keeps visitors engaged and on your site longer. The longer they stay, the more they feel like they know you, the more they feel they are a part of your community, the more they trust you, and the more willing they are to do business with you—and as I've said before, and will say again, people do business with people they know and trust.

Exceeding customers' expectations, online and offline, should be part of every business's culture. Some companies get it and some don't. I stayed at Outrigger Waikiki while speaking at a conference and this note was on the night stand:

Aloha!

Ki-na'ole (flawlessness)—We do the right thing, the right way, at the right time, in the right place, for the right person, for the right reason, with the right feeling, the first time.

They obviously get it.

Ultimately, as with everything related to your Web site and Internet marketing, what is considered to be great content depends upon your objectives t market. In this chapter I will give you an overview of a variety ich, if appropriate for your Web site and implemented correctly, ful in attracting and converting your target market, including:

/OW" factor

media integration

- eBrochures and iBrochures

- Audio and video

- Podcasts

- Interactive maps

- Widgets

- Interactive elements.

The "WOW" Factor

In today's very competitive world your site has to have WOW factor—you need to have your visitors at hello with engaging content, interactivity, originality, some surprise or really cool feature that sets your site apart from your competition. From the second the visitor arrives at your home page or your landing page they need to know that you are different . . . that they have arrived at the perfect place.

Figure 6.1. Links to my social media and social networking profiles are prominently displayed on every page of my Web site, *http://www.susansweeney.com.*

Social Media Links

Provide links to all your social media and social networking profiles from your site (See Figure 6.1). If this is something you want your visitors to do make it prominent and include the links on a consistent place on every page of your site so that no matter where they entered you site they are exposed to the opportunity.

eBrochures and iBrochures

eBrochures are simply electronic brochures. They are similar to paper brochures in that they contain all the information you want your target market to read. An iBrochure is similar again, except that it implements elements of interactivity.

iBrochures implement Macromedia flash and page-turning capability with a simple point-and-click format, as if the viewer is turning the pages of a brochure or magazine. iBrochures can also implement interactive maps and calendars.

Electronic brochures (see Figure 6.2) are a great way of providing an easily accessible, easily updated means of communicating with existing and prospective

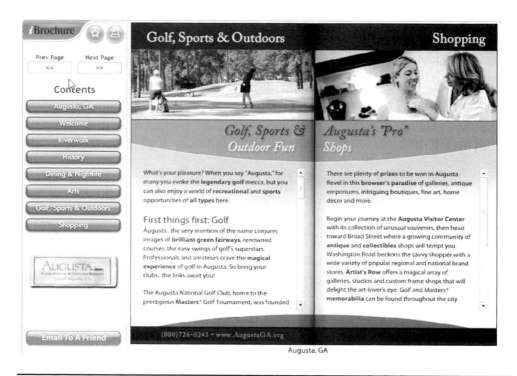

Figure 6.2. An iBrochure for Augusta, Georgia tourism.

customers. Both eBrochures and iBrochures complement your existing Web site and branding strategy and are covered in more depth in Chapter 21.

Audio and Video

Audio and video are great forms of media that can be used to connect to potential customers and communicate exactly why your packages, services, or products are what they need.

Through audio and video, a certain feeling can be communicated that is difficult to attain through text alone—whether it be the blood-pumping adventure of white-water rapids or a warm, welcoming country bed and breakfast. Use these forms of media to your full advantage in communicating the character and customized value of your business, services, and products to your potential customers.

YouTube makes video integration into your Web site very easy. See Chapter 13 for details on using YouTube's embedded code to very quickly and easily add video to your site.

Today we are seeing intriguing blue or green screen video productions where a person appears in video and talks to the Web site visitor as the enter a page. With this technology a subject is recorded in front of a blue or green screen. Actually any solid color will do but blue and green are the most common. Software is then used to replace the solid color with another video clip or a still picture.

Podcasts

Podcasting, in its simplest form, relates to making available a series of audio and/or video files from your Web site. These files can be listened to or viewed on your Web site, downloaded to the visitors personal computer, any MP3 player (not just the Apple iPod), and many mobile devices. You can allow visitors to subscribe to them through an RSS feed.

Podcasts are a great way of keeping your target markets up to date on special events, new package deals, industry news, etc. They are a great way of keeping communications with your target market open and a great way to establish yourself as an expert in your industry. Podcasting is covered in more depth in Chapter 23.

Interactive Maps

A fundamental component that is missing in many online transactions is being able to see where you are going and what is in the surrounding area. This is where the role of interactive maps comes in.

An interactive map is just that—a map that your Web site visitors can interact with. It is a map of a specified region that has integrated interactive multimedia functionality. These interactive multimedia capabilities give users the ability to explore the maps in much more depth. Interactive maps are great for many industries because they give you the opportunity to show consumers where your business is located, as well as other related or complementary businesses in your local area. A hotel, for example, will identify their location on the map and also show where the nearest golf courses, ski hills, skating rinks, basketball courts, football fields, shopping, restaurants, churches, and

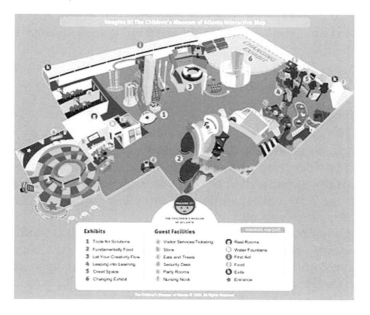

Figure 6.3. An interactive map for the Children's Museum in Atlanta *(http://www. childrensmuseumatlanta.org/visitors/museumfloormap)* incorporates audio and details as you mouse over different locations on the map.

so on, are in relation to the hotel. Interactive maps can link to visual images, a voice-guided tour, videos, or any other marketing component you can dream of. (See an example of an interactive map in Figure 6.3)

Widgets

There are lots of places online to find free tools or shareware to add to your Web site to create some "WOW" factor. Google Gadgets and Widgetbox include great tools like driving directions to your location, weather forecasts for your area, a currency convertor for international customers, countdown clocks for time sensitive purchases, and much, much more. Check out Google Gadgets at *http://www.google.com/webmasters/gadgets/foryourpage/index.html* and Widgetbox at *http://www.widgetbox.com*. Widgetbox has tons of great widgets to incorporate your social media into your Web site.

Interactive Elements

Engaging your Web site visitors with interactive elements is not only a great way to get them to stick around your site longer, but also a great way to keep them coming back—and if you use the viral marketing techniques discussed throughout this book, you could get even more visitors to your site. There are many types of interactive elements. You have to choose the ones that are right for your site given your objectives, your target market, and your products.

The Web site Calories per Hour (*http://www.caloriesperhour.com*) provides great interactivity for its target market. It offers resources, information, and peer support for healthy and sustainable weight loss. It also offers interactive elements such as a food calculator, activity calculators, weight-loss calculators, and BMI, BMR, and RMR calculators. These weight-loss calculators are fun, interactive, and a great way to get Web site visitors to return again and again.

Let's have a closer look at one of the calorie calculators, the running calculator. The running calculator will calculate the calories burned by someone of a particular weight running for a specified distance. This is a great tool for someone who is trying to keep track of the amount of calories he or she burns. It's extremely easy to use; all you have to do is enter your weight in pounds and the distance in the appropriate fields, and the calculator does the rest for you.

Through the many free weight-loss calculators they make available, the Calories per Hour Web site is successful in helping people keep track of their weight loss progress, at the same time creating stickiness and repeat traffic.

Internet Resources for Chapter 6

I have developed a great library of free online resources for you to check out regarding great Web page content. This library is available on my Web site, *http://susansweeney.com*, in the Resources section, where you can find additional tips, tools, techniques, and resources.

I have also developed courses on many of the topics covered in this book. These courses are available on two of my Web sites, *http://www.SusanSweeney. com* and *http://www.eLearningU.com* (which contains other instructors' courses as well). These courses are delivered immediately over the Internet, so you can start whenever is convenient for you.

7

Landing Pages

When you do online promotion, whether it be through social media, online advertising, newsletter promotion, or a pay-to-play campaign, you want to maximize the results of your effort. You want to take the interested visitors directly to the information they are looking for—not to your home page where they may have to navigate to get to the specific information. When done properly, creating a targeted landing page for an ad can greatly increase conversions, or the number of customers who act on your offer. In this chapter, we cover:

- What is a landing page?

- Considerations for landing page content

- Landing page layout

- Testing your landing page.

What Is a Landing Page?

A landing page is a Web page that is created specifically to respond to a marketing campaign you are running. You can't provide all the details and the opportunity to make the purchase in an ad, so you develop a landing page to follow through from the ad. When your target market clicks on the ad, they are taken to the landing page that was developed specifically for that ad. The action you want the target market to take might be to make a purchase, join your e-club, follow you on Twitter, become a fan on Facebook, view a virtual tour, or use your services. The key is that the landing page is usually geared toward a conversion, or converting the browsers into buyers.

The way your landing page is developed depends entirely on your business objectives, your target market, and your offer itself. The landing page should focus on the one thing you want the visitor to do—keep it focused.

The presentation and the content, or copy, of your landing page have a huge impact on the ability of the landing page to close the offer. We begin with a look at content for your landing page. There are a number of points to make note of when preparing content for a landing page:

1. Your landing page should be a continuation of your ad—repeat and expand on the offer presented in your ad. The ad is designed to generate interest and the landing page is designed to close the sale.

2. Your landing page should emphasize the benefits of your offer—this is what justifies the purchase.

3. Your landing page content should flow from the advertisement. If your ad promotes your virtual tour, then when visitors click through to the landing page, they should be given the opportunity to take that virtual tour. Take your target market where you want them to go. Tell them what you want them to do.

4. Your landing page should "speak" to your target market. Use their language and buzz words. Use the appropriate tone for this particular target market.

5. Your landing page should have a dynamite headline. Grab their attention!

6. Your landing page should be written for scanability. Internet users don't read; they scan.

7. Your landing page should promote the "value-added" portion of the offer that will help with your objectives. Free gift on arrival, a coupon, a discount toward a future purchase, or the number of reward points earned with purchase—all of these add to the value of the offer.

8. Your landing page should create a sense of urgency—get your visitors to do what you want them to do NOW! If they leave your site without making the purchase, it is often unlikely you'll get another opportunity. Using appropriate calls to action like "Call Today!," telling the target market that "there are limited quantities" or "limited space available," and techniques like time-stamping the offer with an expiration date create a sense of urgency that encourages the target market to take immediate advantage of the offer.

9. Your landing page content should minimize risk. If you have a money-back guarantee, emphasize it! Anything that helps to close the deal should be prominently displayed.

10. Your landing page should ask for the sale—maybe multiple times and in multiple places. You don't get what you don't ask for.

11. Your landing page should include content that enhances your credibility—things like client testimonials or product or service reviews. Content that helps establish credibility also helps build trust, which is key to doing business online.

12. Your landing page should be optimized for the search engines. If you are running a promotion for just a couple of days, then odds are you do not want your landing page indexed by the search engines. In this case you would use your robot's exclusion protocol in your robots.txt file to tell the search engines not to index the page.

Once you have developed a dynamite landing page, you will want to do some testing to maximize your conversion; very few people get it perfect the first time. You will want to test different page content, format and lengths, different jargon and tones, different layouts, different offers, and a number of other things to find the right balance to best sell your product or service.

Considerations for Landing Page Content

Your most important information on the landing page should be above the fold. The fold is where the bottom of the browser window sits and additional scrolling is required to view the remaining content. This is what your target market sees when they land on your landing page. It is usually this content that encourages them to keep going or to click away.

Your landing page should focus on the one thing you want them to do. You want to eliminate anything that might distract the target market from doing what you want them to do.

Be wary of "banner blindness." People tend to not even notice the information that is in the standard banner ad areas. Stay away from having any content that looks like an ad in shape, size, and color.

Leverage the elements on this landing page. You want to leverage your landing page with your social media marketing—getting them to follow you on Twitter, become a fan or a friend on Facebook, subscribe to your channel on YouTube, etc. You want to give your visitors the option to sign up for your permission-marketing-based newsletter or e-club. You want to make use of the viral marketing tell-a-friend function. You do not want these elements to take over the page and distract the user, but you want to encourage these actions—be subtle!

Give your target market access to anything needed to get them to do what you want them to do. What information do they need? Pricing information? Privacy information? Your contact information? Make sure they have access to whatever they need.

Make sure the landing page looks great. Choose things like font types, styles, and color to your best advantage. Photography should be professionally done; your visitors can always tell the difference.

Provide your target customer with options on how to make the purchase. Prominently display alternative purchase options. Your visitor might be extremely interested in your offer, but not so comfortable making the purchase online.

All of the best-practices techniques that go into building a Web site apply to your landing page as well. The landing page still has to be cross-browser-compatible, easy to use, and quick to load. It should have clean code and effectively brand your business. See Chapter 1 for best practices.

Testing Your Landing Page

There is always something you can do a bit better to maximize your landing page results. There are any number of things you can test and tweak to refine your landing pages. Even the smallest changes can have a big impact. When running a marketing campaign, employ A/B testing to see which landing page techniques generate the best responses from your target market.

When performing A/B testing, you might do a split-run campaign where you run a marketing campaign that directs 50 percent of your target market to landing page A and the other 50 percent to landing page B.

Here are some items to consider when testing your landing pages:

Landing Page Content

1. Is short or long copy more effective?

2. Is it better for you to use bulleted lists to emphasize key points as opposed to paragraphs of information?

3. Does separating content with tag lines or headers increase the number of responses?

4. What happens if you bold or otherwise emphasize key points in your copy?

5. What impact does changing the writing style or tone of your copy have on your landing page's ability to convert?

Landing Page Layout and Presentation

1. What impact does changing the presentation of the offer itself have on results? "Buy one, get one free," "50% off," "1/2 price," "Save $100 off the list price," showing the original $200 price tag with a strikethrough and the new price next to it emphasized in bold red font as $100 are all different ways of presenting the same offer. Which method generates the best response from your target market?

2. Does your landing page perform better with vivid imagery, little imagery, or no imagery? Maybe showing different color shots of the same product if it is available in more than one color will boost sales. Try it.

3. What colors on the page elicit the most favorable responses from your target market? Does the contrast between the page copy and the background influence sales?

4. What font types, styles, and sizes are most effective?

5. How many navigation options work best on the landing page? Are you providing the target market with so many navigation options that they get distracted, or would the page be effective with more navigation options intact?

6. Where is the best position on the landing page to place the "buy," "order," or "reserve" button?

Capitalizing on any great campaign requires a great closing. Your closing is your landing page—a prime reason you never want to put all of your eggs in one basket. It is highly recommended that you test and refine your landing pages over time. This is by no means a complete list of items worth testing, but it is a good place to start.

It is best to test one element at a time so that you can measure results and determine the effectiveness of the new change. If you change too many items at once, it will be difficult to attribute how much of an impact the items you changed had on the effectiveness of that page. If you made three adjustments to your landing page at once, it might be that two of the three components have increased the response rate, but the third might have dragged it down a bit, so you are not quite reaching your potential. If you change just one element at a time, you can tell what impact your change has on the landing page's ability to convert.

This same testing logic applies to the online marketing campaigns you partake in as well. You want your marketing efforts and your landing pages to work together.

Today's Web traffic analytics and Web metrics software provide great information on what's working, what's not, and also the implications of testing elements (see Chapter 28).

Internet Resources for Chapter 7

I have developed a great library of free online resources for you to check out regarding landing pages. This library is available on my Web site, *http://susansweeney.com,* in the Resources section, where you can find additional tips, tools, techniques, and resources.

I have also developed courses on many of the topics covered in this book. These courses are available on two of my Web sites, *http://www.SusanSweeney.com* and *http://www.eLearningU.com* (which contains other instructors' courses as well). These courses are delivered immediately over the Internet, so you can start whenever is convenient for you.

8

Developing Your Pay-to-Play Strategy

It used to be that you could simply optimize your Web site using traditional organic search engine optimization techniques, as described in Chapter 2, which would enable you to place high in the major search engines and would create a great deal of exposure for your product or service offerings. This can still be accomplished; however, with thousands of Web sites competing for the top positions on a given search results page, it is becoming an increasingly more challenging task. This is why many businesses are leaning toward **PPC** online advertising models to generate targeted exposure for their sites, and in turn their services and products. So what options are available to enable businesses to create targeted exposure for their Web sites, and how can businesses with minimal advertising budgets utilize these advertising models to increase their visibility online? In this chapter, we cover:

> **PPC**
>
> *Pay per click refers to the advertising model in which advertisers pay when someone clicks on the ad and is delivered to their Web site.*

- Maximizing exposure through the Google, Yahoo! Search, Bing, and social media advertising networks

- Expanding your reach with contextual advertising

- Geo-targeting ads to better communicate with your target market

- Dayparting and how you can capitalize on increased traffic levels during specific time periods

- Developing effective landing pages for your ads.

Generating Targeted Traffic Using PPC Advertising

At the end of the day, the success of your search engine positioning strategy boils down to one thing—results! Over the past several years, many search engines have adopted various PPC advertising models that enable advertisers to pay for exposure on their search results pages, based on targeted keyword sponsorship. Advertisers pay for click-throughs to their Web site. Ads (or sponsored listings, as they are commonly called) appear on the results page of a search based on keywords.

The concept is very straightforward—advertisers bid on specific keywords or keyword phrases to impact the position of their text ads on search results pages, their ad appears when someone does a search on the chosen keywords or keyword phrases, and if (but only if) someone actually clicks on their ad and is delivered to their site, the advertiser pays. Using PPC, advertisers receive targeted leads delivered to their site, for a fee.

The key is that the lead is "targeted." Using traditional organic search engine optimization techniques can cause your site to appear at the top of search results, generating targeted traffic to your Web site, but even the leading search engines often return results that are not exactly what the searcher desires. What if your Web site always appeared when a searcher conducted a query using a targeted keyword relating to the products or services being promoted on your site? What if you could ensure that everyone interested in your packages, products, or services had the opportunity to click on your search engine listing to learn more about what you have to offer? These are the true benefits of developing your PPC, or pay-to-play, online promotional strategy. By participating in PPC, you generate targeted traffic to your site and you increase brand awareness for your organization, which ultimately results in increased sales for your business. Over the years, some programs have proven successful while others have failed, but at the end of the day, a handful of PPC programs have proven to be extremely successful. These programs include:

- Google AdWords (*http://adwords.google.com*)

- Yahoo! Advertising (*http://advertising.yahoo.com*)

- Bing (*http://advertising.microsoft.com*).

Ads on Facebook and other social media are covered in depth in the social media chapters.

All of the major PPC programs have in-depth tutorials, case studies, white papers, and tools to help you learn more about their programs and make them easy for you to use. Things are changing rapidly in this area, as the competition for your advertising dollar is fierce. Changes to these programs, whether we're talking about program updates, program features, new pricing, new tools, new offerings, or program enhancements, are being made on a regular basis.

In this chapter I provide a very basic overview of Google AdWords and the Yahoo! Advertising programs. Other programs you will want to check out include Bing, Ask, 7Search, and Kanoodle. For information on setting up and managing Facebook ads, see Chapter 20. The information included in this chapter is current as of the date of publication. For the absolute latest information on these programs, I strongly suggest you visit the advertising sections of all the major search engine Web sites.

Exploring PPC Campaigns in Google and Yahoo!

Google AdWords and Yahoo! Advertising have quickly become two of the premier online advertising vehicles for online businesses for several reasons. First and foremost, why wouldn't you want to place targeted ads on the Internet's top search engines to generate exposure for your business and your related products and services? In addition, by sponsoring keywords and phrases on a cost-per-click basis on such prominent Web portals, you are guaranteed one thing—targeted exposure.

Some PPC programs provide businesses with the opportunity to outbid each other for top placement of their ads. This means that businesses with large advertising budgets can dominate the top placements using these particular programs, which is not exactly fair to those businesses that cannot afford a high **CPC**.

Google AdWords and Yahoo! Advertising help to create a level playing field for all advertisers, meaning that even small businesses with a minimal budget can compete with large enterprises for premium listings. Businesses with large advertising budgets can set their CPC for particular keywords well above their competition,

CPC

Cost per click refers to the price paid by the advertiser each time a visitor clicks on the advertiser's ad or sponsored listing.

but this doesn't mean that their ads will appear above the competition. Google AdWords and Yahoo! Advertising rank each ad based on a combination of the ad's CPC and the ad's click-through rate. What this means is that if a business with a high CPC creates an irrelevant ad that does not generate any clicks, that ad slowly moves to the bottom of the listing of ads that appear on Google's search results page and on Yahoo!'s search results page and is ultimately removed. This enables businesses with a lower CPC, but more relevant ads, to position higher—at no extra cost!

How PPC Campaigns Work

Setting up a PPC campaign account in both Google and Yahoo! can be accomplished in 15 to 20 minutes by following a few simple steps. When preparing to launch a campaign, you first determine where you would like your ads to appear on the search engine's network of Web sites, and which languages you plan to target with your ads. You can choose to communicate your ads to the masses, or you can opt to geographically target your ads to specific locations—some even offer advertising to locations within a specific distance from your business's physical location. Now *that's* targeted advertising!

You then need to design an ad group for your PPC campaign in Google or Yahoo!. An ad group is a collection of one or more ads that you wish to display on the network of sites. Each ad consists of a headline and description that, if designed correctly, relate specifically to the keywords that are associated with the overall ad group. Once each ad in a given ad group is designed, you select targeted keywords that you wish to be associated with the ad group.

Why does an ad group contain one or more ads? Google's AdWords program and Yahoo!'s Advertising program are both designed to work effectively for advertisers, weeding out ads that are not generating targeted traffic for them. To illustrate, assume that a given ad group consists of five different ads relating to a specific topic, each with a unique headline and description. When an advertiser launches a campaign, Google AdWords and Yahoo! Advertising randomly display each ad in the ad group to the advertiser's target market. Eventually, certain ads in the ad group perform better than others, generating more click-throughs. When this happens, Google AdWords and Yahoo! Advertising then display only ads within the ad group that are generating results for the client, and they slowly remove the others from the rotation. This helps to maximize the effectiveness of the overall ad campaign.

When launching an ad campaign, you are given the opportunity to set a budget for your campaign. You can set a maximum CPC for each ad group along with a maximum daily budget for your campaigns.

If you are unsure of what your maximum CPC should be, or if you simply do not have the time to spend on such decisions, Google AdWords provides the "automatic bidding" feature. With sutomatic bidding you simply set your target budget, and the Adwords system does the rest, seeking out and delivering the most clicks possible within that budget. The automatic bidding tool considers keywords, competitive bids, ad positions, time of day, and many other factors to give you the most possible clicks for your money—automatically.

Both Google AdWords and Yahoo! Advertising offer excellent traffic-estimation tools that can help you estimate daily traffic for selected keywords and phrases. The traffic-estimation tool helps you fine-tune what your maximum CPC should be, based on your overall online advertising budget and campaign objectives. By manipulating the maximum CPC, you are able to determine what your daily expenditures would be based on traffic patterns associated with the keywords that you have selected, along with where your ads will be positioned during the campaign.

Where Do Your Ads Appear?

These paid listings usually appear separately from the organic results—sometimes these sponsored listings appear at the top of the page, sometimes they appear as a sidebar to the right of the page, and sometimes they appear at the bottom of the page.

When you implement a campaign on the Google AdWords network, your ads appear in more places than just within Google's search results. Through building relationships with some of today's top industry-specific Web sites and search portals, Google expands the reach of your ads to the masses. Popular Web sites such as the New York Times, AOL, Ask.com, and Earthlink all display AdWords' advertisements when a Web surfer conducts a search using those sites' search tools.

Similarly, when you implement a campaign on the Yahoo! Advertising network, your ads appear on all of the advertising partners' sites as well.

The network sites change from time to time, so if you want to appear on a specific site it is best to check for the latest list of sites included in the major search engine's advertising partner network.

Maximize Exposure with Contextual Advertising

Imagine that a consumer is currently in the market for a new speed boat and is viewing a recognized informational Web site to learn more about the latest in speed boats. If you were a salesperson in a traditional bricks-and-mortar store and a consumer wandered into your department, you would approach the consumer as if he or she were already semi-engaged in the sale, just trying to figure out what to buy. In a similar way, the latest advancement in contextual advertising enables you to reach those same consumers, but in the online marketplace.

To further illustrate the example, assume that you are that same consumer on the informational Web site and you are viewing a page of content that provides information on speed boats only. Accompanying the content on this page is a listing of ads for online retailers that are promoting speed boat packages for sale online. Because the ads relate directly to your area of interest, you click on a link, are directed to a Web site, and ultimately purchase the speed boat of your choice from the online retailer.

Similar to the way a Web surfer searches for information using a major search engine and is presented with PPC ads, contextual ads enable advertisers to promote their ad listings on content sites that relate to specific information (for example, speed boats). Contextual advertising provides advertisers with yet another opportunity to target specific customer segments with targeted advertisements. Both AdWords and Yahoo! Advertising currently offer advertisers the ability to take advantage of contextual advertising opportunities by promoting their ad listings on related content sites within their respective advertising networks.

This is even more common on social media networks like Facebook where ads can be very finely targeted based on keywords, interests, geography, age, sex, education, and a range of other criteria. See the details on Facebook advertising in Chapter 20.

Geo-Targeting Your Campaigns

Implementing a PPC strategy enables you to advertise to a mass audience, or to target Internet users in a specific geographic location. Both Google AdWords and Yahoo! Advertising PPC campaigns provide you with the opportunity to target customers not only on a state or provincial level, but also on a local level, by displaying advertisements only to potential customers conducting searches in your business's local area.

With AdWords alone, you can choose to target over 250 different countries in up to 14 different languages. You can also choose to advertise within over 200 different regions throughout the United States. Geo-targeting provides you with an increased level of control over where your ads are displayed and how they figure into your advertising budget. By targeting only those locations where you wish your ads to appear, you can maximize your online advertising dollars, whether you are working with a small or a large budget.

Again, geo-targeting of your ads in social media like Facebook and LinkedIn is covered in those chapters.

Dayparting

When you are analyzing your Web traffic logs, you will most likely notice that your traffic levels spike on a particular day of the week or during a specific time period throughout the day. When monitoring the performance of your PPC strategy, you can also note when searchers are more apt to click on one of your ads to visit your site and learn more about what you have to offer. If you notice a significant increase in your click-through rates at a specific time, you can capitalize on this increased visibility.

Adjusting your PPC advertising strategy to capitalize on traffic during a particular point of the day is what is referred to as "dayparting." Reports reveal that when you capture your target market when they are more apt to visit your Web site (for instance, during a particular time of the day, or on a particular day of the week), they will be more apt to click on your ad and ultimately convert to a customer. This strategy requires in-depth analysis of conversion rates, click-through rates, and general traffic levels (discussed more in Chapter 28). The basic premise behind dayparting is that advertisers increase their CPC during the time of the day when searchers will be most apt to view information on their products and services. By increasing your CPC during this time frame, you maximize the exposure for your services and products—provided that you are presenting the searcher with optimized ads.

Maximizing Your Exposure

Developing ads for your PPC strategy is not just a matter of throwing together a headline and description in the hopes that a customer will click on one of your ads. Well, it could be, but this strategy will not result in your meeting your campaign objectives of click-throughs and conversions. Your ads should be designed to entice the searcher, but be wary that if you create ads that are too inviting, you can rack up your click-through rate quickly without converting any visitors at all. The bottom line is that you do not want to entice uninterested searchers to your Web site, as you would be wasting your online advertising budget.

To avoid this issue, make sure that your ads relate specifically to the keywords they are associated with and make sure your message is clear. When a true potential customer views one of your ads, you want that person to say, "Wow, that's exactly what I am looking for." This ensures that your click-throughs are more targeted.

In addition to developing targeted ads for your campaigns, you also want to be sure that when searchers click on your ad, the page they are directed to provides them with information about what you are promoting. Too often, businesses simply point click-throughs to their Web site's home page, which requires the potential customer to navigate further through the Web site to find more information about the company, services, and products. This often results in wasted clicks and fewer conversions.

Instead, try pointing Web surfers to landing pages that are tailored to specific advertisements. You have to remember that people are not going to initiate contact or sign up for your mailing list or even buy simply by clicking on your ads—they want information. That's why you would never simply point a new customer to your online order form. However, if you develop a landing page that communicates the features and benefits of your services or products and provides the visitor with a clear "Order Now" call to action, you can increase the likelihood that the visitor will convert to a customer.

When developing landing pages for your PPC strategy, you should design various pages and test their effectiveness. (For more on landing pages, see Chapter 7.) The key thing to remember is that if someone is searching for "New York Pretzels," you do not want your landing page to say something unrelated, but rather to include a call to action that says "Click here for New York Pretzels." You want to make sure that you provide the viewer with the information that she or he is looking for. In addition, make sure that you do not overwhelm visitors with navigation options that would distract them from understanding the message you are trying to communicate. Clear communication of your value proposition is the key.

Maximizing Your Budget

One of the biggest mistakes that many businesses make is assuming that they have to bid into the number one position to make their PPC strategy work. Being number one is associated with being the best; thus it is very easy to let your ego get in the way of your marketing objectives. Bidding into the top positions for more competitive keywords generates optimal exposure, but it also blows through your budget more quickly than if your ads were appearing in the lower ranks. When creating the strategy for your PPC campaigns, you should develop a strategy to maximize both your daily budget and exposure for your business. Constantly bidding into top positions can result in having to start and stop your campaigns if the budget is not available to constantly maintain them.

To maximize the effectiveness of your budget, try bidding into the lower ranks to minimize your average CPC. This helps you to stay under your daily budget and lets you implement longer campaigns with your advertising dollars. Also, bidding on the most competitive keywords is not always the best strategy. Use the tools that are available with your PPC program to identify keywords that are proven to be effective but are not being capitalized on by your competitors. These are the words that can help you to drive targeted traffic to your Web site, but will have a minimal CPC as nobody else is sponsoring these words. Advertisers typically focus their efforts on the keywords that are most utilized by their target market and avoid keywords that are less popular.

There have been many books written on pay-per-click advertising, or pay-to-play as some like to call it, and many, if not all, are outdated as soon as they get to market due to the overwhelming rate of enhancements and changes that are occurring with the companies that offer PPC advertising. For the absolute latest information on these programs, I strongly suggest you visit the advertising sections of all the major search engine Web sites to get the more intricate details.

Internet Resources for Chapter 8

I have developed a great library of online resources for you to check out regarding pay-to-play strategies. This library is available on my Web site, *http://www.SusanSweeney.com,* in the Resources section, where you can find additional tips, tools, techniques, and resources.

I have also developed courses on many of the topics covered in this book. These courses are available on two of my Web sites, *http://www.SusanSweeney.com* and *http://www.eLearningU.com* (which contains other instructors' courses as well). These courses are delivered immediately over the Internet, so you can start whenever is convenient for you.

9

Email and Signature Files

Email is one of the most crucial forms of communication you have with your clients, potential customers, suppliers, and colleagues. A widely accessible and generally accepted form of business communication, email is a very cost-effective, time-efficient tool that has a high response rate. Email is used to build your community online, sell your products and services, provide customer service, reinforce brand awareness, and encourage customer loyalty.

In the online community, email is an extremely efficient way to build and maintain relationships. As a marketing tool, email is one of the most cost-effective ways to maintain an ongoing dialogue with your customers and potential customers.

However, with the overabundance of spam, spam-detection software, filtering of email, and anti-spam legislation, things are changing in the email world. It is becoming a challenge to make sure that your email is received, opened, and responded to.

This chapter focuses on individual emails that you send. Mass-marketing emails you send to your target market are more fully discussed in Chapter 12 on private mail list marketing.

In this chapter, we cover:

- Strategies for creating effective email messages

- Email netiquette

- Email marketing tips.

Making the Connection

Email is a communication medium, and as with all forms of communication, you do not get a second chance to leave a first impression. Email must be used appropriately. People receive large amounts of email each day, and the tips in this chapter will help to ensure that your email is taken seriously.

All kinds of files can be sent via email, including audio, video, data, pictures, and text. With an autoresponder, information can immediately be sent automatically to customers and potential customers 24 hours a day, 7 days a week, 365 days a year in response to their online requests. We discuss autoresponders in Chapter 10.

Email Program versus Mail List Software

The time has come where mail list software is essential for sending mass, permission-based, marketing email. In this chapter we talk about regular, day-to-day email. See Chapter 12 for the discussion on marketing email sent to a group and on private mail list marketing.

Effective Email Messages

Most people who use this medium get tons of email, including their share of junk email. Many use organization tools, filters, and blockers to screen incoming emails. The following tips will increase the effectiveness of your email communication to ensure that you have the best opportunity for your email to be opened, read, and responded to.

The Importance of Your Email Subject Line

The first thing most people do when they open their email program is start hitting the delete key. They have an abundance of mail in their inbox and they want to get rid of the clutter, so they delete anything that looks like spam or an ad. How do they determine what is junk? The subject line is usually the deciding factor. It is essential that your email subject line not look like ad copy.

Never send an email message without a subject line. Subject lines should be brief, with the keywords appearing first. The longer the subject line is, the more likely it will not be viewed in its entirety because different people set the viewable subject line space at various widths.

The subject line is equivalent to a headline in a newspaper in terms of attracting reader attention. When you read a newspaper, you don't really read it; generally you skim the headlines and read the articles whose headlines grabbed your attention. The same is true with email. Many recipients, especially those who receive a significant number of emails daily, skim the subject lines and read only the emails whose subject line grabs their attention. The subject line is the most important part of your email message because this phrase alone determines whether or not the reader will decide to open your email or delete it.

Effective subject lines:

- Are brief, yet capture the reader's interest

- Don't look like ad copy

- Build business credibility

- Attract attention with action words

- Highlight the most important benefits

- Are always positive

- Put the most important words first.

Effective subject lines should grab the reader's attention, isolate and qualify your best prospects, and draw your reader into the subheads and the text itself. Avoid SHOUTING! Using CAPITALS in your subject line is the same as SHOUTING AT THE READER! DON'T DO IT! Stay away from ad copy in your subject lines—it is the kiss of death for an email. When opening their email, most people delete all the ads as the first step.

Email "To" and "From" Headings Allow You to Personalize

Use personal names in the "To" and "From" headings whenever possible to create a more personal feeling. People open email from people they know and trust. If your message is coming from 257046@aol.com rather than Jane Doe, will your friends know it is coming from you? Most email programs allow you to attach your own name to your email address.

If you are using Microsoft Outlook, following are the steps to set up your name in the "From" heading:

1. On the menu bar, click "Tools."

2. On the drop-down menu, click "Account Settings."

3. Highlight the email account you want to edit and click "Change."

4. In the "User Information" section, put your name as you want it to appear in your recipient's "From" field in the "Your Name" area. Then click "Next."

5. Click "Finish" and you're done.

For all other email programs, consult the Help file included in the program.

Blind Carbon Copy (BCC)

Have you ever received an email message in which the first screen or first several screens were a string of other people's email addresses to which the message had been sent? Didn't you feel special? Didn't you feel the message was meant just for you? This sort of bulk mailing is very impersonal, and often recipients will delete the message without looking at it.

A few years ago I would have suggested using the BCC feature when sending bulk or group emails. Today, a number of Internet service providers look for multiple addresses in the BCC area to determine if an incoming message is spam. If your message is deemed to be spam, it will probably not get through to your intended recipient. This is one of the reasons I recommend moving to private mail list software for marketing messages that are going out to a group. See Chapter 12 on private mail list marketing.

> **BCC**
>
> *When blind carbon copy is used in an email message, all recipients' names are hidden so that no one sees who else has received the email.*

Effective Email Message Formatting

The content of the message should be focused on one topic. If you need to change the subject in the middle of a message, it is better to send a separate email. Alternatively, if you wish to discuss more than one topic, make sure you begin your message with "I have three questions" or "There are four issues I would like to discuss." People are busy; they read or scan their email quickly and they assume you will cover your main points within the first few sentences of your message.

Email is similar to writing a business letter in that the spelling and grammar should be correct. This includes the proper use of upper- and lowercase lettering, which many people seem to ignore when sending email. However, email is unlike a business letter in that the tone is completely different. Email correspondence is not as formal as business writing. The tone of email is more similar to a polite conversation than a formal letter, which makes it conducive to relationship building.

In general, you should:

- Keep your paragraphs relatively short—no more than four or five lines.

- Make your email scannable.

- Make your point in the first paragraph.

- Make sure that what is likely to be in the preview screen will encourage the recipient to open your email. Many people use the preview screen to determine whether they want to open the email or not, so what appears there is very important if you want your email to be opened and read.

- Be clear and concise.

- Use http:// at the beginning of any Web address to ensure that you make it "live." When you provide the URL starting with the www, the reader sometimes has to copy and paste the Web address into the address field in the browser if he or she wants to visit your site. When you place http:// before the www, the link is always "live" and the reader just has to click on the address to be taken directly to your site. Make it as easy as possible for your reader to visit your Web site.

- Give your reader a call to action.

- Avoid using fancy formatting such as stationery, graphics, different fonts, italics, and bold, because many email programs cannot display those features. Your message that reads: "Play golf today on the best course" could be viewed as "Play <I>golf<I> today on the <B>best course<B>" if the recipient's email software can't handle formatting. That kind of loses the impact!

- Make sure you have turned on the spell-check feature in your email program. If your email software doesn't have a spell-check feature, you might want to consider composing your message first in your word-processing program. Spell-check it there, then cut and paste it into your email package. If your email software does have the spell-check option, turn it on!

- Choose your words carefully. Email is a permanent record of your thoughts, and it can easily be forwarded to others. Whenever you have the urge to send a nasty response, give yourself an hour or two (maybe even 24) to reconsider. Those words can come back to haunt you—and they usually do.

A Call to Action

When you give your readers a call to action, it's amazing how often people will do as they're told. I'll give you an example of something we did. We ran a series of 10 Internet marketing workshops for a large organization. Their staff and selected clients were invited to participate in any, some, or all of the workshops. Their clients could include up to three employees. Because the workshops extended beyond noon, lunch was provided.

Because we were responsible for organizing and managing the project, we needed to know the approximate number of people who would be attending each of the workshops to organize the luncheons. When we contacted each company's representatives by email looking for participation RSVPs, we conducted an experiment. We sent half the representatives one version of the message and the other half a slightly different version. The only difference between the two messages was that in one, we included a call to action. In that message we asked: "RSVP before Wednesday at noon indicating if you will be attending as we must make arrangements for lunch," and in the other, this same line read: "Please let us know if you are planning to attend as we must make arrangements for lunch."

There was a 95 percent response rate from the group who received the first message. This is because we gave people a call to action and a deadline, and they felt obligated to respond more promptly. Meanwhile, fewer than 50 percent of the people in the second group responded to our message. What does this tell us? To improve your response rate, give your readers a call to action when you send them email. People respond when told to do something; they act with more urgency when there is a deadline.

Always Use Your Signature Files

As discussed previously, signature files are a great marketing tool. Always attach your signature file to your online communication. See later in this chapter for information on signature files. Remember to be sure that the signature files are right for the intended audience.

Discerning Use of Attachments

If you are sending a fairly large amount of data, you might want to send it as an attached file to your email message. However, only include an email attachment if the recipient is expecting it. You would never consider going to someone's home, letting yourself in, finding your way into their living room, and then leaving your brochure on the coffee table. However, people do the online equivalent of this when they send an unsolicited attachment. The attachment is sent across the Internet to the recipient's computer and is downloaded and stored on the computer's hard drive. This is considered quite rude and, in most cases, is unwanted.

Also, unless the recipient of your email is aware of the file size and is expecting it, don't send an attachment that is larger than 50K. Although your Internet connection might be a cable modem or a T1 line, and a 3 MB file is sent in seconds, the person who is receiving your message and attachment might be using an old 56 Kbps modem and a slow machine. If you send a 3 MB file, it might take the person with the 56 Kbps modem awhile to download the file. Needless to say, he or she won't be too pleased. Yes, there are still people on dial-up.

Another factor to consider when sending an unsolicited attachment is that the attachment you are sending might be incompatible with the operating system or the software on the recipient's system. You might be using a different platform (Mac/PC) or different operating system, and the recipient might not be able to open and read your file. Even PC to PC or Mac to Mac, the recipient might not be able to open and view the attachment if that particular program is not installed on his or her machine. Someone using an old version of Corel WordPerfect might not be able to read a Microsoft Word 2007 document sent as an attachment. Thus, you have wasted your time sending the file and the recipient's time downloading the file.

Finally, it is a well-known fact that email attachments can act as carriers for computer **viruses.** Many people will not open anything with an attachment, even if it is from someone they know, unless they have specifically requested a file. You might unknowingly send someone an attachment with a virus, and even if the file you send is virus-free, you could still receive blame if recipients find a virus on their system, just because you sent them an

Viruses

A software program capable of reproducing itself and usually capable of causing great harm to files or other programs on the same computer.

attachment. Basically, avoid sending email attachments of any type unless you have the recipient's permission. Be mindful of the size of the file you intend to send, compatibility with other platforms, and computer viruses. One alternative to sending a large attachment is to post the file on a Web server, and in your email message direct users to a URL from which they can download the file.

Email Marketing Tips

Be prepared. You will receive a number of emails requesting information on your company, your products, your locations, and so on, from people who have seen your email address on letterhead, ads, business cards, and sig files. Don't wait for the first inquiry before you begin to develop your company materials. Here are some tips. Following them will make you more prepared to respond.

Include a Brochure and Personal Note

Have an electronic brochure or corporate information available that you can easily access and send via email. Try to send a personal note in your email along with any material requested. Rather than a pdf file, think about sending an interactive brochure (iBrochure) instead; you'll make much more of a statement. There are a number of free tools available to help you convert a pdf into an interactive brochure. *Issuu.com* is one such tool. For others, see my social bookmarks which are accessible from Follow me Online on my Web site, *http://www.SusanSweeney.com.*

Provide Customer Service

Treat your customers right and they will treat you right. Your best referrals come from satisfied customers. If your new customer is taking a cruise, for example, provide a list of details on such things as what the boarding procedure is, what to wear, and what they cannot bring on board.

Gather a Library of Responses

Different people will ask a number of the same questions, and over time you should develop a library of responses to these frequently asked questions. When responding to an email, ask yourself if you are likely to get the question again. If your answer is "yes," then consider developing a document called "Frequently Asked Questions," or "FAQs," and save it. In the future, when you get a question that you have answered before, simply cut and paste your response from your FAQs file into your email message. Always make sure to appropriately edit and personalize your responses.

You can also develop unique signature files for different requests that have the complete email response included in the signature file. This is discussed in the signature files section of this chapter.

Graphic Headers and HTML

For a long time, text emails were the main form of Internet communication. However, the surge in popularity of HTML emails has raised the bar in Internet marketing and communication with its informative imagery, branding opportunity, and easily accessible links. HTML email, or even using HTML and graphics in your email messages, is definitely something that should be taken into consideration by any business. If you are considering using HTML emails, you want to make sure it is done right. Otherwise people will not be able to read your message or it may appear as if you are trying to send them an attachment; as we have said, people tend not to download attachments from people they don't know or are not expecting. HTML emails are covered in more depth in Chapter 12 and HTML signature files are covered later in this chapter.

Reply Promptly

Replying to email inquiries as promptly as possible is very important. The fact of the matter is that people are pressed for time. If someone has decided that on Tuesday night they are going to do their research and finalize their decision on which massage therapist they are going to use, they want their questions answered as soon as possible. If they have to wait 15 or 24 hours for a response from you, you may already have lost their business.

Using Signature Files to Increase Web Site Traffic

A signature file is your electronic business card. Signature files are commonly referred to as sig files and take the form of a short memo that is attached to the end of all your email messages. Businesses and organizations can use signature files in a number of clever ways, from just giving out phone numbers and addresses, to offering more substantial information such as the promotion of your e-club, or to inform people about new specials on your Web site. Signature files can also be used to show off an award or honor your company has received.

Presenting Your e-Business Card

A signature file is your e-business card and should be attached to the end of all your emails including emails that are sent to individuals, forums, discussion groups, newsgroups, and mail lists. If your email program doesn't allow for the use of a signature file, you should consider switching email programs. Sig files are readily accepted online and, when designed properly, comply with netiquette. Sig files can also be quite effective in drawing traffic to your Web site when used appropriately.

Your sig file should always include all basic contact information: your name, organization name, snail mail address, phone, fax, email, and URL. You should provide every way possible for recipients to reach you. The customer is king, and it is the recipients' choice if they would rather call than email you.

URL

Uniform Resource Locator—the address of a Web page.

Some businesses also include a line that reads "Click here to go to our Web site" on their sig file, and when you "click here" you go directly to their Web site. This is a nice idea, but you must also remember to include your actual URL so that the recipients can see it, read it, and have it. Some people print their email to read later or provide a copy to someone else. If your full URL is printed, then they can read it and access your Web site wherever they are. They can't get to your Web site by trying to click on a piece of paper.

It is also a good idea to include a **tag line** in your sig file. Many businesses use **tag lines** to offer information about their operation, their e-club, their specials, an award their company has received, or other marketing-focused information.

Tag line

A variant of a branding slogan typically used in marketing materials and advertising.

When creating your sig file, it is important to always remember to make URLs and email addresses hypertext-linked. This allows readers to click on the URL to take them directly to your Web site or to click on the email address and send you an email without having to copy and paste the address in their browser or email program. To make your URLs and email address hypertext links, place *http://* before Web site URLs and *mailto:* before email addresses. Without the *http://* before the *www*, some older email programs don't recognize it as a link, meaning that to get to your site, recipients have to copy the address, open their browser, and paste the address in the address field to get to the page you are recommending.

How to Develop Your Signature File

Again, if your email program doesn't allow for the use of a signature file, you should consider switching email programs. When preparing the design of your sig file, first you should decide what information you want to include. Once that is done, then you can decide what you want your e-business card to look like. Depending on which email program you are using, you can either create your sig file using Windows Notepad or Microsoft Word and save it as a text file (with a .txt extension), or you can create your sig file within the email program itself.

All email programs have instructions on how to set up your signature file in their "help" file. If you are using Microsoft Outlook, take the following steps to develop your sig file:

1. On the menu bar, click "Tools."

2. In the drop-down menu, click "Options."

3. Click the "Mail Format" tab.

4. Click the "Signatures" button.

5. Then click the "New" button to add your new signature.

6. Enter a name for your signature and click "Next."

7. Enter your signature into the box titled "Edit Signature" and click "Finish."

8. If you have more than one signature, pick one that will be used as a default in the "Choose Default Signature" section.

9. Click "OK."

Graphic Headers and HTML

Using graphics or HTML in your signature file could result in higher brand awareness and more visitors to your Web site. To increase brand power, make sure to match up your logo and colors with what can be found on your Web site and other online and offline promotional material.

If incorporating an HTML header or footer into your sig file is something you are considering, it is very important that it is done correctly. You may even want to look into getting your header professionally developed, because if this is done wrong it could have a negative impact on your business. You should include your telephone number and your Web address.

Once your header image has been designed, make sure that the image is saved as an HTML file with an extension of .htm or .html and make sure it is uploaded to a Web server. You do not want to link to an image that is saved on your computer. If you do it will appear as an attachment—and people tend not to download attachments from people they don't know or are not expecting to hear from.

The Do's and Don'ts of Signature Files

Some businesses and organizations develop different signature files to use with different groups of recipients. It is a good idea to use a different sig file for each different group you are targeting—one that is appropriate for that group. It is also important to update the tag line in your sig file often to reflect current marketing-related information.

Some email programs allow sig files with a maximum of 80 characters per line. No matter what program you are using, you should design your sig file to fit well within the limits of all programs. To ensure that your sig file will be viewed just as you have designed it, a good rule of thumb is to use no more than 65 characters per line. Sometimes people open and view their email in a small window and not the full screen. To help ensure that what you have on one line in your sig file appears on one line (and not two) in your viewer's browser, the fewer characters used the better. See Figure 9.1 for more suggestions on signature files.

Some businesses and organizations get really innovative in the design of their sig files by including sketches, designs, or logos developed by combining keyboard numbers and punctuation. Including graphics, icons, or sketches in your sig file that are developed with numbers and punctuation is not a good idea. It might look quite nice on your screen, but when you send it to another person who has a different email program or is using a different screen resolution, it could look quite different on their monitor.

On the other hand, professionally designed graphics can really reinforce your brand and your identity. Remember: people do business with people they know and trust.

The use of sig files offers a number of benefits to your company. If you use sig files appropriately, you promote your company and your online presence in the following ways:

- The use of sig files increases your company's online exposure. By including a sig file at the end of a posting to a newsgroup, you ensure that your company name will be seen by thousands of people. A great tag line with a call to action can encourage people to visit your site.

- As with any ad, the design and content of your sig file can be used to position your business and create or complement a corporate image.

- Using your sig file can enhance the reputation of your company based upon the email it is attached to. If your postings to newsgroups and

Sig File Do's	Sig File Don'ts
Do list all appropriate contact information.	Don't list prices of any kind.
Keep it short – 4 to 8 lines.	Don't use a sales pitch.
Keep it simple.	Don't use too many symbols.
Provide an appropriate and professional tag line.	Don't list all the company's products
Provide a link to your Web site and social media.	and services.

Figure 9.1.   Some suggested do's and don'ts for signature files.

mailing lists are helpful and continually appreciated, this will become associated with your company name.

- Using appropriate sig files signals to the online community that you are a member who respects proper netiquette.

Sig Files to Bring Traffic to Your Web Site

For many businesses and organizations, the major benefit of sig files is that they can attract visitors to your Web site. Sigvertising is when you use your signature file as a mini-advertisement for your company and its products and services. With sigvertising you can go beyond offering the basic contact information—you can use your sig file as a tool to bring traffic to your Web site. Do this by using your sig file to give the reader some insight into your business and a reason to visit your site—not just to provide your company's phone number and URL.

One of the most important elements of your signature file from a marketing perspective is the tag line. A tag line is a small sentence that is used in branding and is often recognizable without even the mention of the company name.

Do you recognize any of these tag lines?

- "We try harder."

- "It's the real thing."

- "Like a rock."

- "Just do it."

- "Kills bugs dead."

Your signature file should always include a one-line tag line or catch phrase. A catch phrase is simply something that catches the reader's attention and intrigues him or her to find out more. It's a good idea to include a call to action in the catch phrase, wherever possible, to get your reader to take action. I often include the catch phrase "Check out our Internet Marketing Bootcamp" in my signature file, with a hypertext link to my Web site. I get positive results with this, as recipients often do check out our Internet Marketing Bootcamp, ask for additional information on the Bootcamp, and often attend. It works!

Your catch phrase has to be relevant to your objectives and your target market. For example, if your objective is to get more people to your Web site and your target market is people who want to take business courses online, your catch phrase could be something like this: "We've got the largest selection of online business courses on the Web—check us out!" with a hypertext link to your Web site. Or perhaps your objective is to get more people to sign up to your e-club and your target audience is gardening enthusiasts. Your catch phrase could be something like this: "Join my e-club and receive great tips and coupons for the biggest and brightest flowers," with a hypertext link to your e-club sign up.

Consider some of the following tag line or catch phrase possibilities to help increase the traffic to your Web site:

- Tell people about your e-club. Provide a call to action to get people to join.

- Let people know about your e-specials and invite them to your site for more information.

- Let people know about the great content on your site—for instance, your podcasts, videocasts, or articles.

- Announce a contest. If your site is holding a contest, tell readers that they can enter by visiting your site.

- Announce an award or honor. If your company or your Web site has received special recognition, tell people about it through your sig file.

Generally, sig files are accepted everywhere online in email, newsgroups, mail lists, discussion groups, and many consumer-generated media sites. (Consumer-generated media is covered more in depth in Chapter 11.) Be cautious when developing your sig files to ensure that they will be well received. Sig files that are billboards, or sig files that are longer than most of your text messages, are to be avoided. Sig files that are blatant advertisements definitely are not appreciated. The online community reacts unfavorably to hard-sell advertising unless it is done in the proper forum.

Using Signature Files As an Email Template

When replying to routine email inquiries, you can set up signature files as prewritten responses to a specific request in addition to your contact information.

When a routine question comes in, simply click the reply button and choose the appropriate signature with the prewritten response.

Always personalize any emails you send. In the case of a prewritten response, simply highlight the areas that should be personalized with uppercase font and brackets to remind yourself where to customize. For example, [FIRST NAME], [COMPANY NAME] or, if you want to add a full sentence or two, [ADD PERSONALIZED SENTENCE(s) HERE]. This will not only save you time, it will also give you the opportunity to tailor a better response or set up an automated drip campaign.

Following Formalities with Email Netiquette

When writing emails, remember these points:

- Be courteous. Remember to use please and thank-you.

- Reply promptly—within 24 hours at the very latest.

- Be brief.

- Use upper- and lowercase characters appropriately. All capitals indicates SHOUTING!

- Check your grammar and spelling.

- Use attachments sparingly.

- Do not send unsolicited bulk email.

Internet Resources for Chapter 9

I have developed a great library of online resources for you to check out regarding email and signature files. This library is available on my Web site, *http://www.SusanSweeney.com,* in the Resources section, where you can find additional tips, tools, techniques, and resources.

I have also developed courses on many of the topics covered in this book. These courses are available on two of my Web sites, *http://www.SusanSweeney. com* and *http://www.eLearningU.com* (which contains other instructors' courses as well). These courses are delivered immediately over the Internet, so you can start whenever is convenient for you.

10

Autoresponders

Autoresponders, as the name suggests, provide a designated automatic response to an incoming email. You send an email to an autoresponder email address and you get back the requested information via email. In this chapter, you will learn:

- What autoresponders are

- Why you should use autoresponders

- What types of information to send via autoresponders

- Autoresponder features

- Tips on successful marketing through autoresponders.

What Are Autoresponders?

An **autoresponder** is a utility created to work with email programs. It is set up to automatically reply to an email sent to it with a preprogrammed message. The autoresponder reply can be a single email message or a series of preprogrammed messages. Autoresponders are known by many names, such as infobots, responders, mailbots, autobots, automailers, or email-on-demand. They enable you to do drip marketing quickly and easily. Drip marketing is a strategy that involves sending out a number of promotional pieces over a period of time to a subset of your database.

> ## Autoresponder
>
> *A computer program that automatically answers email sent to it.*

Autoresponders have been around for many years. The first generation of autoresponders were basically used to send "Out of Office" notifications. If you were going to be out of the office for a period of time, you would turn on your autoresponder to let people know this in case they were expecting an immediate response to their email. The second generation of autoresponders, while still using very simple technology, were used to send things like price lists and e-brochures.

Today's autoresponders work much the same way—you send an email to a specified email address and you get back the requested information via email. However, over the past few years, we have seen major changes in the technology being used. Today autoresponders are more sophisticated and the enhanced features have provided many opportunities for marketers and merchants alike, as outlined in the next section.

Why Use Autoresponders?

One of the major benefits of using an autoresponder is its immediate response—24 hours a day, 7 days a week, 365 days a year—providing immediate gratification for the recipient. This is particularly valuable in any online business where the faster the response, the better the chance you have of getting the business.

Autoresponders are a real time saver, eliminating the need for manual responses for many mundane and routine requests. They also enable you to track responses to various offers to assist you in your ongoing marketing efforts.

One big advantage with today's autoresponders is the ability to schedule multiple messages at predetermined intervals. The first response can go immediately, with a second message timed to go two days after the first, a third message to go five days after the second, and so on. Market research shows that a prospect needs to be exposed to your message multiple times to become a motivated buyer.

Today's autoresponders are getting even more sophisticated in terms of mail list administration. These programs gather the email addresses of people requesting information and store them in a database. The program adds new names to the database and eliminates email addresses that no longer work.

Today's autoresponder programs also provide reports about site visitors requesting information. This technology is very cost-effective when compared to manual responses by a human, not to mention the associated telephone and fax costs.

Personalization is a standard feature of today's autoresponder programs. Autoresponders are used to send all kinds of information, including:

- Articles on your business, products, or services

- Trivia about your business, products, or services

- Weekly gardening tips, ski tips, or other tips of interest to your target markets

- Movie of the week or featured film series

- Checklists appropriate for your target market—for example:

  - Moving checklists

  - Sailing checklists

- Wedding planning information, where you send a list of items that need to be taken care of, in the month they need to be taken care of.

You can provide a copy of your newsletter so people can read a copy before subscribing, or anything else in which your target market might be interested.

Why use an autoresponder when you could just provide the information on your Web site? There are many reasons. With the autoresponder you have the interested party's name and email address; you don't get that from a visitor to your site. The autoresponder also provides you with the opportunity to send multiple or sequential messages to your potential customer.

You can incorporate viral marketing tactics into your autoresponder messages as well. Use this opportunity to encourage recipients to tell others about the information they are receiving, or present a way for them to provide a copy of the information to their friends. It's important when using viral marketing to provide the recipient with the opportunity to subscribe to receive your information. See Chapter 5 for more on viral marketing.

Types of Autoresponders

There are three different types of autoresponders:

- Free

- Web host

- Other autoresponder providers.

There are many free or minimal-fee autoresponders available that come with an ad on your responder page. Some Web hosting companies provide autoresponders in their Web hosting packages. Some storefront providers are including autoresponders in their product offerings. There also are many autoresponder service providers that offer packages for a fee if you don't want to have ads placed on your responder page.

The important thing is to get the autoresponder that has the features you are looking for. See the Resources section of my Web site, *http://www. SusanSweeney.com,* for appropriate autoresponder resources.

Autoresponder Features

When you are looking for an autoresponder, you want to make sure it has all the features to enable you to make the most of this marketing activity. Today's autoresponders keep getting better—new features are being added all the time. Some of the things you want to look for are discussed in the following sections.

Personalization

Today's autoresponders capture the requester's name as well as email address, allowing personalized responses.

Multiple Responses/Sequential Autoresponders

Studies have shown that a potential customer has to be exposed to your message multiple times before he or she is ready to buy. Many autoresponders allow multiple messages to be sent on a scheduled time line.

Size of Message

Some autoresponders have a limit on the size of the message that can be sent. Ensure that your autoresponder can handle any message you would want to send to prospective customers.

Tracking

You must have access to tracking reports that provide you with information to enable you to track the results of your marketing efforts. You need to be able to determine what is working and what is not.

HTML Messaging

Choose an autoresponder that can handle HTML and plain-text emails. Studies have shown that HTML marketing emails get a higher click-through rate. Autoresponders are constantly being enhanced. Stay current.

Successful Marketing through Autoresponders

The technology itself is only one piece of this marketing technique. The content of the messages sent out by the autoresponder is the determining factor in converting recipients of your message to customers. The following tips will help you produce effective messages:

- *Personalize* your messages using the recipient's name throughout the message and in the subject line.

- Selling is all about relationships. Give your messages a *tone* that builds relationships.

- *Focus* on the reader's needs, and how your product or service provides the solution. Focus on the benefits.

- Have a catchy *subject line,* but don't use ad copy. Ad copy in a subject line is a sure way to get your message deleted before it is read.

- Include a *call to action*. It is amazing how often people do what they are told to do.

- Use *correct spelling,* upper- and lowercase letters, grammar, and punctuation. This correspondence is business correspondence and is a reflection of everything related to how you do business.

- *Get to the point quickly.* Online readers have little patience with verbose messages.

- Write for *scanability.* Have a maximum of four or five lines per paragraph.

Internet Resources for Chapter 10

I have developed a great library of online resources for you to check out regarding autoresponders. This library is available on my Web site, *http://www. SusanSweeney.com,* in the Resources section, where you can find additional tips, tools, techniques, and resources.

I have also developed courses on many of the topics covered in this book. These courses are available on two of my Web sites, *http://www.SusanSweeney. com* and *http://www.eLearningU.com* (which contains other instructors' courses as well). These courses are delivered immediately over the Internet, so you can start whenever is convenient for you.

11

Consumer-Generated Media

The Internet has given consumers a voice like no other form of media. It has provided consumers with a platform where they can publish their opinions for others to read, research, listen to, and share. Consumer-generated media (CGM) encompasses these opinions along with consumers' comments, reviews, critiques, and complaints. It also includes consumer blogs, wikis, videos on YouTube, and the like. CGM is nothing more than the online version of word-of-mouth behavior, but it is quickly becoming an important part in marketing effectively online.

Consumer-generated media is the fastest growing media online and it is one where consumers are in control—in control of what information they want to see on the Web, in control of when they want to see that information, and in control of what information they want to generate on the Web.

The Web has given consumers a voice that simply cannot be ignored. With a massive amount of media being generated across the Internet on a daily basis, they could be talking about your business, products, packages, or services in their blog, or showing your products in their online photo album or through their video on YouTube. In this chapter you will learn:

- What is consumer-generated media?

- Why is it important?

- How will you know what is being said about you and your organization?

- What are the effects of CGM on your corporate reputation?

- Where do you find consumer-generated media?

What Is Consumer-Generated Media?

Unlike paid media, such as print or banner ads, consumer-generated media is created solely by consumers, not professional writers, journalists, or publishers. It is created by consumers, for consumers. It can include anything from facts, opinions, impressions, experiences, rumors, ratings, reviews, complaints, praises—anything. CGM is made available to other Internet users through their participation in groups, review and rating sites, discussion boards, blogs, and other social media networks. CGM encompasses opinions, experiences, advice, and commentary about products, brands, companies, and services, and is usually a result of personal experience.

According to *Pew Internet & American Life Project*, 90 percent of consumers have used the Internet to research a product or a service. Consumers are using the Internet to consult with other consumers. They are reading sites dedicated to consumer opinions, consumer reviews, and personal experiences. They are frequenting discussion boards where they share information, give feedback, ask questions, or simply read what others are saying.

CGM is viewed by consumers as trusted third-party advice and information; they are using this information to form their own opinions on your products, services, and packages and are using this information to help them in their purchasing decision.

Why Consumer-Generated Media Is Important

Consumer-generated media is the fastest growing media online and should be as important to your business as it is to other consumers. Listening to and leveraging consumer-generated media may well be the most important source of competitive advantage for any company. Studies have shown that when it comes to product information, consumers place far more trust in other consumers than they do in manufacturers, marketers, and advertisers. By listening to CGM and to what your customers are saying, you can gain truthful insights as to how they view your business, products, and services.

Consumers consistently rank word-of-mouth as one of the top information sources for making purchasing decisions. According to a recent study, 90 percent of consumers trust recommendations from people they know and 70 percent trust opinions of unknown users, whereas only 27 percent trust experts and 8 percent trust celebrities. The rapid growth of this trend poses both challenges and opportunities for marketing, advertising, and public relation teams.

It is also important to monitor what is being said about your business and key company officials so that you can do damage control for any negative comments and leverage the positive ones.

How to Monitor What Is Being Said about You

There are many tools and services out there that will monitor everything that is being said about anything on the Internet and report it back to you. There are free tools like Google Alerts (*http://www.google.com/alerts*) (Figure 11.1) where, within minutes:

1. You set up an account.

2. Next you define the search terms you want reported back to you—you start with your company name and the names of key company officials.

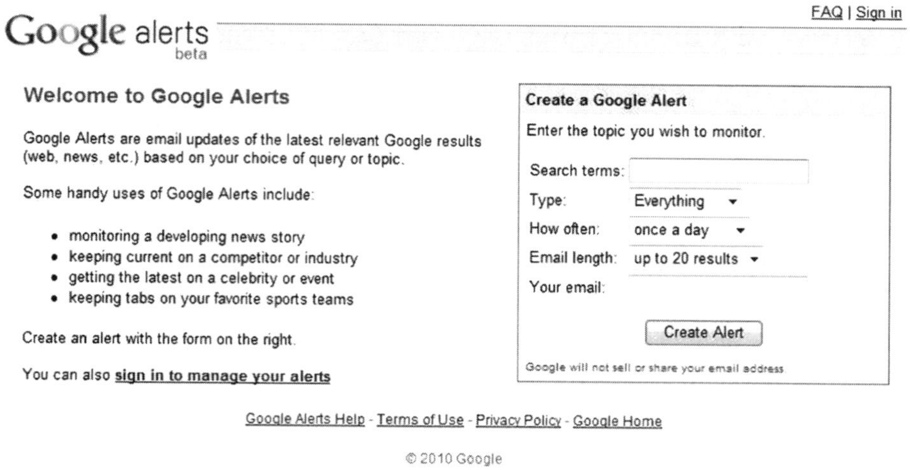

Figure 11.1.   Google Alerts enables you to stay on top of what's being said about you online.

You can manage your account to add other terms later. Some choose to keep a close eye on the competition. Others put in terms that potential customers use. Sometimes you will put in a term from your marketing campaign or one of your videos you hope to go viral.

3. Next you tell Google Alerts where you want them to look for those terms. The options are news, blogs, video, Web groups, or comprehensive.

4. Next you choose from a drop-down menu how often you want to be notified. The options are: as it happens, once a day, or once a week.

5. Next, from a drop-down menu, you choose either up to 20 results or up to 50 results for the email length.

6. Then you provide the email address that you would like to receive these alerts. And you're done.

Now you start to receive the alerts with a short copy of the mention along with a link to where the term was used.

There are similar tools for your social media. You can go to Social Mention and search directly for a term, or you can set up an ongoing Social Mention Alert. Social Mention Alerts (*http://www.socialmention.com/alerts*) (Figure 11.2) works in a very similar way to Google Alerts:

1. First you define the search terms you want reported back to you—again, you start with your company name and the names of key company officials. You can manage your account to add other terms later. Some choose to keep a close eye on the competition. Others put in terms that potential customers use. Sometimes you will put in a term from your marketing campaign or one of your videos you hope to go viral.

2. Next you tell Social Mention where you want them to look for those terms. The options are blogs, microblogs, networks, bookmarks, comments, images, news, video, audio, Q&A, or ALL.

3. Next you choose the language.

4. Next you choose the email type from a drop-down menu. The options are HTML or text.

5. Then you provide the email address that you would like to receive these alerts.

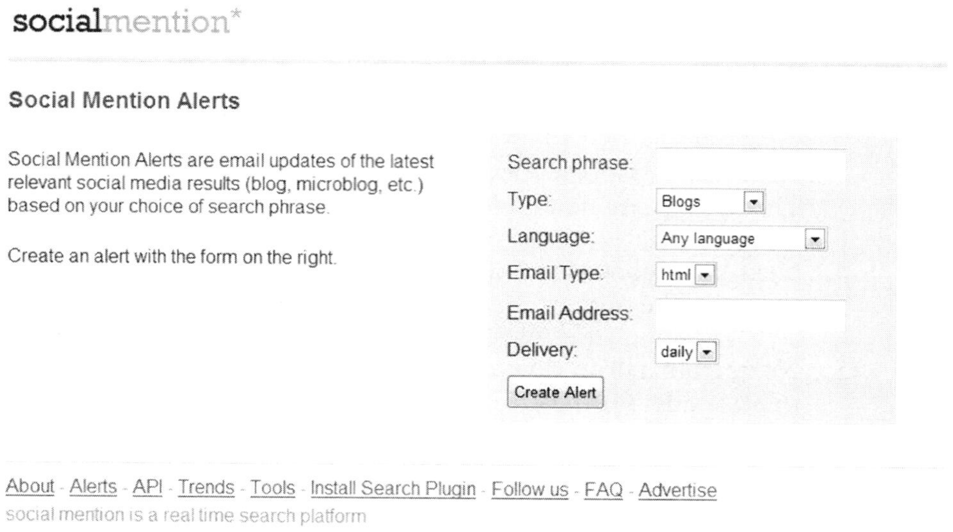

social mention*

Social Mention Alerts

Social Mention Alerts are email updates of the latest relevant social media results (blog, microblog, etc.) based on your choice of search phrase.

Create an alert with the form on the right.

Search phrase:

Type: Blogs

Language: Any language

Email Type: html

Email Address:

Delivery: daily

Create Alert

About - Alerts - API - Trends - Tools - Install Search Plugin - Follow us - FAQ - Advertise
social mention is a real time search platform

Figure 11.2. Social Mention Alerts tracks where you are mentioned in various social media.

6. Then it asks how often you want this delivered. The only option is daily.

7. Once you've completed this, you are sent a verification email. You confirm and you're done.

Again, you will start to receive the alerts with the details of where your defined terms have been used.

The Effect of CGM on Corporate Reputation

The growing popularity of social media networks provides even more opportunities for consumers to give their opinion or complaints. Today, virtually every online consumer creates CGM through their social media channels or their posts on review and rating sites. Because consumer-generated media is everywhere, traditional marketers and advertisers no longer have control over the messages being circulated about their company, products, or services. Nor do they have control over the medium in which those messages are being presented. When a consumer uses a search engine to search for a particular company, brand, or product, it's almost certain that postings created by other consumers will be among the top results.

Understanding and monitoring the impact CGM has on consumers' decision-making process is extremely important for online success. CGM comments are online forever, archived until the person who posted them removes them. It is estimated that the number of comments will grow by about 30 percent each year.

CGM leaves a digital trail, which means it is a highly measurable form of media. It can be converted into market research. It allows companies to gauge their brand equity, reputation, and message effectiveness. It is important for companies to take into account the scope and effect of CGM and use it to help them make more-informed decisions.

There are any number of review sites, rating sites, groups, message boards, and forums where people can post what's on their mind, whether it be to tell of their harrowing experience or the exceptional customer service they received. Any one of these can affect your business. You need to pay close attention to what is being said in both traditional media and consumer-generated media.

Some consumers will go so far as to develop a video to show their displeasure with an organization's response (or lack of response) to their complaint. Check out United Breaks Guitars on YouTube! This video has been shown on CNN as well as on YouTube. At the time of writing this book, United Breaks Guitars had 7,513,364 views and 40,992 ratings where individuals had taken the time after viewing the video to rate it. The video has a 5-star rating, so everyone loved it and many passed it on or told others about it. Rumor has it that United Airlines is now using the video in its customer service training.

You could lose the chance to demonstrate a commitment to customer service by not addressing complaints. The news cycle has accelerated tremendously, and consumers' expectations that companies will frequently and directly communicate with them has been raised, thanks to the Internet. If there is no response from your company on a given issue, consumers are likely to spread the news and further speculate about the issue. Along with other traditional forms, blogging and engaging in social media should now be part of any company's media outreach.

CGM—Opportunity or Threat?

CGM comments have the power to influence anyone who sees them and are a very valuable research tool for any online business. It creates a competitive advantage as it allows you (and everyone else online) to find out how your consumers really feel about your packages, products or services, customer service, staff, and virtually all aspects of your business.

CGM comments give online businesses the opportunity to listen to what consumers are saying and to learn what it was about their products or services that encouraged (or discouraged) the purchasing decision; and it gives them the opportunity to act accordingly. For example, amusement park marketers can gain unfiltered insights into customer experiences that in the past they could have gotten only through surveys and comment cards.

Where Do You Find Consumer-Generated Media?

You will find consumer-generated media everywhere on the Internet. Discussion forums, message boards, and Usenet newsgroups were among the first generation of CGM; blogs, wikis, podcasts, and videos represented the second generation, and now CGM is everywhere—Twitter, Facebook, YouTube, MySpace, LinkedIn, Flickr, Delicious, Digg, Diigo, blogs, rating and review sites—absolutely everywhere online.

CGM can be in the form of text, images, photos, videos, audio, and other forms of media.

There are all kinds of Web sites dedicated to all kinds of CGM that allow consumers to rate products and services, or give feedback. A few such Web sites include:

- Trip Advisor—*http://www.tripadvisor.com*

- Yelp—*http://www.yelp.com*

- Epinions.com—*http://www.epinions.com*

- PlanetFeedback—*http://www.planetfeedback.com.*

Consumer-generated media can give many organizations unfiltered insights into their customers' experiences. It can create interactive relationships with consumers and also provide a new way of advertising and promoting products, services, and packages.

How Do You Use Consumer-Generated Media?

Online businesses should be taking advantage of CGM and adapting their online marketing so that it is interactive with their consumers. To begin adapting to the new CGM, you simply need to:

- Observe, listen to, and engage customers and potential customers in your target market

- Provide your customers and potential customers with a convenient way to communicate with you and participate in your marketing.

Understanding the trends in CGM is what will give you the competitive advantage. Listening to and leveraging such media may be the most important source of competitive advantage for any online business.

Leverage CGM by having systems in place to help you listen to, and understand, what your customers are saying about your company, your products and services, and even your competitors. Pay as much attention to unsolicited commentary as possible. Invite active consumers into a discussion to help gain more control over the buzz that is being generated about your operation.

Different companies use CGM for different reasons. The most important uses of CGM are to:

- Get in sync with consumers—Use CGM to find out what consumers are looking for from related sites and use that information as a way to come up with new content for your site, your social media, or your corporate blog.

- Track your online ads—Use CGM to identify what buzz words people are using to describe your operation and use this information to help you decide what keywords you want to use in your ads and where the best place is to advertise.

- Track your competitors—Use CGM to find out what is being said about your competition. Implement any positive elements from what they are doing and avoid any negative elements.

Consumer-generated media is a great tool in helping online businesses understand their target markets—what they want and what they need.

Internet Resources for Chapter 11

I have developed a great library of online resources for you to check out regarding consumer-generated media. This library is available on my Web site, *http://www.SusanSweeney.com,* in the Resources section, where you can find additional tips, tools, techniques, and resources.

I have also developed courses on many of the topics covered in this book. These courses are available on two of my Web sites, *http://www.SusanSweeney. com* and *http://www.eLearningU.com* (which contains other instructors' courses as well). These courses are delivered immediately over the Internet, so you can start whenever is convenient for you.

12

Establishing Your Private Mailing List

Having your own private mailing list enables you to create one-way communication to your target market. Private mailing lists are also a tremendous vehicle for building relationships and a sense of community. Generating your own private mailing list is highly recommended because a targeted opt-in list has many marketing uses.

Today all the marketing talk has gone to two-way communication and building a community through social media, but it is perhaps more important than ever from a business perspective to get your customers and potential customers into your permission-based database and provide them with valuable content on an ongoing basis. Everything on the Internet has its day, and things evolve. There will always be the next greatest thing. A few years ago people thought that email was dead and everyone would use RSS. That didn't happen, nor was it particularly effective from a marketing perspective. Today everyone is building huge followers on Twitter, fans and friends on Facebook, etc. If you can get these followers, friends, and fans into your permission-based database, you have control, you have their email address and name, you have permission to stay in touch. When the next big thing comes along (and it will . . . ask MySpace), you still have a way to stay in touch. Permission-based marketing and social media marketing are NOT mutually exclusive. You use both.

Your permission-based list can be used to maintain communication with customers and potential customers regarding your products, your specials, and so on. It can also be used to distribute corporate newsletters, last-minute deals, new product packages, e-specials, and upcoming events. In this chapter, we cover:

- Why have your own mailing list?

- The issue of privacy

- Managing your mail list

- Building your mail list

- Promoting your mail list

- Tips to stay under the spam radars

- Recent legislation

- Why email is not dead—the latest.

Why Have Your Own Mailing List?

There are numerous reasons to own and use your own mail list. They include some of the same reasons that make it imperative to join someone else's list. Running a permission-based private mailing list can be beneficial in many ways, including:

- Gets you in front of your current and potential customers on a regular basis

- Conserves contacts—particularly your social media contacts, if you do this right, so that when the next big thing comes along and all your friends, followers, or fans move on, you still have a way to stay in contact

- Builds repeat traffic to your Web site (as discussed in Chapter 3)

- Branding

- Promotion of your products, services, and events

- First-of-mind marketing

- Potential source of revenue.

Permission-Based Marketing

Permission and privacy are critical to the success of any email marketing campaign. Although unsolicited direct "snail mail" might be generally accepted or at least tolerated by many consumers, the rules are completely different online.

Unsolicited email (known as spam) runs the risk of damaging your company's reputation, not to mention the very real possibilities of flames, public blacklisting, hack attacks, or having your Internet services revoked. For serious spammers, recent legislation adds heavy fines and the possibility of prison.

Online consumers are quick to let you know when you have crossed the line, and unsolicited email definitely crosses the line. Because of this, online marketers are using many techniques to get their customers, potential customers, and Web site visitors to give them "permission" to send email on a regular basis.

Permission marketing is really a win-win situation. Recipients receive information that they asked to receive, and the marketer is communicating with an audience that has expressed interest in what is being marketed. Online marketers claim that permission email marketing is one of the best ways to improve customer retention and boost sales.

So how do you get this coveted permission? Generally you have to provide something of value and of interest to your target market. There are many opportunities on your Web site to ask for permission. Make sure you take advantage of them. Make sure your permission marketing is above the fold and grabs the readers' attention.

The more repeat-traffic generators on your site, the more opportunities you can provide for visitors to give you their permission. (See Chapter 3 for more information on repeat-traffic generators.) You should leverage repeat-traffic generators with permission marketing that "sells the sizzle" and accelerates responses with a call to action. Here are some typical examples:

- "We change our coupons every week! Join our e-club to be notified as soon as we update."

- "Join our e-club and receive our biweekly newsletter filled with industry news, updates, and special offers."

- "We have new specials on a regular basis. Join our e-club to be notified by email when we post our new specials."

- "We have a new contest every three weeks. Keep checking back or join our e-club if you'd like to be notified by email every time we begin a new contest."

- "We constantly update our calendar of events. Keep checking back or <u>join our e-club</u> if you'd like to be notified by email every time we update."

- "<u>Join our e-club</u> to receive our e-specials, coupons, our great newsletter, and other great offers available only to our e-club members!"

You get the picture. Almost every page on your Web site provides an opportunity for you to offer permission marketing. Of course, when site visitors click, they are taken to a screen where they add themselves to your email list. It is important not to ask for too much too soon. If your visitors have to fill out a lengthy form to be added to your mailing list, they probably won't.

The two most important things to ask for are the email address and the visitor's first name. You want their first name so that you can personalize any correspondence with them.

If you have more than one permission-based offer, your mail list program should keep track of the element the visitor has given you permission to send. If someone signed up to receive your newsletter, you cannot send them information on your newest product packages unless you have gotten umbrella permission with an e-club.

The best thing to do is to get umbrella permission. When you get umbrella permission you can send out all of your permission-based marketing materials to all the people who signed up. One way of getting umbrella permission is to offer an e-club. When someone signs up for your e-club, tell them that they will receive advance notice of product specials and promotions, company information, and updates of events. Happy Joe's Pizza and Ice Cream, pictured in Figure 12.1, for example, invites its Web site visitors to join its e-club.

Your mail list software should be integrated with the Web site so when someone gives you permission, his or her name is automatically added to your database.

Permission marketing enjoys its success because it is personal, relevant, and anticipated. Your messages should be personalized, enhancing the one-to-one relationship marketing element.

Privacy is a very big issue when a Web site visitor is deciding whether to give you an email address or not. It is very important to assure your visitors that you will not pass on their email address to others or use it for anything but the purpose intended. Your privacy policy should be clearly evident on your Web site on every page that asks for permission. The privacy policy can read like a legal document or be short and to the point.

Figure 12.1. Happy Joe's Pizza and Ice Cream invites its Web site visitors to join its e-club.

The Issue of Privacy

Privacy is a growing concern among many online users. You can boost your mailing list's sign-up rate by guaranteeing that subscribers' email addresses are kept confidential and are not sold to or shared with anyone else. If you cannot assure them that your company will use their email address solely for your correspondence with them, they will not feel comfortable giving their email address to you. Provide people with your privacy policy statement. Make them feel comfortable about divulging their email address to your business. To do this, you should have your privacy policy everywhere you ask permission or, alternatively, place a link to your business's privacy policy in a prominent location on your Web site, especially on your email list sign-up page.

You should never add someone's name to your mailing list without his or her permission. People really resent receiving unsolicited email, even if you give them the option to unsubscribe.

Where We Need to Be

There are only two ways to do more business online:

- Have more people receive your offer.

- Improve your conversion rate of Web site visitors to Web site customers.

There are only a few ways to have more people get your offer:

- Increase the number of visitors to your Web site.

- Increase the number of people you reach through your social media efforts.

- Increase the number of people whom you reach with your online marketing in newsgroups, public mail lists, affiliate marketing, or any of the 101 ways in this book.

Ideally, where we'd like to be in terms of mail list marketing is:

- Have the right mail list technology.

- Grow your targeted mail list through permission-based marketing as big as you can as fast as you can.

- Provide consistently valuable content to your list on an ongoing basis.

- Learn as much as you can about everyone on your list, building a profile on each person, so that you can send more targeted communication through **dynamic personalization**.

> **Dynamic personalization**
>
> *Personalizing communication to your database based on their priorities and preferences.*

The Right Mail List Technology

There are several ways that you can manage your mail list:

- Use your email program (not recommended).

- Use mail list software.

- Outsource your mail list management.

Using Your Email Program

Although managing your mail list through your email program might look like a great option in that it doesn't cost you anything and is run from your desktop, giving you ultimate control, there are severe limitations.

Your email program doesn't easily afford you the opportunity to segment your mail list—those who asked to receive your newsletter versus those who asked to receive notification when you update your What's New section, for example.

Your email program doesn't generally provide the technology to quickly and easily personalize your communication—that is, insert the recipient's first name in designated areas within the email. Email programs do not provide much in the way of tracking information, either.

It would be nice to be able to track such things as how many people opened your email, how many sent a copy to a friend, and how many clicked through and visited your Web site. The tracking technology is generally available only through mail list software or from the third party that manages your mail list marketing if you choose to outsource this activity.

Another drawback is the administrative headache of manually managing all the "Subscribes," "Unsubscribes," and "Changes of Email Address," particularly when you have multiple sign-up opportunities on your Web site—for example, someone wants to unsubscribe from your e-specials but still wants to receive your newsletter and coupons. The time really has come when you need to invest in mail list software or outsource if you want to take this element of online marketing seriously.

Using Mail List Software

There are numerous mail list management software programs available to help you organize your list distribution. (See Internet Resources at *http://www. SusanSweeney.com* for links to mail list software programs.) This software enables you to easily add or remove subscribers. Mail list management software enables you to draft and send properly formatted HTML and text messages directly from within the software, and it generally allows you to personalize your emails quickly and easily.

Most of these programs can be integrated with your Web site so that people can add themselves to your list right from the site. You can also use this software to set up notification mechanisms to reply to subscribers, confirming that they have been added to the list. This makes running your mail list less time-consuming, as the software does most of the work for you.

Using your own mail list software requires an initial investment to purchase the program or an ongoing cost if you use an application service provider (ASP)—a company that develops the mail list software and provides it to you as a monthly or annual service rather than as a product. The major advantage to this model is that as new bells and whistles are introduced, they are immediately available to all users of the software.

The cost to purchase software can range from an entry-level program at $99 to a robust, full-featured program at $2,500. The ASP model could cost you from $30 a month to several thousand dollars if you use an application that charges you per email sent and you have a very large database.

Some of these programs run from your desktop; others have to be run from your server or through your Internet service provider. Many of the ASP model programs are run from the ASP's server. Most of these programs are sophisticated enough to allow you to segment the email addresses in your database so you know who has asked to receive what from your Web site.

Most of these programs have the personalization capability to allow you to insert a recipient's first name throughout the correspondence and in the subject line of the message as well. For this to work, you have to capture the first names for each email address in your database. Keep this in mind when asking people if they'd like to give you permission to send them email for whatever reason—in addition to their email address, have a mandatory field for their first name.

More and more of these programs are incorporating tracking features to let you know what's working and what's not. From an administrative perspective, many of these programs do a great job of adding new "Subscribes," deleting "Unsubscribes," and managing undeliverable addresses. This feature alone is worth its weight in gold.

Features to look for in mail list software include:

- Personalization capability—You want to be able to personalize each email by inserting the recipient's first name in the subject line, in the salutation, and throughout the body of your message.

- HTML capability—You want to be able to send HTML email (email that looks like a Web page rather than text), which gets much higher readership than text email.

- Message editor—You want to be able to bring up a past email, edit it, and resend it to a group.

- Previews—You want to be able to preview your message before you send it to make sure the formatting is correct, the personalization is working, and the message looks great.

- Spam checker—The spam checker is a valuable tool to ensure that your message has the best chance of being received and not being rejected as spam. You want to be able to run your message through the spam checker to see how you score before you send any message. Today, if you score 5.0 or higher in the spam checker, you will want to edit your message to reduce your score before you send.

- Dynamic personalization—Each message is personalized based on the individual's priorities and preferences.

- Filtering—This feature allows you to send specific messages to parts of your list. You could send a message only to those individuals in a specific state by filtering on the name of the state. You could send a message only to those interested in football if you have that information in a field in your database.

- Scheduling—This allows you to prearrange to send your email at a specific future time and date. Great if you want to set up all of your "Tips of the Week" in advance, or if you are going to be traveling when you want your newsletter to be sent out.

- Autoresponders—Some mail list software applications have autoresponders built in. See Chapter 10 for details on their uses.

- Web site integration—You want your mail list software to work with your Web site so when someone subscribes from your site, his or her contact information is automatically included in your mail list software. If someone wants to unsubscribe or change contact information, this can be taken care of through your site or through the emails you have sent. This really cuts down on the administration you have to deal with.

- Reporting and tracking—Some mail list software provides reports on messages sent (audience selected, date sent, clicks, total sent, number of bounces), subscriber activity (subscribes, unsubscribes, emails opened), link tracking, and bounce activity (number of undeliverables, hard bounces, soft bounces).

Outsourcing Your Mail List

A third option is to outsource your mail list management to a third party. There are companies that specialize in this service that have a great depth of experience. One such company that we have had the pleasure to work with is Inbox360.com *(http://www.inbox360.com)*.

When you outsource this activity, of course you have a monthly service fee. The software is run from the outsource company's server or its ISP's server.

Virtually all of the mail list service providers have the latest software, allowing you to personalize your messages, segment your lists, and get great tracking reports. Generally, administrative issues like adding the "Subscribes," deleting "Unsubscribes," and managing the undeliverables are handled by software used by the outsource company.

On the down side, you might lose some control—over content, over your customer, and over timing of your message release. It is imperative to have a clearly laid-out contract with the outsource company, addressing:

- Ownership of email addresses

- Use of email addresses

- Timing of correspondence

- Final approval of content

- Responsibility and timelines for replies to subscribers.

It is important that you retain ownership of all email addresses and that the contract clearly states that all subscribers' names and email addresses are the property of your company. Also include in the contract that you are provided with the current list in digital format every month. This way, if you decide to change service providers, your list goes with you. It takes a lot of effort to build your list, and it is a very valuable asset. Make sure you protect it.

Make sure that your contract clearly states that your email addresses are not to be used by anyone else or provided to anyone else for any purpose whatsoever. People on your list have given you their email addresses in confidence. They trust that you will not abuse the relationship. Make sure it is in your power to live up to that expectation.

Make sure that you have final control over the timing of your communications. It is important that your messages be delivered when you want them delivered. Timing is everything. We discuss timing later in this chapter.

Make sure that your contract has a clause that permits you to approve the final content going out to your list. You want to see and approve everything. You want to make sure the formatting is the way you want it; you want to be sure the personalization is working as it should; and you want to make sure there is no problem with graphics or word wrap.

You want to have a clear understanding with the outsource company regarding replies from messages going out to your list. Often the "From" field, although it looks like it is coming from you, is actually an address that resides with the outsource company. Discuss and agree on what happens when a recipient replies to your communication. Where does it go? When does it go? To receive a batch of replies three weeks after your communication went out is not acceptable.

There are certain benefits to outsourcing this activity to a third party that specializes in mail list marketing. This is their core responsibility. Often the outsource company has been involved in many campaigns—gaining expertise in what works and what doesn't. Often they can help you tweak your content or format to help achieve your objectives. Also, outsourcing this activity to a competent third party frees up your time and allows you to focus on other priorities.

Building Your Database or Mail List

Once you are committed to private mail list marketing, you want to focus on building your database of email addresses. The more people you can reach in your target market with your message, the better.

There are many ways to grow your list:

- Get your fans, followers, and friends in your various social media accounts to join your e-club. Provide some great incentive to have them do so, as it is imperative that you are in control of these relationships—they are extremely valuable. You want to make sure that when the next best thing comes along—and it will—you have a way to stay in touch, and provide them with access to your new accounts. I am sure that many past MySpace users wish they had done this before their friends moved on to Facebook.

- Depending on where your database resides and current legislation, you may be able to import from your existing database. You probably already have a customer or prospective customer list that you can import into your mail list. You may be able to send a one-time message asking them if they'd like to be on your list or join your e-club. Tell them what they'll be receiving and how often, and stress the benefits. Provide them with a link to the sign-up page on your Web site. You need to be careful here with current legislation and where your database members are located (particularly if they reside in Canada).

- Use permission marketing techniques to ask if site visitors would like to be included in your list to receive your newsletter, your e-specials, your coupons, or anything else you want to use to entice them to join your list. See Chapter 4 for more information on permission marketing.

- Collect names and email addresses at all points of contact—registration desk at a hotel, trade shows if you participate, member renewal or registration forms for membership associations or organizations. Ask permission to add them to your e-club—remember to "sell the sizzle."

- Have employee contests and reward the employee who collects the most sign-ups for your e-club.

- Have posters in your bricks-and-mortar location promoting your e-club and letting people know how to join. Think about providing an incentive: "Join our e-club and get a 10 percent off coupon for your next purchase [or a free gift]."

- Promote your e-club in all your direct-mail pieces and ads.

- Use direct email rental lists to ask for sign-ups.

- Use brokers to run campaigns on complementary sites to get targeted sign-ups.

- Promote your e-club in your signature file.

- Encourage viral marketing via existing list members: "Send a copy to a friend" works for a number of repeat-traffic generators such as coupons, newsletters, e-specials, contest information, special offers and promotions, and packages. Make sure that every viral marketing communication includes sign-up information so recipients can add their names and email addresses to your list as well: "If you've received a copy of this newsletter . . . or coupon . . . or e-special from a friend, and would like to join our e-club to receive your own in the future, click here." The link should take them to a sign-up page on your Web site, or open a new message in their email program with "Subscribe" in the subject line and details of what exactly they would like to subscribe to in the body of the email message.

- If you use tele-sales, add to the script a line that promotes your e-club and asks if the person would like to join.

- Partner with other, noncompeting Web sites that have the same target market as you. Choose sites that have lots of traffic and a big database.

Promoting Your Private Mail List

Promote your private mail list wherever you can reach your target market: on your site, online through various online marketing techniques, and offline. You will:

- Encourage your Web site and blog visitors to join your list by making sure you have "Join our e-club—click here" calls to action throughout your site. You might enhance this with an incentive "Join our e-club to receive our biweekly tips, tools, and techniques and to be included in our drawing for a free car wash—click here."

- Encourage your social media friends, fans, and followers to join your e-club. Provide a valuable incentive to have them do this, as it is very important you have these people in your database.

- Include a viral marketing element as previously described to encourage your subscribers to recommend your mail list to others.

- Invite your friends, colleagues, current clients, and potential clients to join your list.

- Remember to mention your e-club in your email signature file. This is an easy way to promote the list.

Your Communication with Your Mail List

To be successful with private mail list marketing, you have to have a great targeted list and you have to know how to communicate effectively with your subscribers. How often should they receive your messages? When do you start to become an irritant? What time and day are your recipients going to be most receptive? How should your communication be formatted? Should it be text or HTML? These all are important questions to be answered if you want to improve the response.

How often should you communicate? It depends on what you're sending and what they asked to receive. Newsletters should generally be sent out every couple of weeks or once a month. Special promotions, coupons, and e-specials generally will be sent out weekly or biweekly at a consistent time. What's-new updates would generally be sent monthly unless you've got something "hot." Tips of the day should be sent . . . daily. Tips of the week should be sent . . . weekly.

The content should always be relevant, valuable, and useful to the recipient. You might consider sending different email content to different target markets. You might also consider doing dynamic personalization where everyone in your database receives different specials or promotions based on their priorities, preferences, interests, or past purchases.

You might also consider sharing the load—making this a joint project with other, related organizations. That way everyone will contribute a little. There are many sources for your email content:

- Create it yourself.

- Find syndicated content online.

- Reprint articles with permission.

- Ask your business partners to contribute an article.

- Recap highlights of interesting articles.

- Interview an expert.

There are many places that offer syndicated content online. A few suggestions on where to find free articles include the following:

- YellowBrix (*http://www.yellowbrix.com*)

- EzineArticles.com (*http://www.ezinearticles.com*)

- IdeaMarketers (*http://www.ideamarketers.com/syndicated*)

- Amazines (*http://www.amazines.com*)

- FreeSticky (*http://www.freesticky.com*).

When should your communication be delivered? There have been many studies on this topic, and consensus has it:

- Never send your message late in the day or first thing in the morning. If you do, your email is included in that large group that is in the recipient's in-box first thing in the morning. You know what happens to all that email because you do it yourself—the first thing is to see how much you can delete, starting with anything that looks remotely like an ad or promotion.

- Don't send after 2 p.m. on Friday or at all in the afternoon on Friday in the summer months. Being buried in that huge pile awaiting a recipient on Monday morning is the kiss of death for your email.

- Lunch hour is best. Generally, people clean out their email first thing in the morning and again before they go to lunch. After their lunch break they are a little more relaxed, and the first thing they do is check their email. This is the best chance for your email to get noticed.

When it comes to the formatting of your correspondence, if you communicate through a newsletter, coupons, e-specials, or similar type of marketing content, an HTML message has a better chance of grabbing the viewer's attention. If your message is meant to look like a personal one-on-one message, then text-based is better. Your communications should be personalized using the recipient's first name appropriately throughout the correspondence and in the subject field.

Your content should always be valuable, fresh, relevant, and succinct. One bad message could result in many "Unsubscribes."

Each paragraph should be written so it can easily be scanned, containing no more than six or seven lines. Include calls to action.

Always encourage viral marketing—"Send a copy to a friend"—and provide instructions for the friend to subscribe to be included on your list.

Use a personal name in the "From" field. You want to build a relationship!

Take time with your subject field:

- Avoid ad copy.

- Avoid gimmicky slogans.

- Build business credibility.

- Use action words.

- Be positive.

Personalize your message with the recipient's first name in the subject field as well as the salutation and throughout the email. Good mail list software makes this easy to do.

More advanced Internet marketers are using dynamic personalization where the various parts of the message are personalized based on each individual's priorities, preferences, past purchases, or other criteria.

Be sure to check the preview screen. Most email programs these days have a preview screen that allows users to get a glimpse of the message before they actually open it. You want the most important information of your email to show up in the preview screen, so be sure to keep it simple and to the point.

Close your email with a P.S. and use the P.S. to restate your offer, give it a sense of urgency, and make it easy for readers to respond. Use phrases like "while supplies last," "in the next 24 hours," "call now," "reply to this email." You should always place your P.S. above your signature, as most people do not read past the signature.

Provide rich content with links back to your Web site. The more time people spend on your site, the more your brand is reinforced and the more people start to get to know you, trust you, and see you as an expert in the field. People do business with people they know and trust. Differentiate yourself. Become the recognized expert.

Stay under the Spam Radar

These days, anywhere between 5 and 20 percent of legitimate, permission-based email is filtered out by the spam detectors and never reaches the intended recipients. Always run your marketing messages through a spam checker before sending them out. The spam checker will give you a spam rating score and tell you how you received that score. Today, if your score is 5.0 or higher, it will be deemed to be spam by most of the spam filters. If your message scores too high, you should edit your message to eliminate or change the items that gave you the score. Then you should run your new message through the spam checker again to make sure you have an acceptable score before sending your message out.

Many ASP mail list software programs have an integrated spam checker, like Professional Cart Solutions (*http://www.profcs.com*) (Figure 12.2) or ConstantContact (*http://www.ConstantContact.com*). If yours does not, there are a number of free spam checkers online and others that charge a fee such as Site Build It! (*http://spamcheck.sitesell.com*) and MailingCheck (*http://www.mailingcheck.com*).

Some email elements that add points to your spam rating include:

- Using software and listservers that are commonly used by spammers. The header identifies the software that you are using.

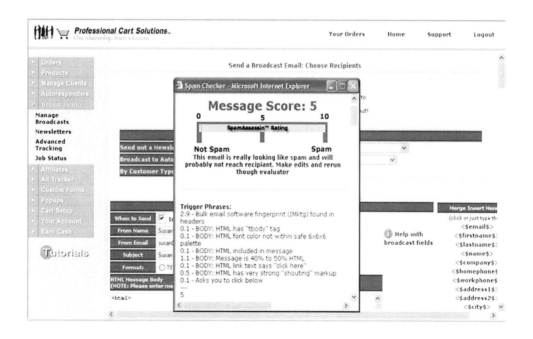

Figure 12.2. Professional Cart Solutions has a spam filter integrated into its software.

- Spam words in the subject line—things such as:

  - FREE in CAPS

  - GUARANTEED

  - Subject talks about saving

  - Starts with "Hello"

  - $.

- Hyperlinks—Using links without the http:// prefix or using IP numbers instead of domain names.

- Color discrimination:

  - Color tags not formatted correctly

  - Using colors not in the 217 Web-safe colors

  - Hidden letters (same color as background).

- Background other than white.

- HTML issues:

  - HTML message with more than 50 percent HTML tags

  - JavaScript within the message

  - HTML forms within your email

  - HTML comments that obfuscate text.

- Using excess capital letters.

- Using large fonts and characters. Fonts larger than +2 or 3 can cause you to have points added to your score. Use H1, H2, H3 instead.

- Using spam words or phrases in the body of your message adds points to your score. There are way too many of these to list. Your spam checker lets you know what words are adding points. The following are the type of words and phrases they are looking for:

– Great offer

– Risk free

– You have been selected

– Guarantee

– Call now

– Amazing

– Act now

– Millions

– Order now.

- Carefully word your "Unsubscribe." Claims that a recipient can be removed, claims that you address removal requests, and list removal information all add points to your score. Use text like "Use this link to unsubscribe."

- If your communication is a newsletter, say so. The spam rating also allows points to be deducted from your score for certain elements. When the subject contains a newsletter header, or contains a newsletter frequency, month name, or date, you might be spared some unwanted points.

- Use a signature file. This is another element that can cause points to be deducted from your score. Spammers never include their signature file.

- Don't mention spam compliance—only spammers do this.

- Always make sure you update your list and do your housekeeping regularly. Remove any addresses that have bounced back to you as undeliverable if your software doesn't automatically do this for you. Remove any "spam flag" addresses in your database—those that begin with spam@, abuse@, postmaster@, or nospam@.

- Set up test accounts for yourself at the popular email hosts to ensure that your mail is getting through. Set up test accounts at gMail, Live, Hotmail, Yahoo!, AOL, and some of the popular ISPs.

- Always monitor the blacklists to make sure you are not included.

Recent Legislation

It is essential to make sure you are in compliance with legislation regarding anti-spam (Can-Spam in the United States), privacy (PIPEDA in Canada), and other rules and regulations related to commercial email throughout the world. It is important that you realize you need to be in compliance with the rules and regulations of the country to which you are sending email.

Measure, Measure Measure

You want to improve your effectiveness as you learn from experience. This can happen only if you keep track of past performance. You want to track such things as delivery rate, number of undeliverables, number of unsubscribes, click-through rates, gross response, and net response. You want to compare response rates within different timings, different types of creativity, different formats, different segments of your list, and different target markets. Once you analyze what is working and what is not, you'll be in a better position to improve your conversion ratios.

Why Email Is Not Dead

There has been lots of a debate recently that with the rise of RSS and everyone communicating through social media that email is, well, dead. While the current situation is showing us that open rates are declining, spam filters are blocking good emails, click-through rates are low, people are experiencing list fatigue, legislation is putting stricter rules and regulations in place concerning sending email, and RSS is an alternative, email is still the killer App. There are a few very important pros to email that RSS and social media just do not deliver:

- Email is trackable (open rates, CTRs, etc.) down to the individual level.

- ROI is easily understood and measurable.

- It is a mature channel with industry-standard metrics.

- Email can be personalized. You can include such elements as the recipient's name, company, and city in the Subject field, in the To field, and in the content of the message. Through dynamic personalization you can also personalize on the recipient's priorities, preferences, and past purchases.

- Email can be segmented.

- Email can be highly targeted, designed, and branded with rich content.

- Email can and should incorporate viral marketing.

With a private mailing list you can plan how you will measure and quantify success before you start. RSS does not allow you to test different elements of your campaign to see which yield the highest conversions. Private mail list marketing allows for such testing of things like:

- Timing—day of the week, time of the day, etc.

- A/B creative

- Format—HTML versus text, long paragraphs versus bullet points

- Segment

- Response rates

- From line—company name, person's name, destination

- Subject line

- Top offer

- Featured offer

- Bottom offer

- Ad copy effectiveness

- Headlines.

Your private mailing list gets you in front of your target customer on a regular basis and it helps build repeat traffic to your site. With private mailing lists you are able to promote your destination, attractions, or operation, which helps bring visitors to your Web site. Private mail list marketing helps reinforce branding and conserves your contact base.

It is important to realize that for business your communication doesn't have to be either/or—either email or social media, either email or RSS; these are not mutually exclusive. You will do both.

Email as the Killer App—The Latest

Email has been around for many years. Just like other Internet marketing techniques, the way in which we go about using it has evolved dramatically since its introduction. When using email today, it is important to have a plan to quantify success, provide consistently valuable content, and build a profile of everyone in your database.

With today's sophisticated mail list programs, you are able to build a profile of everyone in your mail list database. You can do this in one of three ways:

1. Track the click.

2. Ask the question.

3. Track the behavior.

By building a profile, you are able to distinguish which of your customers are interested in the various bits of information you may send out. Once you have these profiles in place, you will be able to send out messages that employ dynamic personalization. With dynamic personalization you can use each customer's profile to send them targeted emails based on their individual preferences.

Dynamic personalization is being used by many businesses to track users' clicks in order to determine their priorities and preferences. Using this information, you are able to send customized emails based on the customer's individual preferences. Let's say we have a bookseller online that sells all kinds of books. If someone in their database has shown interest in the business books and nothing else, then this person would receive customized emails about the business books and nothing else. If, however, someone in their database has shown interest in both their business books and children's books, then this person would receive customized emails that list both business books and children's books. These dynamically personalized emails are customized and personalized to also include the individual's name and other information based on their priorities and preferences; all of this information is provided in their profile.

Another great application of direct mail list marketing is the ability to perform behavioral targeting. While dynamic personalization focuses on the individuals' preferences and priorities, behavioral targeting focuses on the actual behavior. Behavioral marketers target consumers by serving ads to predefined categories. Let's say a user visits several Web pages related to business books. On the next page the user goes to, he or she will be presented with a business-book-related ad. The key for this ad is not the actual profile, but the user's behavior. Had the user visited several pages related to amusement parks, he or she may have been presented with an ad for Six Flags Amusement Parks. Amazon.com uses a type of behavioral targeting. On Amazon.com when you search for, or purchase, a book, you are presented with "people who bought this item also bought. . . ," and a list follows.

The Good News—Social Media, RSS, and Email Are Not Mutually Exclusive

A better alternative to choosing one over the other is to incorporate email, social media, and RSS as parts of your marketing mix. It is not a bad idea to make your content available through all means or offer some of your content through email, some through your social media, and some through RSS.

Internet Resources for Chapter 12

I have developed a great library of online resources for you to check out regarding private mailing lists. This library is available on my Web site, *http://www.SusanSweeney.com,* in the Resources section, where you can find additional tips, tools, techniques, and resources.

I have also developed courses on many of the topics covered in this book. These courses are available on two of my Web sites, *http://www.SusanSweeney.com* and *http://www.eLearningU.com* (which contains other instructors' courses as well). These courses are delivered immediately over the Internet, so you can start whenever is convenient for you.

13

Developing a Dynamite Links Strategy

The more strategically chosen **links** you have to your site, the better. Increase your traffic and improve your search engine ranking by orchestrating links from related Web pages, blogs, and social media venues. In this chapter, we cover:

- Developing a links strategy

- How to arrange links

- Getting noticed—providing an icon and tag line hypertext for links to your site

- Link positioning

- Tools to check your competitors' links

- Social media links

- Meta-indexes

- Getting links to your site

- Reciprocal link pages

- Associate programs

- How links can enhance your search engine placements.

> ## Link
>
> *A reference to a Web site or document that the reader can directly go to by clicking on that reference.*

Links Have an Impact

Developing your links strategy is one of the most crucial elements of Internet marketing. It is a time-consuming task, but it is time well spent. Links are important for several reasons:

1. Strategically placed, they can be a real traffic builder.

2. Most popular search engines use link popularity and link relevancy as part of their ranking criteria. The more links to your site, the more popular it is, so the number of links you have to your site can significantly impact your placement with those search engines.

3. The more links you have to your site, the more opportunities search engine spiders have to find you.

Links Have Staying Power

When you post a message to a social media group where you promote your Web site through your brilliant contributions and your signature file, you receive increased traffic while the message is current and is being read by participants in the social media group. As time passes, your message appears farther and farther down the list until it disappears, and then your traffic level returns to normal. The same goes for a promotional effort in a mail list. You can expect increased traffic for a short while after your mail list posting, but as soon as everyone has read your posting and visited your site, traffic levels return to normal.

This is not the same for links. Traffic from links does not go away as easily as other forms of Internet marketing. Links generally stay active for a long time. When a link to your site is placed on another Web site, you hope people see it and are enticed to click through to visit your site. As long as the site that hosts your link has new traffic, you continue to receive traffic through it. The beauty of links is that in three months that link will still be there and people will still be clicking through!

Links are very important because if you have links placed on a high-traffic Web site, they can turn into traffic builders for your own site. They also are important because they can have a major impact on your ranking in search engines, because all the major search engines use link popularity in their ranking criteria.

Once your links strategy is implemented and you begin to see an increase in the number of sites linking to your Web site, you will see your ranking in the search engines improve. For more information on search engines and their ranking criteria, see Chapter 2.

A Quick Talk about Outbound Links

The more links to your site, the better chance that someone will be enticed to visit. However, a quid pro quo usually applies, and this means providing reciprocal links, giving people the opportunity to leave your site with the click of a button. To minimize this "flight effect," make sure you place outbound links two or three layers down in your site. Never place outbound links on your home page. You want your visitors to come into your site and see and do everything you want them to see and do before they have the opportunity to go elsewhere.

There are two ways you can provide outbound links. The first is by providing a hypertext link, which transports the visitor from your site to someone else's with a single click. The second and preferred method is to have each outbound link open a new browser window when clicked. This way your visitors get to see the referred Web site, but when they are finished and close that window, the original browser window with your Web site is still active. The browser window with your site should still be visible on the task bar during their visit to the referred site.

Regularly test all of the links from your site to ensure that they are "live" and are going to the intended locations. Dead links reflect poorly on your site even if they are out of your control. There are tools available online to help you determine whether you have dead links. These tools include NetMechanic at *http://www.netmechanic.com* (Figure 13.1). NetMechanic is discussed in more depth in the Internet Resources section of my Web site, referenced at the end of this chapter.

Google Webmaster Guidelines on Link Schemes

All things in moderation—including links. We know that link popularity and link relevance are very important in the search engine ranking algorithms. We also

Figure 13.1. The NetMechanic site provides many valuable tools. Its HTML Toolbox can be used to find out if you have dead links on your site or if you have any HTML errors that need correcting.

know that the major search engines hate anything that smells of manipulation. You need to walk a fine line with your links strategy. I provide you with several links strategies in this chapter, but it is important that you know what Google has to say about link schemes before you decide how you will proceed with your links strategy. The following was taken verbatim from Google webmaster guidelines.

LINK SCHEMES

Your site's ranking in Google search results is partly based on analysis of those sites that link to you. The quantity, quality, and relevance of links count towards your rating. The sites that link to you can provide context about the subject matter of your site, and can indicate its quality and popularity. However, some webmasters engage in link exchange schemes and build partner pages exclusively for the sake of cross-linking, disregarding the quality of the links, the sources, and the long-term impact it will have on their sites. This is in violation of Google's webmaster guidelines and can negatively impact your site's ranking in search results. Examples of link schemes can include:

- *Links intended to manipulate PageRank*

- *Links to Web spammers or bad neighborhoods on the Web*

- *Excessive reciprocal links or excessive link exchanging ("Link to me and I'll link to you")*

- *Buying or selling links.*

The best way to get other sites to create relevant links to yours is to create unique, relevant content that can quickly gain popularity in the Internet community. The more useful content you have, the greater the chances someone else will find that content valuable to their readers and link to it. Before making any single decision, you should ask yourself the question: Is this going to be beneficial for my page's visitors?

It is not only the number of links you have pointing to your site that matters, but also the quality and relevance of those links. Creating good content pays off: Links are usually editorial votes given by choice, and the buzzing blogger community can be an excellent place to generate interest.

Links from Social Media Venues

There are two reasons you provide links from your social media efforts:

1. To generate significant targeted traffic to your site.

2. To improve your search engine ranking by improving your link popularity as well as your link relevancy score by having your most important keyword phrases as anchor text in the link or in the text around the link pointing to your Web site.

The objective of generating traffic from the social media links is an easy one to accomplish. The traffic from your social media links will have a positive impact on your search engine optimization (SEO) because more traffic helps your SEO score.

The search engine impact of the links from the social media venue are a source of major discussion and subject to change as the search engines monitor the impact of links from social bookmarking, social voting, and social news sites as well as spamming from social media in an effort to impact the search engine ranking. Some of the social sites are having a major influence on page one ranking, sometimes providing less relevant sites. We all know that the search engines don't like any kind of manipulation, and when they determine specific techniques used just to improve search engine ranking they reduce the weighting of that element in their formula, remove it from their formula, or make it a negative element in their formula.

As things evolve in this area I will be writing about it in my newsletter, so make sure you sign up for the newsletter or review the archive for relevant coverage.

At the time of the writing of this book, the links that are indexed and provided in the search engine results by the major search engines include:

- Facebook profile with very little information provided

- Facebook page

- Facebook groups

- LinkedIn profile—a subset of the profile is indexed

- LinkedIn job postings

- LinkedIn answers

- Twitter

- YouTube videos

- YouTube channel

- YouTube groups

- MySpace profile

- MySpace groups

- MySpace forums

- MySpace events

- MySpace blogs

- Flickr profile

- Flickr photos/videos

- Flickr groups

- Flickr applications

- Digg

- Reddit

- Delicious

- StumbleUpon.

See more on linking in Chapter 2 on search engine optimization.

Strategies for Finding Appropriate Link Sites

Ideally, you should be linked from every high-traffic site that is of interest to your target market. Develop a strategy to find all of these sites and arrange links.

Start with the popular search engines. Most people use search engines and directories to find subjects of interest on the Internet. Most of the people searching never go beyond the first 10 to 20 results that the search engine returns. Thus, these top 10 to 20 sites get a lot of traffic. Search your most relevant keywords in all the popular search engines and directories, and investigate these top sites for link possibilities. Some of these sites will be competitors and might not want to reciprocate links. The best opportunity for links is with noncompeting sites that have the same target market. I suggest you take your most important keywords, do a keyword search in the 20 most popular search engines and directories, and review the top 30 sites in each for potential link sites.

Another strategy to find useful link sites is to see where the leaders in your industry and your competitors are linked. I use the term *competitors* very loosely. It would include your direct competitors, your industry leaders, companies selling noncompeting products to your target market, companies selling similar types of products or services to your target market, and companies that compete with you for search engine ranking. See what your competition is doing. Determine where they are linked from, and decide whether these are sites that you should also be linked from. Learn what they are doing well, and also learn from their mistakes. You should be linked everywhere your competition is appropriately linked, and then some.

Explore These URLs

There are many tools on the Internet to help you identify a Web site's links. These tools can be used to see which sites are linking to your Web site. But they can also be used to see what sites are linking to your competition. This is a great way to research where your site could be linked from but isn't—yet! Let me walk you through a step-by-step process to increase the number of links to your Web site.

When determining which sites you should be linked from, you first have to develop a lengthy list of competitors. A competitor can be any business or site that offers the same or similar products or services as you do or anyone targeting the same demographic group in your geographic area. Because the Internet creates a level playing field for all businesses, you are competing against large and small companies from around the globe. Someone using a search engine to find information on services that your company can provide might see results from companies from all across the world in the top 10 results.

Once you have developed your extensive list of competitors and have gathered their URLs, you must then find out what sites they are linked from. Tools have been developed to assist you in finding who is linking to your site. I have provided a list of some of these tools in the next section. For more resources, visit the Resources section of my Web site at *http://www.SusanSweeney.com*. In most cases, you enter your URL, and then these tools provide a list of sites linking to it. However, by entering the URL for a competitor's site, you can just as easily determine which sites are linking to your competition and industry leaders.

The more organized you are for this exercise, the better. I suggest that you:

1. Gather an extensive list of competitors and their URLs.

2. Choose the tool(s) from the next section that you are going to use for this exercise.

3. Enter the first competitor URL to find the sites linking to it.

4. Copy and paste the results into a Word, Notepad, or other file that you can access later.

5. Enter the next competitor URL to find the sites linking to it.

6. Copy and paste the results into the same Word, Notepad, or other file, adding to your list of potential link sites.

7. Repeat steps 5 and 6 until you have found all the sites linking to your competition. When this is done, you have your potential link sites list.

8. Now develop a link request (see below for details) and keep it open on your desktop so that you can copy and paste it into an email when you find a site you'd like to have a link from.

9. Next, visit every one of the potential link sites to determine whether the site is appropriate for you to be linked from. If so, send your link request. If the site is not appropriate for whatever reason, delete it from your list. Also delete duplicates. When you get to the bottom of your list, it has changed from a potential links list to a request links list.

10. Follow through and follow up. Follow through and provide an appropriate link to those who agree to a reciprocal link. Follow up to make sure that they provide the link to your site as promised, that the link works, and that it is pointing to the correct page on your site.

11. Submit the Internet address of the page that has provided the link to the popular search engines so that they know it's there. This will help boost your link popularity scores.

Tools to Identify Your Competitors' Links

The following tools can be used to obtain a list of locations on the Internet that are linked to your competitors' Web sites:

Google (http://www.google.com)
Enter your competitor's URL in the search box like this: *link: yourcompetitorsURL.com.* The results will contain all Web sites linking to your competitor's Web site.

Link Popularity (http://www.linkpopularity.com)
Simply type in your competitor's URL and it will give you a list of all the sites linking to that particular site.

SEOCentro (http://www.seocentro.com)
In the SEO tools area there is a link popularity tool. You can put in three Web addresses and get a report on links to each of the addresses.

IconInteractive (http://www.iconinteractive.com/tools/pop)
IconInteractive has a link popularity tool which gives you information on links and also an Alexa rating.

Other Potential Link Strategies

Another strategy for finding potential link sites is to visit the many different search engines and do a search on keywords you feel people would search on if they were looking for your site. The top results get a lot of visits from your target market, so they are always good potential link sites.

The following is a step-by-step strategy to get linked from these sites:

1. Make a list of your most important keywords for your Web site using your master keyword list and meta-tags (see Chapter 2).

2. Develop a list of the top search engines (Google, Yahoo!, Bing, Ask).

3. Go to each of the search engines and input your most important keywords as identified in step 1.

4. Copy and paste the top 30 results into a Word, Notepad, or other file that you can access later.

5. Enter the next keyword and copy and paste the results into the same Word, Notepad, or other file, adding to your list of potential link sites.

6. Repeat step 5 until you have used all the keywords in your list. When this is done, you will have 150 potential sites for each keyword. You now have your potential link sites list.

7. Now develop a link request (see the next section for details) and keep it open on your desktop so that you can copy and paste it into an email when you find a site you'd like to have a link from.

8. As stated previously, visit every one of the potential link sites to determine whether the site is appropriate for you to be linked from. If so, send your link request. If the site is not appropriate for whatever reason, delete it from your list. Also delete duplicates. When you get to the bottom of your list, it has changed from a potential links list to a request links list.

9. Again, as already stated, follow through and follow up. Follow through and provide an appropriate link to those who agree to a reciprocal link. Follow up to make sure that they provide the link to your site as promised, that the link works, and that it is pointing to the correct page on your site.

10. Submit the Internet address of the page that has provided the link to the popular search engines so that they know it's there. This will help boost your link popularity scores.

Winning Approval for Potential Links

Now that you have a list of Web sites you would like to be linked from, the next step is to determine from whom to request the link. Usually this can be found on the site. Titles such as Webmaster@ or any variation on that theme are usually a safe bet. If the site does not have an obvious contact, try feedback@. You can either send the request there or ask for the email address of the right person.

Generally, a short note with the appropriate information in the subject line is most suitable. Your note should be courteous; briefly describe your site's content, and provide the rationale for why you think reciprocating links would result in a win-win situation. It doesn't hurt to compliment some aspect of the site that you think is particularly engaging.

It is a good idea to develop a generic "link request" letter that you can have on hand when you are surfing. You should always keep this letter open on your desktop when surfing the Internet so that you can easily copy and paste the letter into an email.

Here is an example of a link request email:

Dear Web Site Owner,

I have just finished viewing your site and found it quite enjoyable. I found the content to be very valuable, particularly [customize here]. My site visitors would appreciate your content as I think we appeal to the same demographic group. My site, http://www. mysitename.com, focuses on [my site content] and would likely be of value to your visitors. I'd like to suggest we trade links.

Sincerely,

John

A typical response might say that they would appreciate the link to their site and offer to provide a reciprocal link. To facilitate this, you should either have the HTML for the link ready to send or have it available on your site, or both. Make sure you have your most important keyword in the text around the link to your site to ensure that you score as high as possible in the link relevancy category.

Make sure to follow through and follow up. If you said that you would provide a reciprocal link, do so within 24 hours. Follow up to make sure that your site has been linked from theirs, the link works properly, and it is linked to the right page on your site.

Then remember to send a thank you. Because they are doing you a favor by adding your site to their Web site, you should strive to develop a good relationship with them. This way they might be more generous with the link they give you. They might place it higher on the page, or even offer you the opportunity of having a small graphic link on their page, which would be dynamite for increasing traffic to your site. These graphic links are explained in more detail later in the chapter.

Another way to get links is to ask for them on your site. You can use the ShareThis or AddThis button as reviewed in Chapter 5 on viral marketing. You can provide the links to Digg, Delicious, StumbleUpon, and other popular social bookmarking and sharing services. In a prominent location on your site, you can place a link that says something like, "Would you like to provide a link to this site? Click here." Link this message to a separate page that holds several options for links. You can provide viewers with several different sizes of graphics they could place on their Web site. You can also provide them with a thumbnail icon, the HTML, and your tag line, which they could simply copy and paste into the HTML code on their Web site. Again, remember to select appropriate keywords to include in the text around the link to increase your link relevancy score with the popular search engines.

Quite often, if you offer viewers these opportunities for links, you have a better chance of receiving these enhanced link features. If you make it easier for them to add the link, they will be more willing to provide it.

You might want to offer an incentive to people who provide you with a link. Include viewers who provide a link to your site in a drawing for a prize. You might run a contest such as "Provide a link to us and win," where you include all those sites linking to you in a drawing once a week or once a month, depending on the size of the prize.

You might need to prompt sites to provide promised links. If you have made an arrangement for a link and find that the link is not there, it is appropriate to send an email reminder. When sending the follow-up email, include your icon, HTML, URL, and any other helpful information.

Other Link Opportunities

There are many link opportunities that are easy to get but are often missed or not optimized with appropriate keyword text in or around the link to your Web site. These include links from:

- Local and business links where you may be a member

- Better Business Bureau

- Chamber of commerce

- Industry associations

- Local directories

- Yellow pages

- Complementary businesses

- Articles you write and upload to syndicated articles sites

- Google Maps

- Interactive maps of others in your geographic area

- Related blog posts—your blog and others' blogs where appropriate.

Making Your Link the Place to Click

There are links and then there are links. Usually links are your company name hyperlinked to your home page, and your company's site link is listed with a number of other companies' links. Sometimes, if you are lucky, there is a brief description attached to the link.

You should take a proactive approach with linking arrangements. Explore every opportunity to have your link placed prominently and, if possible, to have it differentiated from the other links on the page.

Once you have an agreement with a site willing to provide a link, you should ask if you could send them an **icon** and the HTML for the link. The icon (GIF or JPG format) should be visually pleasing and representative of your business. Within the HTML, include a tag line or call to action that entices people to click on the link. With the icon or logo, the tag line, and your company's name, your link will stand out. Again, remember to include appropriate keywords in the text around the link to add to your link relevancy score to improve your search engine ranking.

Icon

An image that represents a logo, an application, a capability, or some other concept.

If another Web site is generous enough to provide a link to your site, your image should be only a thumbnail, for you don't want to take up too much space. This image could be your corporate logo or a graphic from a current promotion for one of your products or services. By having this image and tag line strategically placed on a Web site, the chances that a viewer will click through to visit your Web site are much higher.

To Add or Not to Add with Free-for-All Link Sites

There are thousands of free-for-all links sites on the Net. These sites allow you to submit your URL, and their program in turn adds your URL and link to a long list of sites. These sites will provide little to no traffic and the search engines don't like sites that try to manipulate the link popularity element for search placement. STAY AWAY from these types of link sites.

Links from Meta-Indexes

Meta-indexes are lists of Internet resources pertaining to a specific subject category and are intended as a resource for people who have a specific interest in that topic. These lists consist of a collection of URLs of related Internet resources that are arranged on a Web page by their titles.

Some of these meta-indexes have a "Submit" or "Add Your Site" area; otherwise you have to develop a request-for-inclusion email and send it to the owner of the site. In your inclusion-request email, let the owner know that you visited the site and feel that your site would be appropriate to be included. Give the reasons you think your site is appropriate and request the link. You should provide the HTML for the link as well. Review the techniques discussed in this chapter to have your link stand out with a graphical icon, hypertext link, and tag line, as well as including targeted keywords to enhance your link relevancy scores for enhanced search engine placement.

Meta-indexes are directed at a specific topic, such as "Connecticut fitness centers" or "LA antique car dealerships." Meta-indexes provide easy access to a number of sites on a specific topic, and they are a great way to draw targeted, interested people to your Web site. In addition, some users might rely on meta-indexes as their only search effort. They might not use a search engine to perform a query on Detroit accountants, for example, if they know a certain meta-index contains 200 sites on Detroit accountants. Where search engine results will show links to actual Detroit accountants, they might also show books on accounting, or Web pages relating to accounting software. Experienced Web users know that meta-indexes provide only links to the actual Web sites of Detroit accountants. Meta-indexes can increase your chances of being found by people who are interested in your products or services.

Add Value with Affiliate Programs

Another way of benefiting from links to your Web site is by developing an affiliate program. Affiliate programs (also called reseller, partnership, or associate programs) are revenue-sharing arrangements set up by companies selling products and services. When another site agrees to participate in your affiliate program, it is rewarded for sending customers to your business. These customers are sent to your site through links on your associates' or affiliates' Web sites. By developing and offering this type of program, you generate increased business and increased links to your site and increased link popularity for search engines.

A Word of Caution with Link Trading

You must be aware when trading links that all links are not created equal.

- If you provide a prominent link to another site, make sure you receive a link of equal or greater prominence.

- Be aware, when trading your links with sites that receive substantially less traffic than you do, that you will probably have more people "link out" than "link in" from this trade. Consider trading a banner ad and a link from their site for a link from your site, thus making it more of an equal trade. If their site has more traffic than yours, don't mention it unless they do.

- Never put your outbound links directly on your home page. Have your outbound links located several levels down so that visitors to your site will likely have visited all the pages you want them to visit before they link out.

- When incorporating outbound links, make sure that when the link is clicked, the Web page is opened in a new browser window so that the visitor can easily return to your Web page.

- Sometimes when people update their site, they change the Internet address or delete a page altogether. If you have placed a link on your page to that page, and one of your viewers tries to link out to that page and receives an HTTP 404 error, this reflects badly on your site. You should frequently check your Web site for dead links.

- When you change content on a page within your site, don't create totally new pages; just update the content on your current pages and keep the same file names. There might be links to your pages and if you delete them, anyone trying to click on a link to your site from another site will get an HTTP 404 error. This will result in a dead link on the referring page as well as in any search engine listings you might have.

Internet Resources for Chapter 13

I have developed a great library of online resources for you to check out regarding link strategies. This library is available on my Web site, *http://www. SusanSweeney.com,* in the Resources section, where you can find additional tips, tools, techniques, and resources.

I have also developed courses on many of the topics covered in this book. These courses are available on two of my Web sites, *http://www.SusanSweeney. com* and *http://www.eLearningU.com* (which contains other instructors' courses as well). These courses are delivered immediately over the Internet, so you can start whenever is convenient for you.

14

Winning Awards, Cool Sites, and More

There are literally hundreds of awards and listings for Cool Sites, Sites of the Day, Hot Sites, and Pick-of-the-Week Sites. Sometimes you are required to submit your site for consideration; other times these sites are selected based on such things as:

- Cool apps

- Awesome graphics

- Dynamite content that is useful and interesting

- Uniqueness

- Fun features.

If you are selected for one of these sites, it can mean a huge increase in the number of visitors to your site. You must be prepared for the increased traffic flow as well as the increased demand for online offerings. In this chapter, we cover:

- Where to submit your site for award consideration

- How to win Site of the Day—tips, tools, and techniques

- Getting listed in "What's New"

- Posting your awards on your site

- Hosting your own Site of the Day.

It's an Honor Just to Be Nominated

There are sites that actively find and evaluate other sites on the Internet and recognize those that are outstanding by giving them an award. The award sites are generally quite discriminating in terms of selecting which sites are the recipients of their award. They have established criteria defining what they consider "hot" or "cool" and base their award selection on those criteria. Figure 14.1 shows a variety of popular online awards.

What's New Web sites are designed to inform Internet users of new sites and updates to existing sites, and are often selective in terms of which new

Figure 14.1. A collage of some popular online awards.

sites they promote. The owner of each site also chooses awards for Site of the Day, Week, Month, and Year. As mentioned earlier, some of these sites require you to submit an announcement or site description, and the awards are granted based on criteria such as graphics, dynamic content, uniqueness, and the "fun" quality of your site. Other sites grant their awards based solely on the personal likes and dislikes of the owner of the site and do not adhere to any criteria at all.

Some Web site awards are taken just as seriously as the Academy Awards. The Webby Awards have a very comprehensive nomination procedure. Information regarding the Webby is available at *http://www.webbyawards.com*.

When you win an award, you will be presented with an award icon to post on your site for all to see. The award icon is usually a link back to the site that bestowed the honor on you.

Social Media Awards

Awards are not just for Web sites; social media awards also exist honoring the greatest in social media content. There are many lists on the Internet of things like "The Top 100 Industry Leaders to Follow on Twitter." The Semmys offer awards based on search engine optimization, blogging, reputation, management, and more. Just Google "social media awards" to find these awards.

Choosing Your Awards and Submitting to Win

There are different levels of prestige associated with different award sites. Some are an honor to receive and some are highly competitive because of the number of submissions they receive. To find these award sites, you can do a Google or Yahoo! search with your subject of interest plus the word *awards*—for example, if you have a Web site with multiple games on it, you would look for "entertainment awards." Another option is to visit the awards page on other, related sites and follow the links to awards they have won.

Some awards are easier to receive than others, such as those from commercial sites that give out awards in an attempt to increase the traffic to their own site. They can increase their traffic because the awards they give are graphic links displayed on the winner's site and visitors who visit the award-winning site can follow the link back to the award giver's site. On the other hand, there are webmasters who give out awards to anybody and everybody who makes a submission. The award is granted with the sole purpose of building traffic.

The bottom line is that awards can be valuable assets. The average Web user cannot tell which awards are the prestigious ones and which are given to anyone who submits. So, submit for any awards that you choose to, as long as your site is ready.

Where you place these awards is important. If you win many awards, consider developing an Awards page to house them with a link from your navigation bar.

Always determine if the marketing tools and techniques will increase visitors from your target market before deciding to include them in your online marketing strategy.

Getting mentioned on one of the popular Cool Sites lists is probably a way to draw a tremendous amount of traffic to your site. However, that traffic is like a flash flood—fast and furious. Be careful what you wish for—you just might get it. Be prepared! Have a plan that you can implement on a moment's notice. If you offer something free from your site, be sure that you can access a huge volume of whatever it is and that you have a plan to distribute quickly. If you offer a free download from your site, plan to have a number of alternative **file transfer protocol** (FTP) sites available to your visitors. If you have a call-in offer, make sure you have a telephone response system in place and staff to handle the huge volume of calls you might receive. You need a plan to handle a huge volume of emails as well.

> **File transfer protocol (FTP)**
>
> *A standard Internet protocol is the simplest way to exchange files between computers on the Internet.*

Once you have decided that the type of traffic that comes along with winning awards fits with your marketing strategy, make sure your site has the makings of a winner and then submit to as many award sites as you can.

- First, make a list of the URLs of the award sites you are interested in.

- Understand the submission form and guidelines. Review a number of forms to determine the information commonly requested.

- To save time, develop a document with the answers to the various questions from which you can copy and paste into the different submission forms.

- Submission forms capture the following types of information:

  - URL

  - Title of your site

  – Contact person (name, email, phone, address)

  – Owner of the site.

- Submission guidelines tell you what types of sites can be submitted. (Some awards do not accept personal pages; others do not include commercial sites; others are just for your social media.) The submission guidelines also tell you what meets the definition of "cool" or "new" or "award winning" and what doesn't.

- Some award sites require that you display their award icon on your site. Posting an award on your site can provide a number of positive results—including enhanced credibility.

What's Hot and What's Not

Most of the award sites provide their selection criteria. Some base their selection on valuable content; others look for innovative and unique capabilities. Sites vary on what they consider "hot" or "cool," but they are fairly consistent on what doesn't make the grade, as summarized next.

What's Hot	What's Not
Great graphics, animation, video, interactivity	Single-page sites
Innovative original content	Single-product promotion
Innovative apps	Offensive language or graphics
Broad appeal	Lengthy download time
Fun features	

Posting Your Awards on Your Site

If you have managed to collect a few awards for your Web site, you want to display them. After all, any award is a good award, and the site that granted you one expects you to display it in return for the recognition.

Posting the awards on your home page might not be the best idea, though. By posting the awards on your home page, you are placing links leading out of your site on the very first page people land on. Thus, you are giving people the opportunity to leave your site before they have even had a chance to explore it.

Where should you post your well-deserved awards, then? The simplest way is to create an Awards section on your Web site. Here, you can list all of your awards without losing traffic.

Becoming the Host of Your Own Awards Gala

You can also create your own awards program to draw traffic to your site; however, this requires a considerable amount of work to maintain.

The benefit of having your own awards program includes having links to your site from the awards placed on winners' sites. Having links back to your site is important for search engine placement because of link popularity. If you are the host of the awards program, you control the text around the link that takes people back to your site, so make sure you include your most important keywords to enhance your link relevancy score to further improve your search engine ranking.

There are also great opportunities for permission ("Click here to be notified via email when we have a new award winner") and viral marketing ("Tell a friend about this award—click here").

In addition, having your own awards program provides you with "bragging rights" and the opportunity for press releases to announce your awards, which gain exposure for your Web site and increase traffic. You need to work at it daily or weekly, so you must be committed to it.

Be sure there is a benefit from a marketing perspective before you design and develop your own awards program. You must also be prepared to conduct your own searches to find sites worthy of your award if the quality of sites being submitted to you is not up to your standard.

There are a number of steps involved in getting your awards program up and running:

- Develop the criteria to use in your site selection.

- Develop several Web pages related to the award, including information on selection criteria, submission forms, today's or this week's award winner, and a past award recipients' page, in order to promote the award. (Be sure that you stipulate whether you are looking for submissions from commercial sites or personal pages and what criteria will be used in judging submissions.)

- Develop your award icon. Have this icon link back to your site. The award distinguishes the winner; thus, the link might be displayed prominently on its site. This is a great traffic builder.

- Finally, announce the award and market, market, market.

Internet Resources for Chapter 14

I have developed a great library of online resources for you to check out regarding winning awards. This library is available on my Web site, *http://www. SusanSweeney.com,* in the Resources section, where you can find additional tips, tools, techniques, and resources.

I have also developed courses on many of the topics covered in this book. These courses are available on two of my Web sites, *http://www.SusanSweeney. com* and *http://www.eLearningU.com* (which contains other instructors' courses as well). These courses are delivered immediately over the Internet, so you can start whenever is convenient for you.

15

Online Advertising

The world of online advertising is changing rapidly. In the very early days when banner advertising was in vogue, visitors were clicking through, good banner space was hard to find, and prices were rising. Then we saw the big decline. Click-through rates were poor and, as a result, advertisers were looking at alternative online advertising mediums. We saw banner advertising prices decline significantly. Quality space was not difficult to obtain and banner advertising was being used primarily to meet branding objectives.

Over the past few years we have seen more and more pay-per-click targeted advertising opportunities, and this type of advertising is now on the rise. I have chosen to discuss the different types of online advertising in different areas of this book—search engine pay-per-click advertising in Chapter 8, e-zine advertising in Chapter 17, Facebook advertising in Chapter 20—and deal with other forms of online advertising, including traditional online advertising, in this chapter.

Despite all the doom and gloom and bad press, traditional online ads can still be an effective advertising medium for online businesses if the ad is properly developed and is placed on a well-chosen site.

We are seeing a shift toward ads using rich media. Advertising online provides visibility—just as offline advertising does. You must develop an online advertising strategy that works with your products, your services, your marketing objectives, and your budget.

In this chapter, we cover:

- Your online advertising strategy

- Advertising opportunities on the Web

- Ad design and impact on click-throughs

- Ad sizes and locations

- Placing classifieds

- Tips for creating dynamite ads that work

- The cost of advertising online

- Measuring ad effectiveness

- Using an online advertising agency

- Sources of Internet advertising information

- Behavioral advertising

- Re-targeting

- Content integration.

Expanding Your Exposure through Internet Advertising

Today, Internet advertising is being recognized in the advertising budgets of businesses around the globe. Advertising is a way to create awareness of your Web site and increase the traffic to it. Ads are placed on the sites that your target market is likely to frequent, thus encouraging this market to click through and visit you.

The Internet offers many different advertising spaces. Ads can be placed on search engines, content sites, advertising sites, portals, and online magazines. The choice of where your ad is displayed is based on the objectives you wish to achieve with your online advertising strategy.

There are a number of advantages to online advertising:

- The response from these ads can easily be measured within one day through Web traffic analysis.

- The amount of information that can be delivered, if your Web site is visited, far surpasses that of a traditional advertising campaign.

- The cost of developing and running an online advertising campaign is much less than using traditional media.

Let's compare online advertising to traditional advertising. In traditional offline advertising, you generally work with a public relations (PR) firm or advertising company to come up with your marketing concept. As a client, you would review and approve the concepts (usually after several attempts) before they are ever released to the public. The PR firm or advertising company is responsible for developing TV, radio, and print ads for your business. They come up with the media-buy strategy after reviewing appropriate publications, editorial calendars, pricing, and the discounts that they receive for multiple placements. The ads are then gradually released over the period of the campaign and finally are viewed by the public. At the end of the campaign, the PR firm or advertising company evaluates the success of the marketing campaign. This is very easy if the objective of the campaign is to achieve X number of sales, but it is much more difficult if the goal of your campaign is to generate company awareness.

Today, online ads are developed in much less time and are placed on Web sites quickly. Web traffic analysis software can tell you the next day if the ad is working or not by tracking the number of visitors who clicked through and visited your site through the ad. This provides you with the opportunity to change the site on which you are advertising or to change the ad to see if it attracts a larger audience.

Maximize Advertising with Your Objectives in Mind

When developing your online advertising strategy, start with the objectives of your overall advertising campaign. The most common objectives for an online advertising campaign include:

- Building awareness

- Increasing Web site traffic

- Promoting your social media

- Growing your fans, friends, and followers in your social media accounts

- Generating Web site traffic, leads, and sales.

You have a number of choices to make, such as what type of advertising to use and where to advertise. These decisions should be based on your objectives. If your objective is to increase overall company recognition, a nicely designed ad on several of the high-traffic search engines would be effective. If you would like to develop leads and find new customers, then a more-targeted approach should be taken, such as placing an ad on a high-traffic Web site that is frequented by your target market.

When deciding how to proceed with your online advertising strategy, consider how many people you want to reach. Do you want a high-quality response from a small number of highly-targeted people, or do you want to reach a mass audience of grand proportions?

Always keep your budget in mind when you are devising your online advertising strategy. If you have a reasonable budget, you may want to work with several online advertising agencies. If your budget is small or nonexistent, there are many ways to stretch your advertising dollar. If you have the time, you can find promising sites to trade banners with.

Online Advertising Terminology

Click-Throughs

When viewers click on an ad with their mouse and go to the site advertised, it is called a "click-through." Sometimes advertising prices are determined by the number of click-throughs. You don't pay every time your ad is displayed; you pay only when someone actually clicks on your ad and is delivered to the appropriate page on your Web site.

Hits

Hits to your site are the number of times that another computer has accessed your site (or a file on a site). This does not mean that if a page on your site has 1,000 hits, 1,000 people have visited it. If your home page has a number of graphic files on it, this number could be misleading. A hit is counted when the home page main file is accessed, but a hit is also counted for every other file that loads along with the home page. Each one of your pages will have a number of files on it—you have a file for each graphic, a file for each ad you display, and often a different file for each navigation button on the page. So if a person visits 10 pages on a site and each page has 15 files included on it, then at least 150 hits would be generated.

Impressions or Page Views

When an ad is viewed, it is called an impression. Advertising prices often are calculated by impressions. If a person visits a page where your ad is displayed six times, this generates six impressions.

CPM

Cost per thousand, or CPM, is a standard advertising term. CPM often is used to calculate the cost of advertising if a site sells advertising based on impressions. If the CPM of advertising your computer software on another site is US$40 (that is, $40 per thousand impressions) and the number of impressions your ad generates is 2,000, then you, the advertiser, would have to pay US$80 for displaying the ad.

CPA

Cost per action, or cost per acquisition, is an ad payment model in which advertisers pay only when their ad leads to a complete conversion—sale, registration, download, or booking. Almost all affiliate advertising is based on the CPA model. This type of advertising model is best suited to high-volume sites as a large number of ad displays are needed to generate actual sales.

Online Advertising Trends

Advertising online has become more strategic over the years as lessons have been learned, technology has advanced, bandwidth has increased, and new venues and channels have emerged. Some of the trends we are seeing today are discussed next.

Keyword Advertising

You can purchase keyword advertising on search engine sites (see Chapter 8) that have sophisticated advertising programs, or sites whose advertising real estate is maintained by online advertising agencies that have sophisticated advertising programs. Your ad appears when someone does a search on the keyword that you purchased. This is good for zooming in on your target market.

Geo-targeting

Purchasing geographically targeted advertising is one of the trends in Internet marketing. This is done by purchasing advertising for a range of IP addresses. Every device that connects to the Internet has its own unique IP address. These are assigned centrally by a designated authority for each country. Sites sell advertising by IP addresses to help businesses pinpoint their target geographic group. For example, John Doe is planning to purchase a motorcycle in Florida and is searching for a dealership in his area. Cycle Riders, a new- and used-motorcycle dealership in Orlando, happens to be marketing over the Internet, and as part of Cycle Riders' advertising campaign they have purchased ads by keyword and by IP address. Simply stated, they have said that they want their ad to appear only when the keyword *motorcycle* is searched on by individuals whose IP address is within a certain range (the range being those existing in Florida). When John Doe does his search on the word *motorcycle,* the Cycle Riders ad is displayed at the top of the page holding the search results. Someone in Michigan searching for *motorcycle* would see a different ad.

Behavioral Advertising

Behavioral advertising, also known as behavioral targeting, is advertising to Web site visitors based on their own behavior and the behavior of others who are searching for the same things on the Internet.

Behavioral marketers target consumers by following Web site users around and categorizing them based on their searches. For example, if a user visits several Web pages related to skates and hockey and then visits a car dealership Web site, on that Web site there will be an ad for hockey skates. The key for this ad is not the actual profile, but the user's behavior. Had the user visited several pages related to amusement parks, there may have been an ad for Six Flags Amusement Parks.

Re-targeting

Targeting, in terms of advertising, refers to an advertiser's attempt to reach a desired audience. Re-targeting, also called re-marketing, is the process of targeting those visitors who have been to your site but left without completing the desired conversion.

Re-targeting works by observing your Web visitors' behavior while they are on your site. If the Web site visitor leaves your site without completing the desired conversion, purchasing one of your products, or signing up for your newsletter, then targeted messages are delivered to these visitors when they visit other areas of your site or when they visit any other site in the advertising network.

The possibilities of re-targeting can be enormous. Re-targeting can also be done with Web site visitors who have been to your site and completed the desired conversion. These customers can be re-targeted with ads for products or services that complement their previous purchase or they can be re-targeted with new related products and services.

Advertising through Content Integration

Today's online consumer does not want to be advertised to. A new trend for advertisers now is content integration. Content integration takes product placement one step farther than ever before.

With content integration, your products and services become part of an article or part of the topic of discussion in an e-magazine (an e-zine), newsletter, or other online publication. For example, if *Popular Woodworking*'s online magazine was running an article on the best wood-finishing products, the article would incorporate links to various Web sites such as Minwax (*http://www.minwax.com*). The article would either recommend or simply inform the reader of Minwax and the link out would allow the visitor to link to its Web site for more information.

Video Advertising

Another growing advertising vehicle is video. Online video advertising is generating quite a bit of excitement as more and more businesses are recognizing the combined branding and direct response value. See Chapter 23 for information on video promotion and video syndication.

Social Media Advertising

There is a lot of discussion among Internet marketers about the pros and cons of advertising in social media and social networking sites. For every person who says people don't look at ads when they are participating in their social sites, there is a great story of someone who has had phenomenal success.

The opportunities abound in social media and social networking sites. The targeted advertising provided through Facebook enables you to get your ad to your target market on a granular level. You can advertise your wedding planning services and have your ad appear ONLY to the female, age 20–25, within 15 miles of Witchita, Kansas, who is engaged using the keyword *wedding*. And you only pay when the ad is clicked on and that person is delivered directly to the landing page of your choice. See the social media chapters in this book to learn more about social media and social networking opportunities.

Ad basics

Ads often have an enticing message or call to action that coaxes the viewer to click on it. "What is on the other side?" you ask. The advertiser's Web site, of course. Online ads can be static, just displaying the advertiser's logo and slogan, or can be animated with graphics and movement.

If you use an advertising or PR company to develop your offline ads, quite often they can provide you with a library of ads that you can use for your online advertising campaign. If you choose not to use an advertising or PR company, you can outsource the creation of your ad to another company or create your own.

The ad should be designed to have a direct impact on the number of click-throughs it achieves. There are a number of resources online to assist you in developing dynamic ads. Animation Online at *http://www.animationonline. com* allows you to create banners online at no charge. Other resources to assist you in designing and building banner ads are identified in the Internet Resources section of my Web site, referenced at the end of this chapter.

The objective of your banner ad is to have someone click on it. Do not try to include all of your information in your ad. An ad that is too small and cluttered is difficult to read and is not visually appealing. Many ads simply include a logo and a tag line enticing the user to click on it. Free offers or contest giveaways are also quite effective for click-throughs because they tend to appeal to the user's curiosity.

Banner Ad Tips

Follow these tips to ensure that your banner ad achieves your marketing objectives:

- Make sure that your ad is quick to load. If the Web page loads in its entirety before the ad, then the viewer might click away before ever seeing it. Ideally, you should have a very fast loading ad on a relatively slow loading site. This way, your viewers have nothing to do but read your ad while they are waiting for the site to load. You should always try to keep your ad size under 5K.

- Keep it simple! If your ad contains too much text or animation, or too many colors and fonts, viewers experience information overload and will not be encouraged to read or click on your ad.

- If you are using animated ads, limit your ads to two to four frames.

- You should always include a call to action such as "Click here." It is amazing how many people do what they are told. However, you still have to make your ad interesting and one that grabs their attention. Don't simply say "Click here"—give your audience a compelling reason to do so.

- Test your ads with the different browsers, the different versions of these browsers, and at different screen resolutions to make sure that they look the way you want them to.

- If you know absolutely nothing about advertising and graphic design, do not try to create an ad on your own. Go to a professional. If you do design your own, get a second opinion and maybe a third.

- Have your link send your target customer to an appropriate landing page rather than your home page. (See Chapter 7 for tips on landing pages.)

Interesting Ads

The following are more technology-advanced forms of advertising. They are interesting to viewers because they have attributes that are unique or unusual in some way. These attributes might be more apt to grab viewers' attention and entice them to click on the ad.

- **Expanding ads.** An expanding banner ad (Figures 15.1) is one that looks like a normal ad but expands when you click on it, keeping you on the same site rather than transporting you to another site on the Internet. Usually these say "Click to Expand," and the viewer then can learn more about what the banner is promoting.

- **Animated ads.** Animated ads contain a group of images in one file that rotate in a specific order. These ads are more likely to receive a higher click-through than a normal ad because moving images increase the chance of viewers being attracted to and reading the ad. These ads also allow you to deliver more information than in a normal ad because you can show different files, which contain different data. Limit your ads to two to four frames to keep your load time fast and to make sure your viewers read your information.

Figure 15.1. This is an example of an expanding advertisement. It displays the ad and then prompts the viewer to scroll to see more. When the banner expands, it prompts the viewer to click through to the advertiser's site.

- **Drop-down menu ads containing embedded HTML.** We are seeing an increase in ads containing embedded HTML. These allow viewers to select from a drop-down menu which site they want to visit. These ads are great because instead of making viewers click through and then navigate through your site, as with a conventional ad, these direct your viewers to the page of interest on your site. This type of ad also is great for co-op advertising programs. Several companies targeting the same target market, in a noncompeting way, can use this type of advertising to get more exposure for their dollar.

- **Interstitial ads.** These are advertisements that appear in a separate browser window while your visitors wait for a Web page to load. Interstitial ads are more likely to contain large graphics, streaming presentations, and more applets than a conventional ad. However, some users have complained that interstitial ads slow access to destination pages.

- **Flash ads.** These ads allow you to use rich media in your advertisements. By using this technology, you can incorporate animation and sound into your advertisement.

- **Floating ads and DHTML.** These ads appear when you first view a Web page, and they appear to "fly" or "float" over the page for anywhere from 5 to 30 seconds. They tend to obscure your view of the page, and they often disable mouse input until the ad is finished loading so that you must watch it before being able to access the page content. They have a high click-through rate and are great for branding, although their intrusiveness has been questioned.

- **Unicast ads.** A unicast ad is basically like a television commercial that runs in a pop-up window. It has animation and sound and can last fro 10 to 30 seconds. Although they are like television commercials, the a step farther in that a viewer can then click on the ad to obtain fu information. They have a higher-than-average click-through rate

- **Rich media ads.** These advertisements use dynamic tools such HTML forms, Java, ASP, Javascript, or other programming or applications that increase the appearance or the fun the ad. A rich media ad may include sound or a registra usually commands higher CPM levels than other banne

Location, Location, Location

As with all types of advertising, the location of the ad is extremely important. There are any number of targeted sites where you can place your ads. Always make sure that your advertising location is consistent with your objectives and always make sure your ads appear above the fold or above the scroll. That is, be sure your ad is positioned on a Web page so that it can be viewed without having to scroll.

Ad Price Factors

The price of ad space varies from site to site. Ads are most often sold based on the number of impressions or number of click-throughs. However, they may also be sold on the cost per acquisition. As stated earlier, an impression is an ad view, and a click-through is the actual clicking on the banner ad and being sent to the advertiser's Web site. The price per impression should be less than the price per click-through, whereas the price per acquisition should be much greater than either to make it worthwhile for the Web publisher.

When site owners charge per impression, there is usually a guarantee that your ad will be seen by a certain number of people. The burden is on the seller to generate traffic to its site. When the charges are per click-through or per acquisition, the responsibility is on you, the advertiser, to design an ad that encourages visitors to click on it and then follow through with the desired version. Sites that charge per impression are more common than those that click-through or per acquisition.

obvious advantages to you, the advertiser, when paying per click-not have to pay a cent for the 10,000 people who saw the ad link. Sites that do not have a large volume of traffic often ecified period of time.

g Advertising

to purchase advertising, there are a few

your site is the target market of the site you

- How many sites are there like the one you are considering advertising on? Are there other sites you could use to reach the same audience?

- What size ads are allowed? Generally, the larger the ad, the more it costs.

- How many ads are on each page? The more ads on a page, the lower the click-through rate for any particular ad on that page. Generally, the more ads on a page, the lower the price per ad.

- Where on the page will your ad appear? Top? Bottom? Side? Above the fold or below?

- What ad rotation system is being used? Is there a comprehensive program that automatically profiles the visitors and provides the best ad? The more targeted the audience, the more expensive the ad; these profiling systems can provide ads to a very targeted audience.

- What are the site's competitors charging?

- Does the site have a sliding-scale ad rate?

Making It Easy with Online Advertising Networks

If your objective is to reach a large number of users through a wide variety of sites, Internet ad networks could be right for you. Ad networks manage the advertising real estate on a wide range of different Web sites that people look at everyday. If you are going to join an ad network, you are known as an advertiser. You supply your ads to the ad network and determine how you want it to promote you.

ValueClick Media (*http://www.valueclickmedia.com*) is an example of a popular ad network (Figure 15.2). ValueClick Media manages the advertising for over 13,000 sites in its network and is an ad network leader. It can target any specific industry of your choice, or run your ad to a mass audience. For a more-targeted audience, your CPM would be higher. Even though you have to pay a little more initially, it saves you in the long run.

"Run of network" (RON) or "run of network buy" means that you, as the advertiser, purchase inventory across an ad network's entire range of sites or a cluster of specified sites in the network designed to reach a specific audience.

The benefit of joining an ad network is that the network not only targets your audience, it also provides you with real-time reports that indicate the

Figure 15.2.   ValueClick Media is a large ad network offering advertisers the opportunity to target their audience using ValueClick Media's network of over 13,000 sites.

success of your ads. This allows you to evaluate the success of your current campaign and offers you the chance to change your marketing strategy if you are not happy with your results. Maybe you want to take a different approach, or maybe a different ad might work better for you. Whatever it might be, the data that the ad network can provide to you is beneficial in determining the strength of your advertising campaign.

You can also join an ad network as a publisher. Publishers are the Web sites that ads are placed on. If you would like to make some additional online revenue from your site without the administrative and technical headaches, you can join an ad network, which will place ads on your site and pay you for the usage of this space. Very similar to an affiliate program, when you join an ad network you can dramatically increase your online revenue.

Bartering for Mutual Benefits with Ad Trading

When you use this technique, you barter with other Web sites to trade ads with their sites. If you are browsing the Internet and find a site that you think appeals to your target market but is not a direct competitor, then ask for a trade. Send the Webmaster an email outlining your proposition. Include the reason you think it would be mutually beneficial, a description of your site, where you would place that site's ad on your site, and where you think your ad might best go on their site.

When you make arrangements like this, be sure to monitor the results. If the other site has low traffic, then more visitors could be leaving your site through its ad than are being attracted. Also, check the other site regularly to make sure that your ads are still being displayed for the duration agreed upon.

Form Lasting Relationships with Sponsorships

Sponsorships are another form of advertising that usually involve strong, long-lasting relationships between the sponsors and the owners of the sites. Sponsors might donate money, Web development, Web hosting, Web site maintenance, or other products and services to Web site owners in exchange for advertising on their site—this creates a mutually beneficial relationship. By sponsoring other Web sites on the Internet, you can achieve great exposure for your own site. The benefits of sponsorships on the Internet are that you can target a specific audience, you usually get first call on ad placement, and you show your target market that you care about their interests. Overall, by sponsoring other sites on the Internet, you have the opportunity to get directly in the face of your target market.

There are a number of ways in which you can advertise online through sponsorships. The following is a list of the more common forms of online sponsorship:

- **E-zines and newsletters.** An example would be Lee Valley Tools sponsoring a woodworking e-zine.

- **Content sites.** An example would be Web MD sponsoring a health and fitness Web site.

- **Online chat sessions.** An example would be Honda sponsoring a chat on the ATVFrontier.com forum.

- **Events.** An example would be an airline such as Continental Airlines sponsoring a seminar on vacation planning and booking.

Commercial Links

Another form of online advertising is commercial links. A number of targeted sites provide lengthy lists of URLs related to a specific topic. These sites sometimes provide your listing for free but charge a fee to have a hypertext link activated from their site to yours. These are great sites, especially because they are targeted toward your demographic group.

Sponsoring a Mailing List

Another online advertising opportunity is presented by mailing lists. Mailing lists provide a highly-targeted advertising vehicle. Mailing list subscribers are all interested in the list topic and are therefore potential clients, if you select the mailing list carefully.

The rates for sponsoring lists can be quite low. The cost would be determined on a price-per-reader basis and is usually between one and ten cents per reader. Subscribe to the lists that appeal to your target market and read the FAQ files to determine whether advertising or sponsorship opportunities exist for each mailing list. If the mailing list allows sponsorship, contact the mailing list administrator to inquire about the cost of sponsoring and, if the cost is reasonable, check availability and sponsors.

All of the members of the mailing list have subscribed and want to be on the list; therefore, they are likely to read your email. This is an excellent opportunity for you to expose your product specials, packages, or services to these potential consumers. A good example would be Kraft.com sponsoring a mailing list about outdoor cooking, recipes, and how to prepare a particular item. Readers are interested in the topic, so they might be encouraged to click through and purchase Kraft products.

A Few Final Thoughts to Remember

Before any advertising campaign goes live, make sure you have prepared your landing pages appropriately. A landing page is a Web page that is created specifically to respond to a marketing campaign you are running; when done properly it can greatly increase conversions, or the number of customers who act on your offer. For more information on landing pages, see Chapter 7.

Now more than ever it is important to track your ROI, or return on investment. ROI will help you determine whether or not an ad campaign has generated more, or less, revenue than it costs. The Web metrics software systems available today allow you to track your ROI pretty easily. They even allow you to track the different ads you have running at the same time. For more on Web metrics, see Chapter 28.

Internet Resources for Chapter 15

I have developed a great library of online resources for you to check out regarding online advertising. This library is available on my Web site, *http:// www.SusanSweeney.com,* in the Resources section, where you can find additional tips, tools, techniques, and resources.

I have also developed courses on many of the topics covered in this book. These courses are available on two of my Web sites, *http://www.SusanSweeney. com* and *http://www.eLearningU.com* (which contains other instructors' courses as well). These courses are delivered immediately over the Internet, so you can start whenever is convenient for you.

16

Maximizing Media Relations

Your online media strategy can be extremely effective in building targeted traffic to your site. News release distribution can be done easily. Build the right list of email addresses or make use of one of the online news release distribution services. All reporters and writers have email addresses. While there are still a few that don't like to receive emailed news releases, many others prefer the email versions. When email news releases are sent out, reporters reply by email. They will expect your response within 24 hours. Develop a media kit that you can email to editors. In this chapter, we cover:

- Developing your online media strategy

- Public relations versus advertising

- Online public relations versus traditional public relations

- Effective news releases

- Social media news releases

- News release and distribution services online

- How to distribute news releases online

- Providing an area for media on your site

- How to find reporters online

- How these reporters want to receive your information

- Encouraging republication of your article with a direct link to your site or the article

- Providing press kits online

- Electronic newsletters.

Managing Effective Public Relations

Media relations can be very important to your marketing efforts. The best results are achieved when you integrate both online and offline publicity campaigns. News release distribution can be accomplished easily if you have an established list of reporters and editors, or if you make use of a news distribution service.

Maintaining effective public relations delivers a number of benefits to your company. Your company, your products, and your services gain exposure through news releases. Your relationship with current customers is reinforced, and new relationships are formed.

Benefits of Publicity versus Advertising

Media coverage, or publicity, has a major advantage over paid advertisements. Articles written by a reporter carry more weight with the public than ads do because the media and reporters are seen as unbiased third parties; the public gives articles printed in media publications more credibility than they do paid advertisements. Another advantage of distributing news releases is that it is more cost-effective than advertising. You have to pay for advertising space on a Web site or time on the radio, but the costs of writing and distributing news releases are minimal.

One of the disadvantages of news releases compared to advertising is that you don't have control over what is published. If the editor decides to cast your company in a negative light, there is nothing you can do to stop him or her. If the writer of the piece does not like your company, for whatever reason, this might come across in the article. Basically, after your news release is distributed, you have no control over what will be written about your business.

It is important to note that when generating publicity, you might lose control over the timing of your release as well. For example, you might want an article released the day before your product launch or event, but the editor could relegate it to a date the following week. There is nothing you can do about this. It is not a good idea to rely exclusively on publicity for important or newsworthy events, because if the release is not reviewed or is not considered newsworthy, you might be stuck with no promotion at all.

What Is a News Release?

Before you begin your media campaign, you should know what news releases are and how to write them. News releases are designed to inform reporters of events concerning your product offers, your business, or your services that the public might consider newsworthy. News releases can get your company free public attention.

A news release is a standard form of communication with the media. News releases must contain newsworthy information. Companies that continually send worthless information in a blatant attempt to get their name in the press do not establish a good relationship with the media.

Writing a News Release

Journalists are bombarded with volumes of news releases. To improve the chances that your story will interest a journalist enough to publish it, you must make the journalist's job easier by presenting your news release in an appealing format and style. Your news release should be written as if it were prepared by an unbiased third party. The news release should follow a standard format, which is described in the following paragraphs.

Notice of Release

The first thing the reader sees should be . . .

FOR IMMEDIATE RELEASE

. . . unless you have sent the information in advance of the time you would like it published. In that case, state it as follows:

FOR RELEASE: Wednesday, December 12, 2010 (using the date you want it released).

Remember that no matter what date you put here, the publication can release the information before or after that date. If the news is really big, it is unlikely that the publication will hold it until the date you have specified.

Header

The header should be in the upper-left corner. It should contain all of the contact information for one or two key people. These contacts should be able to answer any questions regarding the news release. If reporters cannot get in touch with someone to answer their questions, they might print incorrect information or even drop the article altogether.

Contact:

Susan Sweeney

Connex Network, Inc.

(902) 468-2578

susan@susansweeney.com

http://www.SusanSweeney.com

Headline

Your headline is critically important. If you get it right, it will attract the attention you are looking for. Your headline should be powerful, summarizing your message and making the reader want to continue reading. Keep the headline short—fewer than 10 words.

City and Date

Name the city you are reporting from and the date you want the news to be released.

The Body

Your first sentence within the body of the news release should sum up your headline and immediately inform the reader why this is newsworthy. With the number of news releases reporters receive, if you don't grab their attention immediately, they won't read your release. Begin by listing all of the most relevant information first, leaving the supporting information for later in the article.

Ask yourself the five W's (who, what, where, when, and why) and answer them up front. Write the news release just as if you were writing a newspaper article for publication. Include some quotes from key individuals in your company and any other relevant, credible outside sources. If there are any statistics that support your main message, include them as well, providing references.

Your last paragraph should be a short company description.

The Close

If your release is two pages long, center the word *more* at the bottom of the first page. To end your release, center the word *end* or the symbol ### at the end of your message. A sample news release is shown in Figure 16.1.

Google to Announce Fourth Quarter 2009 Financial Results

MOUNTAIN VIEW, Calif. (January 12, 2010) – Google Inc. (NASDAQ: GOOG) today announced that it will hold its quarterly conference call to discuss fourth quarter 2009 financial results on Thursday, January 21, 2010 at 1:30 p.m. Pacific Time (4:30 p.m. Eastern Time).

The live webcast of Google's earnings conference call can be accessed at http://investor.google.com/webcast.html. The webcast version of the conference call will be available through the same link following the conference call.

Following the earnings conference call, Google will host an additional question-and-answer session at 3:00 p.m. Pacific Time (6:00 p.m. Eastern Time) to provide an opportunity for financial analysts to ask more detailed product and financial questions. This follow-up call will also be webcast and available at http://investor.google.com/webcast.html.

About Google Inc.
Google's innovative search technologies connect millions of people around the world with information every day. Founded in 1998 by Stanford Ph.D. students Larry Page and Sergey Brin, Google today is a top web property in all major global markets. Google's targeted advertising program provides businesses of all sizes with measurable results, while enhancing the overall web experience for users. Google is headquartered in Silicon Valley with offices throughout the Americas, Europe and Asia. For more information, visit www.google.com.

###

Google and AdSense are trademarks of Google Inc. All other company and product names may be trademarks of the respective companies with which they are associated.

Contacts:

Maria Shim   Jane Penner
Investor Relations   Corporate Communications
650.253.7663   650.214.1624
marias@google.com   jcpenner@google.com

Figure 16.1.   This news release from Google is written in the traditional format with hypertext links to access relevant content.

Advantages of Interactive News Releases

Online news releases take the same standard format as offline news releases, but the online news release can be interactive, with links to a variety of interesting information that supports your message. When your news release is provided by email and you provide a hypertext link in that email, the journalist is just a click away from accessing all the information he or she needs to complete the story. Helpful links to include in your interactive news releases are:

- A link to the email address of the media contact person in your organization so that with the click of the mouse a journalist can ask a question via email. All contact information should be provided—telephone, cell, email—so the journalist can make the contact and you can get the coverage.

- A link to the company Web site, blog, and social media accounts so that the journalist can quickly and easily access additional information as part of his or her due diligence, or can find required information.

- Links to articles that have been written about the company and related issues, both on the corporate Web site and on other sites. Don't provide a link to the site of a magazine that has written the article; rather, get a copy of the article and place it on your own Web site to ensure a live link.

- Links to graphics, pictures, and videos for illustration. If your story relates to your product, have a link to a graphic that can be used. Provide a link to your YouTube channel, Facebook page photos, and your Flickr photostream to provide easy access.

- Links to key corporate players, their biographies, their photos, their social media accounts, and possibly some quotes. Journalists usually include quotes in their stories.

- A link to an FAQ section where you can have frequently asked questions and a few that you wish were frequently asked.

Social Media News Releases

We are starting to see the emergence of a new social media news release that has a completely different format. Although we have not reached the point of a standard format at this point, the new format takes a very different approach

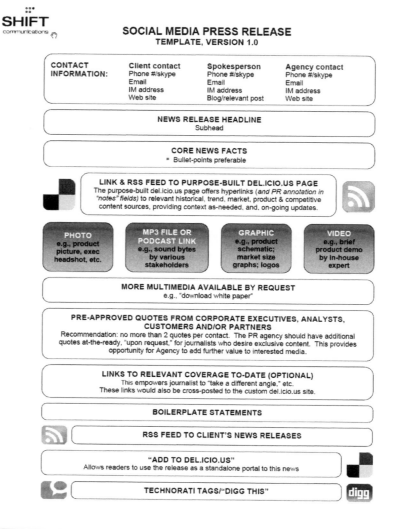

Figure 16.2. Shift Communications has provided a template for a social media news release.

than the text; it is written as you would see it in a magazine, written in third person, with links to appropriate content for the journalist to do due diligence. See Figure 16.2 for a social media news release template developed and made available as a free download from Shift Communications.

Sending News Releases on Your Own versus Using a Distribution Service

When distributing news releases on your own, you save the money it would cost to have a service do it. You can also be more targeted in your efforts than a service would be. Some services' lists could be outdated or incomplete. Their lists of reporters and editors might not be comprehensive and might not have been updated. On the other hand, some services could make sure your news release is taken more seriously. A reporter who recognizes the name of the service might be more receptive than if the release were to come from an unknown company. Using a service is bound to save you a lot of time.

If you decide to send your news releases on your own, you have to build a list of journalists. When reading publications that you'd like to be covered in, look for the names of reporters and find out their contact information. If you don't know whom to send a news release to at any publication, you can always call and ask for the name of the appropriate editor. Subscribe to a personalized news service to receive articles about your industry. This is a great way to find the names of journalists who might be interested in what you have to say.

There are a number of online resources to assist you in building your news-distribution list. Mediafinder (*http://www.mediafinder.com*) is a Web site that provides access to a database of thousands of media outlets including magazines, journals, newspapers, newsletters, and catalogues. Cision (*http://us.cision.com*) is a public relations resource that has detailed profiles on more than 20,000 media contacts, including their phone numbers, fax numbers, email addresses, and work preferences. They also have editorial calendars that tell you who will be writing a scheduled story, what the topic of the story is, and when it will be written.

There are a number of news release distribution services online. Several of them are listed in the Internet Resources section of my Web site, referenced at the end of this chapter.

Golden Tips for News Release Distribution

When distributing your news releases, don't send them to the news desk unaddressed. Know which editor handles the type of news in your release, and address the news release to that person. Don't send the news release to more than one editor in any organization unless there is more than one angle to the information in the news release.

Call ahead, if possible, to discuss and solicit the editor's interest in your news release before sending it. Also, follow-up with a phone call a few days later to make sure that it was received and to answer any questions.

Be sure to review editorial calendars of related publications to see if there are upcoming articles where your story could make a contribution.

News Release Timing and Deadlines

One of the most important things to remember when sending a news release or advisory is the deadline. Know how far in advance you should send your information for each of the media. Here are some time guidelines for your news release distribution.

Monthly Magazines

For popular monthly magazines, you should submit your news releases at least two to three months before the issue in which you want it to appear. Magazines are planned far in advance, because it often takes a number of weeks to have the magazine printed and in subscribers' mailboxes.

Daily Newspapers

It is a good idea to have your news release arrive on the editor's desk at least several weeks in advance. If it concerns a special holiday, you should send it even earlier.

TV and Radio

When submitting news releases to TV and radio, remember that you might be asked to appear on a show as a guest. Be prepared for this before you submit the release. TV and radio move very quickly; a story that has been given to the news director in the morning might appear on that evening's news.

Formatting Your Email News Release

Keep your emailed news releases to one or two pages with short paragraphs. It is best to insert the news release in the body of the email. Do not send your news release as an attachment. You don't know which platform or word-processing program the reporter is using. You might be using the latest Microsoft Word program on a PC, but the reporter could be using an incompatible program on a Mac and may not be able to open the file. There could also be problems downloading, which would prevent your release from being read.

Make sure the subject line of your email is compelling. Journalists can easily delete emailed releases unopened, and quite often they do, because they receive large volumes of these daily. Make sure your email is clear and concise. Get to the point with the first sentence. If you don't grab the reader's attention at the beginning of the release, the recipient might not keep reading to find out what your news is.

It's important to be able to send news release information in digital format within the body of the email. With a quick copy-and-paste, the journalist would then have the "first draft" of the story. You have made it easy for him or her to then edit the draft and have a story quickly. Everybody loves to save time, and nearly all journalists are under tight deadlines.

What Is Considered Newsworthy

Your news release has to contain newsworthy information for it to be published. One of the main concerns for public relations representatives is figuring out what is considered newsworthy and what isn't. You have to have a catch, and, if possible, the story should appeal to some sort of emotion. Here is a list of newsworthy items:

- The appearance of a celebrity at a company event or upcoming online promotions

- A special event your business is hosting

- A charitable contribution by your company

- History-related information on your company for certain magazines

- A milestone anniversary that your business is celebrating

- An award presented to your company

- Holiday event tie-ins

- Tips, articles, or advice

- Stories with a human interest element.

Developing an Online Media Center for Public Relations

If publicity is a significant part of your public relations strategy, you should consider developing an online media center as part of your site (Figure 16.3). The media center should be easily accessible from your navigation bar. It would include all the components a journalist needs when doing a story on your company. Journalists should be able to find pictures to include in the story and all the information necessary to do their due diligence. They should be able to send a question to the appropriate media contact within the organization with one click. The media center should include:

- A chronology of news releases distributed by the company. Make sure you put the latest news release at the top.

Figure 16.3. Nu Skin provides a media center on its Web site.

- The company history and background information.

- An electronic brochure.

- Links to other articles written about your operation. Make sure you have these on your site and not as a link to the magazine site that published the article.

- Links to story ideas for future articles.

- Links to pictures that can be used by journalists in their story. Perhaps have a gallery where journalists can choose the pictures they want to include in their story. Alternatively, you can provide a link to your Flickr photostream or photos on your Facebook page.

- Background information on key company personnel, along with their pictures, bios, and quotes.

- A link to your company's media contact and all contact information.

- FAQs and answers to anticipated questions.

By having a media center on your site, you are sending a clear message to the journalist. You are saying, "You're important to me! I want to provide you with everything you need to quickly and easily complete your story on our operation or our products and services." With the media center you are providing all the information, in a format that journalists can use, to enable them to do the story no matter when they choose to do it.

You will want to encourage permission marketing by offering visitors the opportunity to be notified to receive your news releases "hot off the press." Place a "Click here to join our media list and to receive notification of our news releases" link on your Web site. In addition, make it easy for visitors to send a copy of your news release to a friend. Sometimes journalists work on stories together, so give the journalist the option to send the news release to a colleague, or even to his or her editor, through viral marketing.

Internet Resources for Chapter 16

I have developed a great library of online resources for you to check out regarding media relations. This library is available on my Web site, *http://www.*

SusanSweeney.com, in the Resources section, where you can find additional tips, tools, techniques, and resources.

I have also developed courses on many of the topics covered in this book. These courses are available on two of my Web sites, *http://www.SusanSweeney. com* and *http://www.eLearningU.com* (which contains other instructors' courses as well). These courses are delivered immediately over the Internet, so you can start whenever is convenient for you.

17

Increasing Traffic through Online Publications

More than 60 percent of Internet users frequently read online publications, or e-zines. You can identify marketing opportunities for your business by searching for and reading e-zines that are relevant to your business. In this chapter, we cover:

- What electronic magazines are

- How to find appropriate e-zines for marketing purposes

- Submitting articles to e-zines

- Advertising in e-zines

- E-zine resources online

- Both eBrochures and iBrochures—the latest in online publications.

Appealing to Magazine Subscribers on the Net

Many Web users frequently read e-zines. This is one of the reasons they are among the most popular marketing tools on the Internet. Five years ago there were a few hundred e-zines in publication. Now there are thousands of e-zines dedicated to a wide variety of topics such as family relations, travel, business, finance, health, you name it. For any topic you are interested in, there quite likely are several e-zines dedicated to it.

What Exactly Are E-zines?

E-zines, or electronic magazines, are the online version of magazines. They are content-rich and contain information regarding a certain topic in the form of magazine articles and features. Many e-zines display ads as well. Some e-zines are Web-site-based and others are email-based.

Many offline magazines provide a version online as well (Figure 17.1). *TIME* magazine, *Seventeen, Business Travel News,* and *National Geographic* are all accessible via the Internet. Some of these sites provide the full version of their traditional magazine; others are selective about the articles they provide; and still others provide the previous month's edition.

Figure 17.1. Time Magazine is an example of a traditional magazine that has an online version.

Figure 17.2. SnowRider provides a great ezine of interest to those who enjoy snowmobiles and ATVs.

Web-Based E-zines

There are many Web-based e-zines that have only an online presence (Figure 17.2). These e-zines are accessed through Web sites by browsing from page to page. They have the look and feel of traditional magazines and include lots of pictures and advertisements. Usually there is no charge to view Web-based e-zines, but some do charge a subscription fee. These Web-based e-zines tend to be as graphically pleasing as offline magazines.

Email E-zines

Although email e-zines can come as text or as HTML, these days we are seeing most in HTML as they get a much higher readership. Today we are seeing a blur between newsletters and email e-zines as most newsletters now are sent as HTML and most are content-rich on a specific subject.

Email-based e-zines tend to be very content-rich and, as such, tend to be more of a target-marketing mechanism. Email e-zines tend to be several screens in length with one main article or several short articles and, sometimes, they include classified advertising. The benchmark is that these e-zines should be able to be read in about five minutes. Circulation is often in the thousands. Most run weekly or biweekly editions and are free to subscribers.

People interested in the subject of the e-zine have taken the time to subscribe and have asked to receive the information directly in their email box. Once you have found an e-zine that caters to your target market, that e-zine could be a valuable marketing vehicle.

A major advantage when you advertise in this type of medium and place your Internet address in the ad is that your prospective customer is not more than a couple of clicks away from your site.

People subscribe to e-zines because they are interested in the information that is provided. Even if they don't read it immediately when it is received, they usually read it eventually. Otherwise, they would not have subscribed. No matter when they take the time to read it, if you advertise in these e-zines or have your business, products, or services profiled, subscribers will see your URL and advertisements. For this reason, email e-zines are a great marketing tool.

Using E-zines as Marketing Tools

Online publications are superior marketing tools for online businesses for several reasons. They can be used in a number of ways to increase the traffic to your Web site. You can:

- Advertise directly

- Be a sponsor

- Submit articles

- Send press releases

- Be a contributing editor

- Start your own e-zine.

Finding Appropriate E-zines for Your Marketing Effort

There are many locations online to find lists and links to both Web-based and email e-zines. A number of these resources are listed in the Internet Resources section of my Web site, referenced at the end of this chapter.

You evaluate an e-zine's marketing potential by its audience, reach, and effectiveness. The most important thing when choosing an e-zine is to find one that reaches your target market. E-zine ads are effective because there is a high correlation between the target customer and the magazine's subscribers. If you advertise in an e-zine simply because it has the largest subscriber rate, you will probably be disappointed unless your products and services have mass-market appeal.

You should review a number of the e-zine-listing sites, such as the one shown in Figure 17.3. Some of these sites have keyword search capabilities. Others have their e-zines listed by category. Once you have a list of e-zines you feel fit well with your marketing objectives, you should subscribe and begin reviewing these e-zines.

Figure 17.3. BestEzines.com allows e-zine publishers to list their e-zines and visitors to write reviews/rate them.

The Multiple Advantages of E-zine Advertising

One of the major advantages of e-zine advertising is the lifespan of your ads. E-zines that are delivered to email addresses are read by the recipient and sometimes saved for future reference. Many e-zines archive their issues with the ads intact. Advertisers have received responses to ads that are several months old!

When you place an ad in an e-zine, you see it in a relatively short period of time, perhaps the next day or the next week, depending on how often the e-zine is published. Most traditional magazines close out their ad space months before the issue is available on the newsstand.

Your ad in an e-zine is also much more likely to be noticed because there are so few of them. In a traditional magazine every second page is an ad, whereas e-zines have a much greater focus on content and far fewer ads.

When your ad appears in an e-zine, your customer is just a click away because your ad is usually hyperlinked to your Web site. This brings your customer that much closer to being able to purchase your products and services.

Another advantage of e-zine advertising is that they are often shared with friends and associates. Most e-zines use viral marketing effectively, encouraging readers to send a copy to a friend. Your ad might be passed around a number of times after it first enters the mailbox of the subscriber. You are being charged for the ad based on the number of email subscribers. Therefore, the extra viewers of your ad cost you nothing.

One of the most tangible advantages of e-zine advertising is the relatively low cost, due, in part, to the low overhead for development, production, and delivery. E-zines need to fill all of their available space. If an e-zine advertising section has empty spaces, the publisher might be willing to negotiate. Some will even barter with you—advertising space at a discounted price in exchange for their e-zine promotion on your Web site.

E-zines provide a very targeted advertising medium. People subscribe to various e-zines because they have a genuine interest in the topics covered. This provides a major advantage over other advertising mediums. E-zine ads have been shown to have very high response rates due to their targeted nature.

Because they are distributed via the Internet, e-zines reach a far wider audience geographically than most traditional magazines. It is not uncommon for an e-zine to have subscribers from all around the world.

Another advantage is the link for search engine ranking purposes.

There are thousands of e-zines out there. Most e-zines have thousands of subscribers. When you couple the low cost to advertise in these e-zines and the many e-zines that might reach your target market, it is no wonder many companies are allocating more and more of their advertising budgets to online activities.

Guidelines for Your Advertising

Once you have found e-zines that reach your target market, you should consider a number of other factors before you make a final decision on placing your ad, including:

- Check the ads displayed in the e-zine for repetition. If advertisers have not advertised more than once, then they probably did not see very positive results.

- Respond to some of the ads and ask the advertisers what their experiences were with advertising in that particular e-zine. Be sure to tell them who you are and why you are contacting them. If you are up front, they will probably be receptive to your inquiry.

- Talk to the e-zine publisher and ask questions (for example, how many subscribers there are). Ask what other advertisers have had to say about their results. Find out what types of ads they accept and if there are any restrictions. Check to see if the publisher has a policy of never running competing ads. Maybe the e-zine has a set of advertising policies that you can receive via email.

- Find out if the publisher provides tracking information and, if so, what specific reports you will have access to.

- Find out if your ad can have a hyperlink to your Web site. If the e-zine allows hyperlinks, make sure you link to an effective landing page (see Chapter 7 on landing pages)—one that is a continuation of the advertisement or a page that provides details on the product or service you were advertising. Provide a link to your order form from this page to assist with the transaction.

- In some cases e-zines have an editorial calendar available to assist you with the timing of your ad. The editorial calendar will tell you what articles will be included in upcoming issues. If an upcoming issue will have an article relating to your products or services, you could choose to advertise in that issue. You might contact the editor regarding a review of the services you offer or submit an article relevant to the issue topics.

- Make sure that the advertising rates are reasonable based on the number of subscribers, and ask yourself if you can afford it. Find out the "open" rate, or the rate charged for advertising once in the e-zine. Ask what the rate is for multiple placements. If you are not in a position to pay for the advertising now, ask if there are other arrangements that could be made. For example, the publisher might accept a link on your Web site in exchange for the ad.

- Develop your ads with your target customer in mind. They should attract your best prospects. Wherever possible, you should link to your site or provide an email link to the right individual within your organization.

- Develop a mechanism to track advertising responses. You could use different email accounts for different ads to determine which ads are bringing you the responses. You can also use different URLs to point viewers to different pages within your site. If you have a good traffic-analysis package, you can track the increase in visitors as a result of your ad.

- Make sure you are versed in the publication's advertising deadlines and ad format preferences.

- Check to see if your ad can be integrated into the content of the articles in the magazine. These types of ads are often seen more as part of the article and less as an advertisement. They are also in front of your target market as they are reading the article if there is a close correlation between your ad and the content of the article.

Providing Articles and News Releases to E-zines

Besides advertising, a number of other marketing opportunities can be explored with e-zines. Once you have found the e-zines that cater to your target market, these e-zines could be fruitful recipients for your news releases. Refer to Chapter 16 for recommendations on news release development and distribution. The editors might also accept articles of interest to their readers. You might be able to incorporate information on your organization, your products, or your services in an interesting article that would fit the editor's guidelines.

There are many e-zines looking for great content. If you can write articles that provide great content for their readers and at the same time provide a little exposure for your organization, it's a real win-win situation. You'll want to target those e-zines that have the same target market you do and have a broad subscriber base. You'll want to make sure the e-zine includes a resource box at the end of the article crediting you as the author and providing a hyperlink to your Web site or your email address. Having articles published enhances your reputation as an expert, and people like to do business with people who are experts in their field. You might see if you can be a contributing editor or have a regular column or feature in their e-zine.

Besides sending your articles directly to targeted e-zines, you can also submit them to "article banks" online. Article banks are online resource sites for e-zine publishers. E-zine publishers search through these banks for appropriate articles for their e-zine and, if they use one, they include the resource box of the author.

Reasons You Might Start Your Own E-zine

Today, it is relatively easy to start your own e-zine. There are lots of resources online regarding e-zine development and administration. Don't make this decision without much thought, though, as you can damage your reputation if you don't deliver consistent, valuable content.

There are a multitude of reasons that you should consider developing and distributing your own e-zine. E-zines can be an extremely effective online marketing tool for the following reasons:

- You become established as an "expert." By providing your readers with valuable articles related to your area of expertise, you become, in their eyes, a valued and trusted expert.

- You establish trust. The first time someone visits your Web site, he or she has no idea who you are, how capable you are, or how professional you are. Sure, visitors get an impression from the look and feel and content of your site, but are they ready to do business with you? By providing them with free, valuable content over a period of time, you earn your visitors' trust, and they are more likely to turn to you when they are ready to purchase.

- You generate significant traffic to your Web site. Your e-zine should always reference and provide a hyperlink to something available from your Web site. Once your visitor links through, there should be elements that encourage him or her to stay awhile and visit a number of pages on your site. The more often people visit your site, the more likely they are to do business with you.

- You build loyalty. Relationship marketing is what it's all about on the Web. You want to build relationships over time, and your e-zine will help you do just that; if your subscribers receive something free from you every month, with whom are they going to do business when they have a need for your services or products? People prefer to spend their money with businesses they know and trust.

- You stay current with your customers and potential customers. When you are in front of your subscribers every month, you're not too easy to forget. You can keep them up to date on what's new with your company and your products, packages, and services, or what's new in the industry.

- You grow your database. See Chapter 12 for tips on how to build your database.

Developing Your Own E-zine

If you do start your own e-zine, you should spend sufficient time planning and testing before you publish to ensure that you do it right. You don't get a second chance to make a first impression, and you want your readers to subscribe and tell others about the great e-zine they found. You want them to be excited to read your e-zine every time it is delivered to their email box. The following tips will help you in your email-based e-zine planning and preparation:

- Provide great content. This goes without saying. If you have content that people want to read, they will remain subscribers. Don't think that shameless self-promotion is great content; your target audience certainly won't. As a rough guide, make sure your e-zine is 80 percent rich content and no more than 20 percent promotion and ads. Your e-zine should be full of what your target market considers useful information.

- Consider the length of your e-zine. You want your e-zine to be read relatively soon after it has been delivered. You do not want it consistently put aside for later because it is always too long to read quickly. In this case, less is more. Subscribers should be able to read your e-zine in five minutes or less. If you do have a lengthy article, you might give a synopsis in the e-zine with a hyperlink to more detail on your Web site.

- Limit your content to four or five dynamite articles for an email-based e-zine. Provide a brief table of contents at the beginning of the e-zine. Keep the copy short and to the point.

- Encourage your readers to send a copy to others they feel might be interested in your great content. Make sure you provide subscribing instructions as well for those who receive these forwarded copies. You should also provide instructions on how to opt out, or unsubscribe.

- Make sure you run your e-zine through a current spam checker to ensure that your e-zine will not be seen as spam by the spam filters.

- Have an unsubscribe button at the bottom of every email, enabling anyone in your database to opt out.

- Keep your subscriber addresses private and let subscribers know your privacy policy.

As word about your e-zine spreads, a large community of people who fit your target market will be reading it.

Once you have your own e-zine, you'll have to:

- Promote it to your target market through your social media accounts—tweets in Twitter, posts to your Facebook page; and also through the traditional methods—your private mail lists, your Web site, and your email signature file.

- Provide an opportunity for subscribers to let others know. In your online e-zine, have a form that allows subscribers to email a copy of the e-zine to their friends and colleagues. Use a call-to-action statement such as "Do you know someone who might be interested in this e-zine? Click here to send them a copy." This is a great way to pick up additional subscribers because some of the nonsubscribers who read your e-zine might then become subscribers if your content is interesting to them.

- Make it easy for people to subscribe to your e-zine. Provide clear subscription instructions in each email version of your e-zine and on the online version. Have a form handy on your site to collect email addresses from people who wish to subscribe. Always ask for the first name so that you can personalize your e-zine.

- Provide an archive of past issues on your Web site so that visitors can sample your wares before subscribing. Make sure you provide an option for visitors to subscribe from that page as well.

- Don't provide your list of subscribers to anyone. This protects your subscribers' privacy and keeps your list spam-free. People will not be happy if they start receiving spam as a result of your e-zine.

eBrochures and iBrochures—The Latest in Online Publications

An eBrochure is similar to a paper brochure. It contains all of the information you want your target market to read.

An iBrochure is similar to the eBrochure except that it implements elements of macromedia flash and page-turning capability. The iBrochures also use a simple point-and-click format, as if you were turning the pages of a brochure or magazine.

These iBrochures can be developed by you or you can have a professional develop them. There are free online sites like Issuu (*http://www.issuu.com*) where you can upload any pdf file and they turn it into an iBrochure within seconds. Madden Media is one of the leaders in the travel industry, developing amazing iBrochures.

Madden Media's iBrochure for Tucson, AZ, featured in Figure 17.4, is an excellent example of how to get the most out of an iBrochure. There is the option of clicking on the specific parts of the iBrochure you are interested in reading, or you can flip through and read all pages. They have also integrated other Internet marketing techniques into their iBrochures as well, such as viral marketing with their "tell a friend" button. They have integrated the reservation software with the "book a room" button so that those who are ready to purchase do not have to go to a separate Web site. They have also used the call to action "bookmark this site" element we talked about earlier in this book. They are also giving something away for free with their "free visitor info" button.

Some iBrochures use interactive maps and calendars. Most eBrochures and iBrochures may, depending on the file size, easily be downloaded from your site, sent to customers or prospective customers via email, or handed out on CD or DVD. Both complement your existing Web site and branding strategy and open up a whole new way of communicating with existing and prospective customers. Both eBrochures and iBrochures have the advantage of easily being updated or corrected.

Figure 17.4. Madden Media's iBrochure for Tucson, AZ.

Internet Resources for Chapter 17

I have developed a great library of online resources for you to check out regarding online publications. This library is available on my Web site, *http://www. SusanSweeney.com,* in the Resources section, where you can find additional tips, tools, techniques, and resources.

I have also developed courses on many of the topics covered in this book. These courses are available on two of my Web sites, *http://www.SusanSweeney. com* and *http://www.eLearningU.com* (which contains other instructors' courses as well). These courses are delivered immediately over the Internet, so you can start whenever is convenient for you.

18

Marketing through Blogs

Blogs can be used to provide your potential and existing customers with the latest news on your products and services, industry news, updates, tips, or other content relevant to your target market. But be careful. Always go back to your objectives and target market to determine the proper application, if any, of a blog for your operation. If you don't have time to update your Web site or generate traffic to your site, you probably don't have time to blog. Many people jumped on the blog bandwagon when it first began, and since then many have fallen off as 82 percent of blogs have been abandoned.

Blogs have changed over the last few years with businesses using them for different purposes. Many businesses have gone to a blog engine with a template for their main Web site because they are easy for non-technical people to update.

In this chapter, we cover:

- What are blogs and how do they work?

- To blog or not to blog?

- The many uses of blogs.

- Blog promotion.

What Are Blogs?

Wikipedia defines a blog as "A **blog** (a *contraction* of the term 'web log') is a type of *Web site*, usually maintained by an individual with regular entries of commentary, descriptions of events, or other material such as graphics or video. Entries are commonly displayed in reverse-chronological order. 'Blog' can also be used as a verb, meaning *to maintain or add content to a blog*."

Sometimes blogs look like an ongoing diary or a journal on a site. Sometimes they look just like a traditional Web site. Traditional blogs have one author and are usually written in more conversational or informal style than most business materials and can include text, images, and links to other content such as podcasts, video files, or even Web sites. Web sites that are built on a blog engine have the look and feel of a traditional Web site, as well as the typical text, photos, and videos that you would find there.

Writing the actual content for your blog is referred to as blogging. Each article that you add to your blog is called a blog post, a post, or an entry in your blog. You are a blogger if you write and add entries or posts to your blog.

Blogs usually focus on one topic or area of interest, or at least they *should* focus on one type or area of interest. For example:

- A person might have a personal blog about his or her trip through South Africa.

- A market analyst might have a blog on his or her findings in the finance and investment industry—what's happening in the industry, or news or articles on his or her latest research.

When setting up your blog, you have several options:

1. There are a number of free blogging platforms. WordPress (*http://wordpress.org*) and Blogger.com (Figure 18.1) are the most popular. Both are very easy to use and have wizards to get your blog up and running in short order.

3. You can also create your own blog using HTML.

The Many Uses of Blogs

Before you decide to blog, you should go back to your objectives. Why do you want to blog? What do you hope to accomplish? Is this the fastest, easiest, cheapest way to achieve that objective?

Figure 18.1.   Blogger is a free blog publishing tool owned by Google.

There are different reasons businesses decide to blog or use a blog platform:

- To have another vehicle to reach their target market—if you have a hard time finding time to update your existing Web site, realize that you will have a hard time finding the time to blog.

- To give key company officials a voice online

- To improve their search engine ranking

- To replace their traditional Web site—a Web site template on a blog engine makes it easy for the small-business person to update and maintain the Web site without outside help.

- To feed their social media.

Go back to your objectives first to determine if a blog is the best solution to achieve your objectives.

Blog marketing can take several forms:

- You can have your blog in addition to your Web site.

- You can have the blog as your Web site or Web presence.

- You can post on others' blogs.

To Blog or Not to Blog?

Blogs were the rage in Internet marketing several years ago. Because of this, there was a lot of buzz created around them, and just about everyone jumped on the bandwagon. Since then about 82 percent of blogs have been abandoned.

As with everything related to your Web site content, you must go back to your objectives and your target markets when trying to determine whether a blog is right for your business.

What are you hoping to accomplish with your Web site content? Whom are you hoping to interact with on your site? Is a blog the most effective technique to "speak to" your target market and get them to do what you want them to do? Is there a more-effective mechanism? How much work is involved? Is this time well spent, or are there other techniques that would be more effective given the time commitment?

You don't add Web site content just because it is the latest trend or because you can. Always go back to your objectives and your target market to see if this type of content is the most effective and most efficient way to accomplish what you want to do online.

Pros and Cons of Blogging

Some pros of blogging are:

- Blogs are an easy way to add new content, thus keeping your Web site current.

- Blogs can be used to provide your potential and existing customers with the latest news on your products and services, industry news, updates, tips, or other relevant content.

- Using keyword-rich content can help your search engine placement.

- Blogs can be updated from anywhere. You can even send camera phone photos or videos straight to your blog while you're on the go with Blogger Mobile.

- You can create an RSS feed to syndicate your blog, giving you instant access to your subscribers and the opportunity to have your blog content appear on your social media and relevant partner sites.

Some cons of blogging are:

- Blogs need to be constantly updated, a minimum of three times per week. You need to have the discipline to keep it current.

- You have to have enough news or new content to make it worthwhile for both you and your readers.

- Updates usually get done on your own personal time.

- The time spent updating blogs could be used toward something more productive.

- The time commitment needed to update is often underestimated.

- The marketing impact is often overestimated—how many times have you bookmarked a blog and gone back on a regular basis?

Again, it is important to be cautious when considering whether or not a blog is right for you. Don't jump on the blog bandwagon—just because it's easy doesn't mean it's right.

Avoiding Classic Blog Mistakes

While blogs can be an easy way to communicate with your target audience, there are many common mistakes that people make when taking on such an endeavor.

Underestimating the Time Commitment

One of the biggest mistakes people make when deciding to start a blog is underestimating the time commitment. While it's convenient to know that blogs *can* be updated from anywhere, it is more important to know that they *have to* be updated.

Blogs should be updated at least two or three times per week, and you need to have the discipline to keep it current. That means at least two or three times every week you have to research your topic or put your thoughts into words in a way that is interesting to read (both very time-consuming tasks), and post them online.

Overestimating the Marketing Impact

The second biggest mistake people make when deciding to start a blog is overestimating the marketing impact. It takes time and effort to build an audience for a blog—again, when was the last time you bookmarked a blog and went back to it on a regular basis? And if you did, did it influence you to make a purchase?

Irregular or Infrequent Updating

Users must be able to anticipate when and how often updates to your blog will occur. People are busy and they do not have the time to keep checking your blog to see if it has been updated—always provide an RSS feed.

Your readers need to know that everyday, or every two days, or whatever the case may be, there is going to be a new post they can read. Otherwise you will lose many of your readers. Pick a posting schedule and stick to it—a blog that isn't updated regularly will simply be ignored.

Writing for the Search Engines and Not for the Blog

There is the growing tendency by many bloggers to write for search engines rather than focusing on the needs of their "human" readers. Putting search engines first rather than putting your readers first will almost certainly lead to bad decisions that will make your blog less usable, even if it is optimized for search spiders.

While blogs can be a great way to speak to your target market and keep them up to date on all the latest news on your business products and services, you must determine if there is a more effective, time-efficient way to communicate.

Promoting Your Blog

Just like your Web site, once you have a blog, you want to maximize its exposure; you want to have as much of your target market reading or reviewing your blog on a regular basis as possible.

There are many ways to get your blog noticed. The most obvious place to start is your own Web site. However, there are many other ways to promote your blog:

- Use your blog to feed or update your social media accounts. Make sure you provide links from your blog to your social media accounts to grow your friends, fans, and followers.

- Generate links to your blog from other, related sites.

- Promote your blog in your email signature file, on your Web site, in your newsletter or e-zine.

- Submit your blog to all of the major search engines.

Another way to promote your blog is to register it with all the major blog directories such as Blogarama (*http://www.blogarama.com*) and Blogcatalog (*http://www.blogcatalog.com*).

Get your blog listed and high in the search results for your important keyword phrases in Technorati (*http://www.technorati.com*), Google Blog Search (*http://blogsearch.google.com*), Blog Search Engine (*http://www.blogsearchengine.com*), and other popular blog search engines.

Resources for Chapter 18

I have developed a great library of online resources for you to check out regarding blogs. This library is available on my Web site, *http://www.SusanSweeney.com*, in the Resources section, where you can find additional tips, tools, techniques, and resources.

I have also developed courses on many of the topics covered in this book. These courses are available on two of my Web sites, *http://www.SusanSweeney. com* and *http://www.eLearningU.com* (which contains other instructors' courses as well). These courses are delivered immediately over the Internet, so you can start whenever is convenient for you.

19

Social Media

Social media is changing the way we do business. Your business is either already doing social media marketing or is considering it. Many businesses are spinning their wheels wanting to figure out how to do it, how to manage it, how to measure it, and where to start. I have chosen to address marketing in the most popular social media channels in separate chapters. There are some issues that cross all channels, however. In this chapter, we cover:

- What is social media? Social networking?

- The changing consumer

- How to know what's being said about you, your business, your products and services, and what to do about it

- Why social media is right for your business

- How to develop a social media strategy

- Can social media management be outsourced?

What Is Social Media? Social Networking?

There is a lot of confusion over the terminology—social media, social networks, social networking—are they all they same thing?

Social media is a technology type. It is media that is easily shared. Blogs, podcasts, video, photos, microblogging, and online communities are all types of social media.

Social network services are online communities of people who share interests and activities. These online communities are Web based and provide a number of different ways for members of the community to interact and share social media with each other. LinkedIn and Facebook would be included in social network services.

Social networking refers to the use of social media technology and a social networking service to form new relationships and strengthen old relationships online.

Many people use the term *social media* as a general all-inclusive term.

The Changing Consumer

The consumer online has changed the way business is conducted. Gone are the days when businesses could advertise and issue press releases to influence their customers.

Back in the olden days (last year in Internet terms ☺), consumers would do research through the search engines, then visit the top-ranked sites to continue their research; based on the content found on the site, they would make their buying decision and then they would make their purchase.

Today consumers sometimes use social media to do their research. Sometimes they use the search engines to do their initial research, visit the top-ranked sites to do their more-detailed research, and then go to social media to see what their friends (or the social world in general) have to say about the product, service, or company they are thinking about purchasing from before making their buying decision.

Today the business that builds the relationship, that is accessible, that engages and connects, that "helps" its customers rather than "sells" its customers is the one that will get the business. Social sites like Facebook, LinkedIn, and Twitter enable a whole new type of communication to take place between the business and the consumer.

Today's consumer is less trusting of what he or she finds on a Web site. Consumers want to hear from other people just like them about their experience, their recommendations, and their suggestions. They ask their friends on Facebook; they visit review and ratings sites; they talk with others in groups on Facebook, LinkedIn, and other social media and social networking sites.

It has become paramount that you know and react to what is being said about you, your business, your brand, and your products and services.

Know What's Being Said about You

There are many tools available online to track what is being said about you and your business. There are free simple tools like Google Alerts (Figure 19.1; *http://www.google.com/alerts*) that, once you set up an account and identify the phrases you want to be alerted on, will email you links to where that phrase has been used on Web sites or in blogs, news, video, and groups. Social Mention (*http://www.socialmention.com*) is another tool that searches user-generated content such as blogs, comments, bookmarks, events, news, videos, and microblogging services.

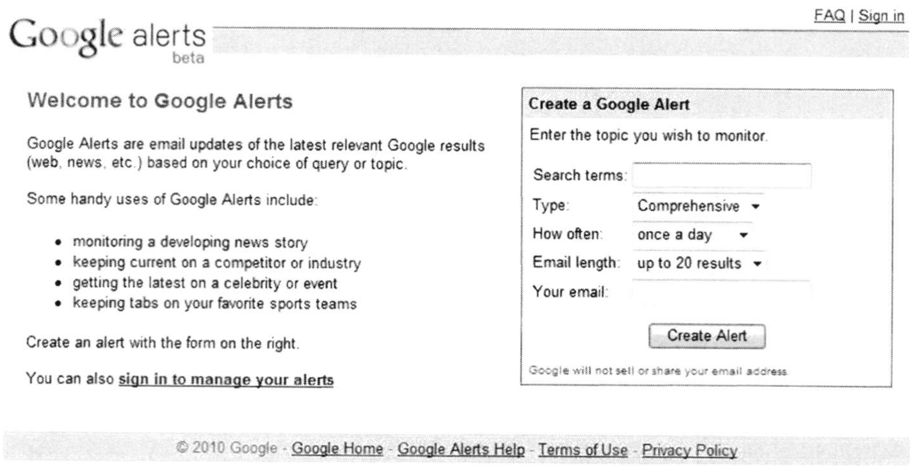

Figure 19.1.   Google Alerts is a great tool to let you know who is saying what about your business.

If the comment is positive, you can choose to do nothing or communicate appreciation or add additional content. If the comment is negative, you will want to do some damage control.

Why Use Social Media?

Social media provides an opportunity for all businesses to achieve some of their online objectives. Given the changing online consumer, the low cost of entry, and the fact that everyone can do it, it is no wonder we are seeing the social media marketing explosion. Social media can be used to:

- Generate significant targeted traffic

- Generate exposure for your business

- Build new business relationships

- Generate leads and sales

- Increase permission-based subscribers

- Improve search engine ranking

- Reduce marketing expenses

- Build an online reputation

- Increase customer trust and loyalty

- Increase referrals

- Maintain connections and relationships.

Businesses that choose to embrace the new way of doing business through building relationships and communicating with their target consumers and customers in an engaging and interactive fashion will take market share away from their competitors that choose to ignore this changing business environment.

How to Develop a Social Media Strategy

Many people are wasting a lot of valuable marketing time when they visit Facebook, LinkedIn, YouTube, and other social media sites. They get distracted with funny videos, a post from an old friend, or a family member's recent photos and have wasted an hour or two before they realize it. Some get overwhelmed because they don't know where to start. It is vitally important to document your social media strategy and also to separate your business and personal use of social media.

In working with organizations, helping them with their social media strategies, I find that many are overwhelmed and don't know where to start. Developing a social media strategy is a logical step-by-step process. It doesn't have to take a lot of time—with most organizations I work with we hammer out a high-level strategy in one day. The process is always the same:

1. First you need to determine and document your objectives, your target markets, and the products or services you are looking to promote.

2. You need to document the resources you are willing to invest—human and financial.

3. One by one, you take each objective and pair it to the segments of your target markets and then determine which social media venue(s) would be most appropriate.

4. Next, for each objective and target market identified in step 3 you look within that social media venue to determine which element will best fit with your objective given your resources. For instance, if you have determined that Facebook is the right venue but you don't have the resources to manage a fan page on an ongoing basis, perhaps participation in groups, or posting on others' fan pages, or Facebook targeted advertising might be the best choice to include in your strategy.

5. For each tactic identified in step 4, you need to specify exactly what will be done, how often it will be done, who will take responsibility for making sure it gets done, and what "success" looks like. You also need to know how you will measure to determine if you are getting a good ROI (return on investment) and ROE (return on effort).

It is important to have this documented because what doesn't get documented doesn't get done.

Even If You're Not Ready to Jump In

Make sure you reserve your business name in the various social media venues before someone else does. Even if you're not ready to fully participate, you want to grab your name just to make sure you have it.

There are tools to help you with this. Go to UserNameCheck *(http://www.usernamecheck.com)* or KnowEm *(http://www.knowem.com)* to do a search for your business name to see if it is still available in the popular social media venues. If it is available—grab it.

Social Media Policies and Procedures

Businesses must walk a fine line between being open and transparent on the one hand and having the personal lives of their employees influence customers' opinions of the business.

You need to have policies and procedures in place for what is and isn't acceptable use, what employees can and cannot do in social media when representing the company. It amazes me how many organizations don't address this issue because it just hasn't crossed their mind.

Think about it. You have no policies and procedures for your employees. You are an accounting firm or law firm or travel agency. A few younger staff members (not to pick on young people ☺) accept clients as friends on their personal Facebook account. The staff person or the staff person's friend uploads a video of a crazy Friday night party.

Can Social Media Be Outsourced?

This question is very dependent on your organization and industry. For some organizations, outsourcing can work wonderfully, but for others it may not be possible. It depends on your objectives, your target market, and your products and services.

For organizations that really want to give an inside look at their company, providing direct access to the CEO and answering detailed customer service questions on a regular basis, social media may need to be done internally. If your social media objectives include aspects that are very specific to the company and cannot be accomplished by a third party, such as providing internal company information, it would be best to perform this work internally.

For other organizations, however, outsourcing social media can be a very attractive option. Many businesses may not have the time, resources, or expertise to manage their own social media marketing. Although some people say that it can't be done, it is being done and done very successfully. I'm close to a prime example of how this can work as my daughter owns a social media management business, Miss Mediosa (*http://www.missmediosa.com*), that performs social media services for its clients. In speaking with her and the clients I've referred to her, it has been easy to see that outsourcing is possible and works very well; most often, customers and followers can't tell who is doing the updating.

When choosing an outsourcing company, it is important to make sure they keep up to date with the latest resources and tools in social media as new tools appear daily. It is also important that they develop documented strategic plans with their clients. Social media management businesses should have experience setting up profiles and frequent updates with appropriate keyword phrases to improve your search engine results. The company should work with you to develop a clear understanding of your business and your objectives in order to produce relevant and engaging updates for your followers.

Miss Mediosa provides three main services, and clients can choose to use any or all of the services. A thorough social media strategy is developed first in order to clearly lay out a strategy that works with the client's objectives, target markets, and products or services. A clear understanding of the strategic plan is vital for both the outsourced company and the client for the social media campaign to be successful. Miss Mediosa also offers a set-up service so that clients receive detailed profiles in the social media networks that are right for their business, which include search-engine-optimized keywords and other brand-aligned customizations. Finally, an ongoing implementation of the strategic plan is offered where Miss Mediosa provides frequent updates that meet the client's objectives and that follow the frequency schedule outlined within the strategy. Reports are then provided that show the progress and results of the effort.

For someone to do these tasks internally, it may be difficult to keep up with the latest changes in social media including the latest tools and resources available. If you do choose to manage social media internally, you may want to outsource the strategic planning so that someone with experience in social media and marketing can help your staff develop a detailed plan to be followed in order to meet your objectives. Above all, in choosing a social media management company, be sure that the importance of developing a social media strategy is understood and that sufficient time is dedicated to this process of gaining a better understanding of your business and your objectives.

Internet Resources for Chapter 19

I have developed a great library of online resources for you to check out regarding social media. This library is available on my Web site, *http://www. SusanSweeney.com,* in the Resources section, where you can find additional tips, tools, techniques, and resources.

I have also developed courses on many of the topics covered in this book. These courses are available on two of my Web sites, *http://www.SusanSweeney. com* and *http://www.eLearningU.com* (which contains other instructors' courses as well). These courses are delivered immediately over the Internet, so you can start whenever is convenient for you.

20

Facebook

Facebook is one of the most popular social networking Web sites that exists today. With more than 350 million active users, and more than 35 million status updates posted each day, it's difficult to find people who aren't using Facebook. In fact, if Facebook were a country, it would be the world's fourth largest.

As a business marketing tool, Facebook has a number of features and applications that can be used for a variety of objectives and goals. Some features require a lot of effort and maintenance, while others can be as simple as a one-time set-up. Be careful when making your decision on which features your business will engage in. As always with Internet marketing, it is important to return to your objectives, target market, and products and services when deciding whether or not Facebook is right for your business.

Businesses can set up fan pages, groups, or advertisements in order to interact with their target market and build a community online. Different elements can be used to achieve different objectives. Facebook pages can be used to build a community online, reinforce the brand, and sell more products or services. Facebook groups can be used to find your target market and create exposure. Ads can be used to drive targeted traffic to your Web site. In this chapter we cover the various opportunities that businesses can take advantage of within Facebook, including:

- Personal profiles

- Fan pages

- Advertising

- Groups

- Applications.

Look before You Leap

Be sure to adequately research the opportunities within Facebook available for your company, and to carefully consider the pros and cons of having a Facebook presence before you jump in. Some elements of Facebook require an ongoing commitment, while others are more on an ad hoc basis. Consider how much time you have available to spend working on this social media account and choose your activities accordingly. As always, refer back to your objectives, target market, and products or services when deciding whether or not Facebook is right for you. You may want to grab your username if it is available in order to ensure this online real estate in case you decide to get involved with Facebook somewhere down the road.

Facebook and SEO

It is important to always keep search engine optimization in mind as you engage in social media networks. Updates should include links back to your Web site and should include important keywords in the anchor text or text around the link. Make the most of your updates by not only providing valuable content to your fans, but also boosting yourself up on the search engines while you're at it.

Within Facebook, elements that are indexed by the major search engines include fan pages and Facebook groups. Facebook profiles are also indexed, but only very limited information is shown, especially depending on your own personal privacy settings that you've established. Facebook advertising and Facebook applications are not, at the time of writing this book, indexed by major search engines.

Personal Profiles

It is important to recognize the difference between personal profiles and fan pages on Facebook. Personal profiles are meant for personal use only—not for businesses. There are a number of entrepreneurs (particularly singers, professional speakers, and authors) whose brand is centered around their own first and last name.

Some people have gone the route of setting up a personal profile with their own first and last name for the purpose of promoting their brand—perhaps even mixing their personal networks with their professional networks. However, this is not the preferred route. Personal profiles are limited to 5,000 friends, while Facebook pages allow for unlimited fans. If you were to set up a personal profile, grow your friends to 5,000, and then switch over to a fan page, it would be very difficult to transfer all 5,000 of your friends to become your fans on your fan page.

Personal profiles require a first and last name, email address, and date of birth. This feature is intended for real people, not for businesses, so don't try typing in the first word of your business name as your "first name" and other words as your "last name." Registering a personal profile in your business name is against Facebook's terms of use—you will get kicked out.

Setting up a personal profile is relatively easy. Go to the Facebook homepage (*http://www.facebook.com*) and fill in your first name, last name, email address, and a password and select your gender and birthdate in order to sign up. From here you will receive a confirmation email. Simply click on the confirmation email to confirm your registration, and you now have a Facebook personal profile (Figure 20.1).

There are a number of features on Facebook that can be used only if you have a personal profile. For example, in order to participate in groups for the purpose of making comments, answering questions, or providing advice, you must have a personal profile. With a personal profile, you have the ability to post on walls, comment on groups, use the "like" button—whereas these functions are not possible with a fan page account. Basically, any of the posting that you would like to do within Facebook, whether it's on a personal profile, fan page, event, or group, you will need a personal profile to do so.

Your company should have corporate policies and procedures in place regarding the use of social media. Be sure that your employees understand the restrictions that you have set. If one of your employees, say your newly hired college intern, adds your clients, co-workers, and business partners to his or her personal account, how will you keep them from seeing the intern's photo albums of college parties and bar outings? She or he may have pictures that are inappropriate for your clients and business partners to see. Be sure to outline in your policies and procedures whether or not you allow employees to communicate with clients and business partners through their personal social media accounts.

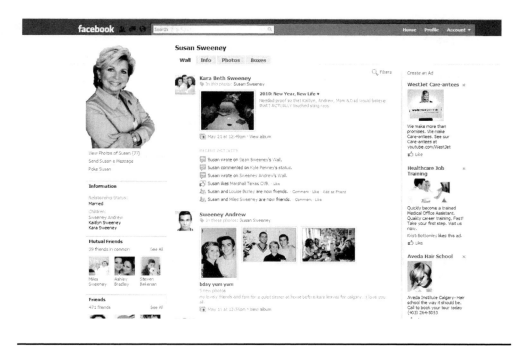

Figure 20.1. Your personal Facebook profile shows your updates as well as any of your friends' updates that involve you.

Fan Pages

As discussed, fan pages are created for the purpose of promoting business organizations, sports teams, public figures, brands, celebrities, or bands. Close to a million businesses have active fan pages on Facebook. Users can add themselves as fans, write on your wall, purchase products, learn about promotions, upload photos, and join others in discussion—all from your fan page.

To set up your own fan page, visit *http://www.facebook.com* and click on the link to "Create a page for a celebrity, band, or business" (Figure 20.2). This will take you through the process of developing a page name, location, and account. Be sure to type the page name exactly as you'd like it to appear, as you won't be able to change this later. You will also select a category for your fan page to help users find you, and to provide you with more relevant features preinstalled on your page. We recommend setting up your account with a specified email address such as *socialmedia@yourbusinessname.com* so that the email address is not connected to any particular staff member. Once

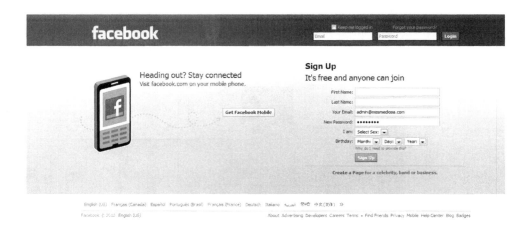

Figure 20.2.   Click "Create a Page" on the Facebook homepage in order to create your own fan page.

you've gone through this set-up process, you're ready to upload content and publish your page.

One great feature of fan pages is that multiple administrators can be assigned (Figure 20.3). This way, if there are a number of people in your organization providing updates to your fan page, there is no need to share an email address and password for log-in with the whole team. Employees can use their own individual accounts to log in and access the fan page.

Administrators of fan pages are not shown, so if you choose to have one of your staff members, or many of your staff members, monitor and maintain your fan page, your fans will not be able to see who personally provided the update. The privacy of your fans is also protected. With fan pages, the profiles of your fans are not visible, whereas the profiles of your friends on your personal profile can be seen by the public.

Fan pages are public; personal profiles are more private. Fan pages are indexed by the major search engines and are viewable by anyone. Even those without Facebook accounts can view your fan page—there is no need to sign in to Facebook to view the page content.

There are a number of ways to interact with your fans once you've developed a fan base. You can send updates to your fans, upload videos and photos, stimulate discussions, ask questions, write notes, upload flash content, and more. It is important to keep in mind your objectives and target market when updating your fan page. Actively engaging fans and building an online

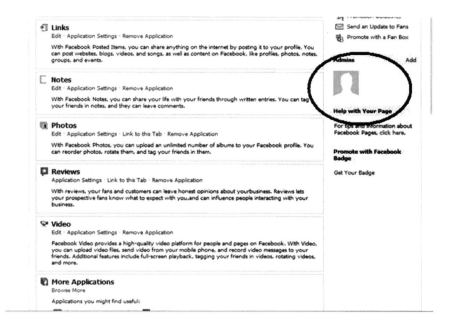

Figure 20.3. Click "Add" to add administrators who can have access to your Facebook page.

community will help with brand exposure, brand recognition, and generating traffic.

You can also choose to add on applications from the Facebook application directory in order to provide unique and engaging experiences for your visitors. Examples include restaurant reservations, events, and more. There are all kinds of applications that can be found in the directory—if you can imagine it, there's probably an application for it. We talk more about applications later in this chapter.

There are a number of things that should also be considered when deciding whether or not fan pages are right for your business. Fan pages are unable to join groups or attend events.

You must have a strategy to build fans. You may consider adding links to your fan page from your newsletters, emails, Web site, other social media accounts, or any other promotional material that you use. Once you've developed a fan base, it is very important that you direct your fans to your Web site in order to generate another copy of who they are and how you can reach them. Use permission marketing in order to develop your own personal database of these potential customers. Before you know it, Facebook could be replaced with the next big social media network. If you've already worked to transfer your fans to your own personal database, you won't have any trouble redeveloping your target market of fans or followers with your new account. For more information on permission marketing, see Chapter 4.

Fan pages provide access to metrics, which can help you track who your fans are, where they're coming from, and how often they visit. Take note that metrics are only available after you've reached 10 fans, and that more-detailed data is available as you gain more fans.

If you decide that setting up a fan page is right for your business, here are a few tips:

- Update your Facebook page frequently. If it isn't updated, you will lose your fans or your fans will stop visiting your page to look for updates. If you don't have many fans or your fans don't return to the page, what is the point of having it?

- Build your fan base.

- Provide links to your Web site in order to generate traffic from your fans and followers. Get important keywords in the anchor text or text around the link for search engine optimization.

- Provide valuable content to get fans to tell others about your fan page, and so that they return to your page often.

- Encourage participation and engagement with your fans. Participation will often show up on their walls, for their other friends to see.

- Send updates to your fans to provide relevant information that helps you achieve your objectives.

- Harness the power of news feeds. The news feeds on users' home pages tell them what their friends are doing. When users become your fan, news feed tells their friends. In turn, this can lead to the friends' becoming fans, and the friends of their friends finding out about your business through their news feeds, and so on.

- If you have trouble with any of the features on Facebook, they have a great Help section on their Web site: *http://facebook.com/help.php*. You can also reach them by email at: info@facebook.com.

Advertising

Facebook advertisements provide one of most targeted advertising opportunities online today. With the ability to set up the ads on a pay-per-click basis, you pay only for the ads that users actually click on. Alternatively, you can choose to pay based on CPM, or cost per thousand impressions. Advertising with Facebook is easy to set up through their step-by-step process for developing a highly targeted ad.

To set up an advertisement, log in to your account and click on the advertising icon or "Advertisers" link at the bottom of any page (Figure 20.4). This will take you to the ad development area. Click on "Create an Ad" on the top right, and fill in the form to create your ad. You will be asked for a number of things, including:

- An ad title—Maximum of 25 characters. Develop a "grabber title" to give people a reason to click on your ad. Calls to action work well.

- Ad description—Maximum of 135 characters. Go niche to get a better click through. Provide a call to action and grab the attention of users.

- Photo—Adding a photo or logo is optional, but it may help to attract people to click on your ad.

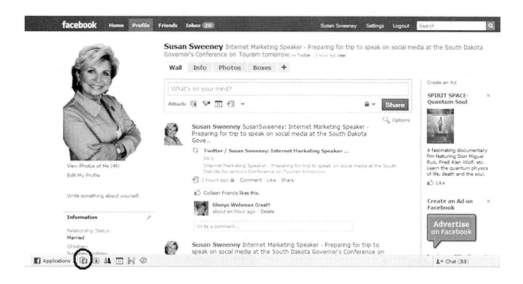

Figure 20.4. Click on the advertising image in order to create a Facebook page or advertisement.

- Destination URL—Choose a landing page rather than your homepage and try to make sure that the ad is brand aligned, so that the Web site and the ad look like they belong to the same company. See Chapter 7 on landing pages to make sure your link is optimized before letting your ad go live.

As you develop your ad, you can see what it looks like in the side panel. Once you've developed these elements of your ad, from there you will target exactly who will see your ad. You can choose any combination of the following fields:

- Geographic location of the user—You can go as broad or as narrow as you want—right down to within 10 miles of a specific city.

- Age of users.

- Birthday—You can target people on their birthdays.

- Gender.

- Keywords—The keywords are taken from information in the users' profile, their interests, and listed favorites. Keywords are available after 2,000 users have used it in their profile. When you list multiple keywords, Facebook reads this as "or" rather than "and."

- Education—You can target by education level or status.

- Workplace—You can target users by company or organization.

- Relationship—You can target singles, those in a relationship, those who are engaged or married.

- Interested in male or female.

- Language.

- Connections—You can target users who are connected to, or users who are NOT connected to, your page, a particular group, users of a particular application, or users invited to a particular event.

- Friends of connections—You can target users whose friends are connected to your page, a particular group, users of a particular application, or users invited to a particular event.

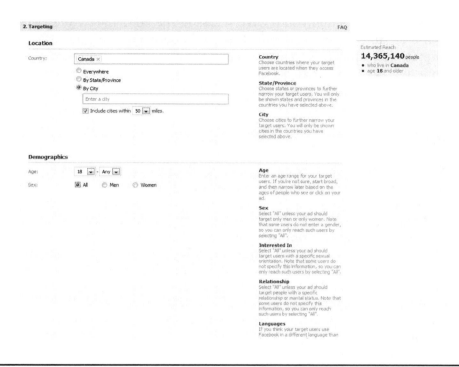

Figure 20.5. An estimate is provided of the total number of people on Facebook that fit your targeted customizations.

As you fill in these details, you will see the number at the bottom of the page change to portray an estimate of how many people fit the profile you've selected—how many people will be exposed to your advertisement (Figure 20.5).

From there, it's on to money issues. You will select the currency you'd like to pay in, the name of your campaign, your daily budget, dates and times you'd like your ad displayed, and more.

You can schedule when your ad will run so that you can avoid times when your target customers are not likely to click through. You can choose whether you want your ad to run on a cost-per-click or cost-per-impression basis. Facebook will provide you with a suggested bid for your advertisement, and you can choose what your maximum bid is for your particular ad. Your bid will influence the position of your ad.

Finally, you'll see a complete view of how your ad will appear and who will see it. You have a final opportunity to edit your ad. You will then provide your credit card information in order to pay for the advertisement. Once your ad is up and running, you'll have access to the ad manager on Facebook. Here you'll be able to access detailed metrics about your ad, including how many impressions you ad has had, as well as the number of clicks you've received and your average cost per click.

Groups

When it comes to Facebook groups, you have a number of options. You have the opportunity to join existing groups where groups are accessing the same target market that you're trying to reach, or you can start your own group to update and maintain in order to reach your target market. There are advantages and disadvantages of each option, so be sure that you make your decision carefully. Having your own group requires updates, conversation stimulation, and group member engagement, as well as an active search in order to build your group members and reach your targeted customers. Opting for membership in established groups, however, leaves you with less control. If the current group administrator decides to close down the group, there's nothing you can do about it.

Groups are relatively simple to set up within Facebook, but they require a personal profile to do so. Once you're logged in to your account, click on "Profile" in the top toolbar. Next, click on the "Info" tab within your profile and scroll to the bottom where your groups are listed. From here, select "See All" and choose "Create a New Group" at the top of your page (Figure 20.6). You will then be able to choose a group name, network, description, category, subcategory, contact information, and privacy settings for your group.

Businesses may create groups in order to foster a stronger sense of community, to promote something quickly, or for greater control over participants. If you decide to set up a Facebook group, be sure to include valuable keywords in order to be sure you appear in the search engine results, and be ready for the time commitment required for updates and maintenance.

Groups should be updated frequently in order to provide valuable content to group members so that they remain members. Post links, videos, and photos to your groups to engage your members. Ask questions and stimulate conversations. Another great promotional feature for administrators is the use of "Events." This allows you to invite all of your group members to an upcoming sale or special event that your business is hosting. As always, refer back to your objectives and have a clear plan of what you are trying to accomplish with your group.

Groups are fairly high-maintenance in that if you post a question, comment, photo, or video, you will need to return to the group in order to view your members' comments and continue the interaction through a response.

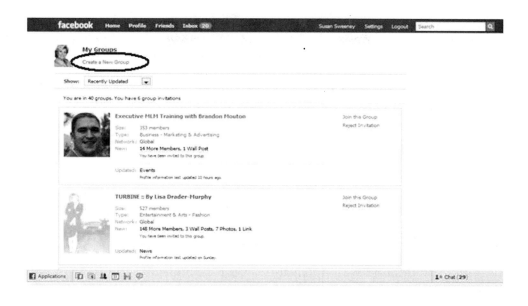

Figure 20.6. Click on "Create a New Group" to start your own Facebook Group.

On the other hand, groups can be a great way to interact with your members on a more personal basis. As postings require a personal profile, showing the first and last name of who is making the post, your members have the opportunity to put a face to the name and communicate with a real person rather than a corporate logo. Aside from having your own group, you may also consider participating in other groups based on similar interests and activities. A golf course may participate in common-interest golf groups in order to provide golf tips or specials, with a link back to your Web site. This can be a great way to access your target market without the commitment of managing your own group.

Email blasts are possible through the use of groups—but only if there are fewer than 5,000 members in the group. Only group owners are able to send these out. Unlike fan pages, groups list your personal name when you are a group administrator or when you contribute comments and postings to the group wall. Groups also allow a high degree of control over who can participate. Group administrators can set restrictions in terms of the ages and locations of participants.

Groups do not have access to the unique applications that are available for fan pages and personal profiles. Another disadvantage of groups versus fan pages involves the metrics and monitoring that is available with fan pages.

Groups do not have access to the visitor statistics that fan pages have. Also, Facebook groups are accessible to only those with a Facebook account. With fan pages, anyone can view the page on the Internet, but with groups, users must sign in to view the content.

Finally, groups do not provide as much visibility on members' personal profiles as you may receive through fan pages. In the Info section of a personal profile, the groups that they are a member of appear in a long list of links, whereas the fan pages that they are a fan of appear with photos in a more spread-out fashion. It is more eye-catching to see a fan page in this section than it is to see the title of a group.

Applications

There are thousands of applications on Facebook that can be used with your personal profile or fan page. Applications can be hosted by fan pages or personal profiles, but not by groups. When you set up a fan page, it comes with the basics:

- A wall where you and your fans can post content and make comments

- An info section where you can post the company address, hours of operation, etc.

- A photos section for you to post photos

- A discussion board where you can stimulate conversation and ask questions

- A reviews section where fans can leave reviews of your company.

Aside from these basic applications, Facebook has an application directory (Figure 20.7) with thousands of additional applications that you can add to your fan page. These may include things like an online take-out and delivery ordering service for restaurants or an online reservation system for hotels and events. If you can't find the specific application you'd like to have for your business in the directory, you can also create your own (or outsource this activity to an expert) in order to provide fans with a unique service, game, or gadget to use in relation to your business.

There are a number of ways that you can make use of Facebook applications. First of all, you can find applications in the directory and use them on your own

Figure 20.7. Facebook's application directory provides applications for business, games, sports, and more.

page or profile. Second, you can design your own application or hire someone to design an application to be used on your page or profile that will help you achieve one of your social media objectives. Another option is to advertise in applications that are used by your target market. When deciding how to make the best use of Facebook applications, refer back to your objectives, your target market, and your product or service.

Internet Resources for Chapter 20

I have developed a great library of online resources for you to check out regarding Facebook. This library is available on my Web site, *http://www. SusanSweeney.com*, in the Resources section, where you can find additional tips, tools, techniques, and resources.

I have also developed courses on many of the topics covered in this book. These courses are available on two of my Web sites, *http://www.SusanSweeney. com* and *http://www.eLearningU.com* (which contains other instructors' courses as well). These courses are delivered immediately over the Internet, so you can start whenever is convenient for you.

21

LinkedIn

LinkedIn is another popular social networking Web site. Mostly used for professional networking, LinkedIn has over 55 million members in over 200 countries and territories across the world. Executives from all Fortune 500 companies use LinkedIn, and a new member joins approximately every second.

LinkedIn allows you to set up a personal profile that outlines your current and past job positions. It is a great way to keep in touch with your network of business contacts. Aside from your personal profile, there are a number of elements that you can use within LinkedIn. In this chapter, we discuss:

- LinkedIn set-up

- LinkedIn and SEO

- Groups

- Recommendations

- Answers

- Events

- Jobs

- Advertising

- Applications.

Maintenance and time commitments of LinkedIn are less demanding compared with other social networking sites. Aside from the initial task of setting up your profile, other time-consuming tasks such as updates and postings are not absolutely vital. Simple maintenance of accepting connection requests and answering inbox messages could be sufficient. For those looking to have a prominent presence on LinkedIn, however, maintenance could take significantly more time.

LinkedIn Set-up

In order to set up an account with LinkedIn, visit *http://www.linkedin.com* and fill in the section called "Join LinkedIn today" by providing your first name, last name, email address, and password (Figure 21.1). Next you will be asked for some information to get your professional profile started, including your

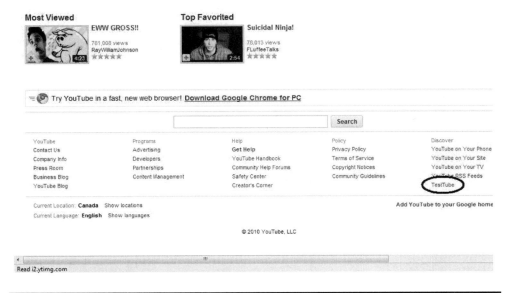

Figure 21.1. Fill in your first name, last name, email, and password from the LinkedIn homepage to get started with your own account.

current employment status, company, job title, country, and zip code. You can then import contacts from your email program, or you can skip this step to continue on. You will need to confirm your email address. Once you are all set up, click on "Profile" and "Edit my Profile" in order to complete all of your information.

Fields include your industry, geographic area, current workplace, past workplaces, education, Web sites, contact information, and any additional information you'd like to provide. You can also link your Twitter account to your LinkedIn profile so that tweets that you post to Twitter will automatically be posted to LinkedIn as well. Your "Updates" section, located beneath your profile picture and title on your personal profile, allows you to update your status to let your connections know what's new with you. As this is a professional profile, keep your status professional—no one cares what you had for breakfast, but a promotion, the release of your latest newsletter, or a new position or new product offering might be interesting to your connections. How much information you provide is up to you. Including information about your past work experiences and education can help others to find you. It can also serve as an online resume where users can view your experience (Figure 21.2).

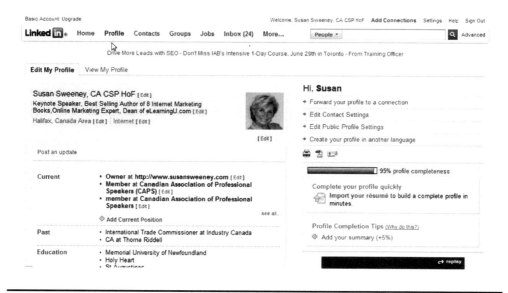

Figure 21.2. Your LinkedIn profile lists your current and past job positions, education, contact information, recommendations, and Web site.

A profile picture should also be uploaded so that people can put a face to the name. If you met someone at a large conference or if you have a common name, this can help users be sure they've found the right person.

After your profile is set up, you should search for some connections. Often you will receive suggestions for people that you may know based on your past workplaces and education. You can search for people by entering their name in the top search bar. (Make sure you've selected "people" and not "groups" or "jobs.") You should add only people that you know. If you can't specify a direct connection to the user, you will need to know his or her email address in order to request to connect.

Basic accounts with LinkedIn are free. Business accounts are also available, for various fees, in order to gain access to additional features and increase the regular limits. There are three options: Business, Business Plus, and Business Pro. Business accounts, at $24.95 per month, allow for 15 requests for introductions rather than the usual five, three InMails per month (no InMails available with the basic account), five folders in the Profile Organizer (none with basic), unlimited OpenLink messages (none with basic), reference searches, 300 person search results (100 with basic), five saved searches (three with basic), expanded profile views, upcoming feature sneak peeks, and priority customer service. Business Plus and Business Pro accounts have further increased limits and cost $49.95 per month and $499.95 per month, respectively. Businesses can also set up recruiter accounts in order to find candidates for job positions.

LinkedIn and SEO

LinkedIn profiles, job postings, and answers are indexed by the major search engines. A subset of company profiles is also indexed. In order to make the most of your search engine optimization, be sure to include strategic keywords in your profile and, if possible, show your expertise by providing answers to questions related to your industry in the LinkedIn Answers area. If you're providing links, make sure that you include keywords in both the anchor text and the text around the link.

LinkedIn Groups

LinkedIn groups allow members with similar interests to join together for discussions and updates. The LinkedIn Groups Directory can be found at: *http://*

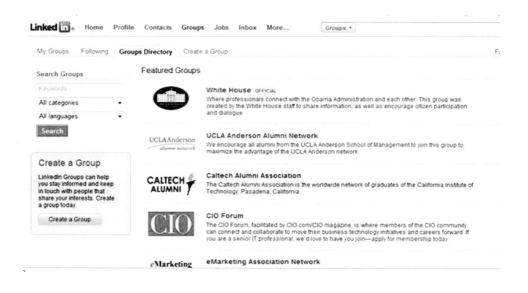

Figure 21.3. To access the Groups Directory, click on the Groups tab at the top of the page and then click on the "Groups Directory."

www.linkedin.com/groupsDirectory or by clicking on the Groups tab at the top of the page and then on the "Groups Directory" (Figure 21.3). To find groups that you might be interested in, simply search for relevant keywords or browse through groups by category, and then request to join any groups that interest you. Once you've joined groups, they will be accessible through the "Groups" section at the top of your LinkedIn page when you're signed in. This page will provide you with the latest updates from the groups that you've joined. You can also choose whether or not you'd like to receive updates by email.

When you click on one of the groups that you're a member of, you can see the discussions, members, and updates of that particular group. You can join the conversations by clicking on the "Discussions" tab within the group, and then clicking on any of the discussions that interest you. When you participate in discussions, keep in mind your goals and objectives. Include a link to your Web site in your signature to drive traffic to your site. Get your important keywords in the link itself or in the text around the link to maximize your search engine optimization.

You can also create your own group on LinkedIn to gain access to your target market. Maintaining a group is much more time-consuming than commenting on other groups, as frequent updates and discussions should be maintained. However, you have much more control as the owner of a group than you do as a member of a group. To create a group, click on "Groups" on the top of the page when you are signed in to your account. Then click on "Create a Group." From here, you can upload a photo and set a group name, group type, summary, description, and accessibility settings. You can adjust the privacy settings so that users will have to receive your approval in order to join the group, if you prefer.

Once you've joined groups, the group logo will appear on your profile page for others to see.

LinkedIn Recommendations

Another thing that will show up on your profile page will be recommendations from current or past colleagues. Recommendations provide the opportunity for past co-workers to recommend your services to other, potential clients. Similar to the usual phone-call reference that usually takes place post-interview, these references appear on your profile at all times for users to see how much others have appreciated your work. Users with recommendations are three times more likely to come up in search results. It is easy to request a recommendation from your personal profile page by scrolling down to the "Recommendations" section and clicking "Request a Recommendation." You can choose to show, hide, or even request new or revised recommendations.

You can write recommendations about those that you've worked with as well. In order to make a recommendation, click on the "Request a Recommendation" link on your profile in the "Recommendations" section. Scroll down to the "Make a Recommendation" part and enter a name or select a name from your connections list.

LinkedIn Answers

LinkedIn Answers give you the opportunity to demonstrate your expertise in your industry, and to help drive traffic to your personal profile and your Web site. You can adjust your settings to determine whether or not the answers that you provide are displayed in your profile. To find the Q&A section on LinkedIn, click on the "More" button at the top of your page once you're signed in to your account, then click on "Answers." You will then be taken to Answers Home, where you can ask questions or view the latest questions that have been asked from your network. At the bottom of the page, the week's top experts are listed. If you provide answers to questions and one or more are selected as a best answer, you earn expertise. You can also browse questions by category along the right-hand side of the page. These answers are search engine optimized, so be sure to use strategic keywords and links.

LinkedIn Events

LinkedIn Events are also accessible through the "More" section at the top of your page. Events allow you to view the events that your connections are attending, as well as the most popular events on LinkedIn. From here you can access the events that you're attending, find events, or add your own event.

LinkedIn Jobs

Job seekers and recruiters often turn to LinkedIn to find high-quality positions and candidates. To access the jobs section of LinkedIn, click on "Jobs" at the top of the page. From here, you can search for jobs by keyword, location, experience level, or job title, or you can post and manage job listings.

Job listings on LinkedIn cost $195 for a 30-day posting, or you can purchase five job credits for $145 per job or 10 job credits for $115 per job. LinkedIn provides great services for those looking to hire, including LinkedInsight, which displays resumes, work history, and potential references within your network. You can also send your job posting to your connections and request referrals for qualified candidates. Companies like PayPal, Microsoft, Expedia.com, and Adobe are some of LinkedIn's recruiting clients.

LinkedIn Advertising

There are two categories of advertising with LinkedIn—Large Budgets ($25,000+), which can be seen at *http://advertising.linkedin.com* and Direct Ads (for small to medium advertisers), which can be seen at *http://www.linkedin.com/directads*.

To set up a Direct Ad, visit *http://www.linkedin.com/directads* and click on "Start Advertising Now." Your first step will be to design your ad. You will need to provide an ad name, headline, ad line 1 & 2, URL, destination URL, profile link, and logo.

Once you've designed your ad, you will choose how it will be targeted. You can select for your ad to be shown to all LinkedIn members or you can target your ad by up to three of the following categories: company size, job function, industry, seniority, gender, age, or geography. As you update the targeting for your ad, the estimated number of people that match your targeted audience criteria will update to show you the reach of your advertisement.

Finally, you will need to determine payment options for your advertisement. Here you will select a daily budget, which will determine how many times per day your ad is shown. You can then select whether you'd rather pay by click or by impressions. You will have to select a maximum bid—LinkedIn will provide you with a suggested bid. You also have the opportunity to show your advertisement to LinkedIn's collection of partner Web sites, called their LinkedIn Audience Network. Selecting this option will make your advertisement eligible to be delivered to LinkedIn members within your target audience when they are visiting partner sites. Once you've selected your pricing options, you will then be prompted to provide your credit card information, which will be periodically charged for clicks and impressions.

LinkedIn Applications

LinkedIn has a directory of applications, which can be found under the "More" tab at the top of your page (Figure 21.4). Some of the most popular applications include Amazon Reading List (allows you to show others in your network what books you're reading and recommend), Huddle Workspaces (allows you to collaborate and exchange ideas with your connections in a private area), Box.net (helps you share and exchange documents with your connections), SlideShare (allows you to share presentation slides), Company Buzz (provides you with information about what people are saying about your company), TripIt (share your travel plans with connections), and Google Presentations (demonstrate your presentations or videos on your LinkedIn profile). You can also use Polls to conduct market research from your own profile. Refer back to your social media goals and objectives when determining whether or not any of the LinkedIn applications are right for your business.

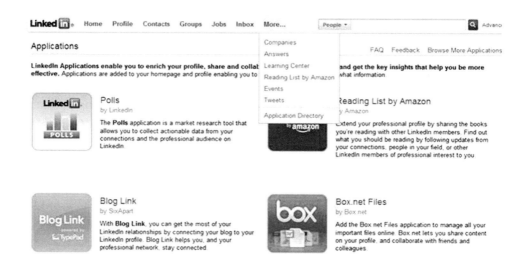

Figure 21.4. Access the LinkedIn application directory through the "More" tab at the top of your page.

Internet Resources for Chapter 21

I have developed a great library of online resources for you to check out regarding LinkedIn. This library is available on my Web site, *http://www.SusanSweeney.com,* in the Resources section, where you can find additional tips, tools, techniques, and resources.

I have also developed courses on many of the topics covered in this book. These courses are available on two of my Web sites, *http://www.SusanSweeney.com* and *http://www.eLearningU.com* (which contains other instructors' courses as well). These courses are delivered immediately over the Internet, so you can start whenever is convenient for you.

22

Twitter

Another popular social networking site is Twitter. Originally invented out of Jack Dorsey's curiosity of what his friends were doing, Twitter has grown tremendously to millions of users. Twitter started out asking "where are you and what are you doing?" and users' answers must be under 140 characters. Your answers (your "tweets") are shown on the Twitter home pages of all of your followers. It's an easy way for people to stay connected, and Twitter has taken off with businesses for the purpose of staying connected with their customers in all kinds of interesting and innovative ways.

Although some people choose to answer this question with information on what they had for breakfast, or what flavor of coffee they like the best, from a business perspective, no one cares. Using Twitter for business purposes means tweeting for business purposes. Tweet about things that are new at your company, upcoming events or specials, keeping up with the latest news in your industry, or asking your followers questions in order to engage conversation. Go back to your objectives.

Twitter is indexed for the major search engines, so use relevant keywords and provide links to drive traffic to your Web site.

In this chapter, we cover:

- Twitter set-up

- Twitter lingo

- Business use of Twitter

- Twitter and SEO

- Management tools and applications

- URL shorteners

- Building your list of followers.

Twitter Set-up

If you decide to set up Twitter for your business, you may want to consider having multiple accounts, depending on your objectives and your target market. An example might be a resort where the restaurant has a separate account for daily specials, the golf course has a separate account to announce available tee times, and the spa has a separate account to promote its spa packages. Ford has at least seven different Twitter accounts, including FordCustService, FordDriveGreen, FordTrucks, and FordRacing.

Getting set up is easy. Visit *http://www.twitter.com* and click on the "Sign up now" button. You will need to fill out a quick form with your full name, username, password, and email address. You'll then receive a confirmation email, and once confirmed, you'll be ready to go. With Twitter growing so quickly, it may be difficult to find the username you'd like, so even if you're not planning on using Twitter right away, you may want to consider grabbing your username (if it's available) just so that you have access to it in case you decide to start using Twitter later.

Once you're set up, you'll want to upload a photo for your Twitter account. On the top toolbar, click on "Settings." From here, you'll see another toolbar across the top. Click on "Picture" to change the picture that currently shows up next to your username. Many people choose to use a personal photo here, so that customers get a personal experience with their company. Next to the "Picture" button, there is also a "Design" button. You can go here to change the colors of your text, links, and sidebar or to change your Twitter background. Use colors that are brand aligned with your company so that it looks consistent if your followers click your Web site link from your account.

Another feature you'll want to update will be the "Profile" section of your Twitter account. This can be found in the "Account" subsection of the "Settings" section. Fill in your Web site URL and one-line bio; be sure to include strategic keywords in your bio so that your customers or potential customers will have no trouble finding you. You should also include a location and name, which helps with Twitter search results.

There are many Web sites online, both free and for a fee, that provide custom Twitter background design services. Backgrounds come in various designs, including those with company information, photo collages, brand colors, and logos. It is important that your Twitter account is brand aligned.

Twitter Lingo

Twitter has a language of its own. There is a bit of lingo you might want to become familiar with before getting involved with Twitter. Here are some of the most common terms:

- *Tweet*: A Tweet is a Twitter posting; maximum 140 characters.

- *Re-Tweet (RT):* Whenever a person forwards a Tweet onward, an RT provides attribution to the original poster.

- *Direct Message (DM):* This is a special Tweet that goes to one (or more) specific people privately; this contrasts to regular Tweets, which are 100 percent public.

- *Mention (@username):* Each person has a unique username. When the @name (such as @susansweeney) is put within a Tweet, a copy of that message appears in that person's account.

- *Hashtags (#):* Hashtags are a shorthand to allow people to search on a particular topic. If you search on #oprah, for example, it will bring up all posts that have the #oprah hashtag.

Business Use of Twitter

There are a number of big-brand businesses using Twitter. Dell employees have built one of the largest employee bases on Twitter. Other companies include JetBlue and Starbucks, which frequently offer specials and deals exclusively to their Twitter followers. ComCast also offers support to its customers through Twitter.

Companies can also set up Twitter accounts that are private—only to be used internally. In order to keep your Twitter account private, click on "Settings" and scroll down on the "Account" page, to click on "Protect my Tweets." This will allow only followers that you have authorized to view your Tweets. Your Tweets will not be publicly visible.

Twitter and SEO

Be sure to keep search engine optimization in mind with all of your Twitter updates. Whether you're providing information in your profile or in your actual tweets, be sure to use strategic keywords, especially in the anchor text and words around links. Twitter is indexed by the search engines, so it is important that your tweets are consistent with your goals and objectives.

Management Tools and Applications

The Internet is filled with all sorts of applications and programs to be used with social media, especially Twitter. If you're looking to save time with your tweets, consider using a program like TweetDeck or HootSuite. HootSuite allows you to schedule your tweets—consider choosing one day a week, or biweekly, to spend filling in your scheduled tweets for the upcoming week. This can be a great application when you are going on vacation or have a week filled with meetings coming up. This way you won't have to squeeze in time on your lunch hour or at the end of your day to keep your tweets going, but you also won't have any down time, which could result in losing some of your followers.

TweetDeck is a desktop application that allows you to keep track of multiple social media accounts in one place. You can keep track of the most interesting people that you follow by creating a list of the people you're most interested in receiving tweets from. You can also easily see who has mentioned, direct-messaged, or re-tweeted you. If you're interested in keeping track of what's being said about your company, you can create a saved search of your business name in order to routinely monitor where your name comes up in tweets.

Many people tweet their trains of thought; complaints about companies, products, and customer service are common on Twitter. With the convenience of tweeting from your phone, angry customers often don't waste any time sharing their opinions. It's important to keep your eyes peeled for any disgruntled customers on Twitter so that you can respond promptly. You don't necessarily

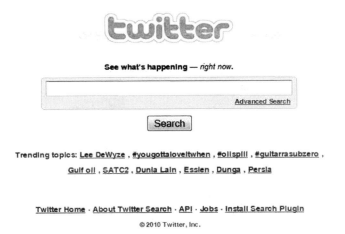

Figure 22.1. Use Twitter search to search for tweets using specific keywords or topics.

need a Twitter account, however, to see what people are saying about your business. Using Twitter search (*http://search.twitter.com*) allows you to search for keywords that Twitter users are talking about (Figure 22.1). Although you won't be able to respond without a Twitter account, you'll be able to see what's being said. Other sources such as Social Mention (*http://www.socialmention. com*) are useful when tracking what people are saying about you online. There are tons of Twitter resources in my social media bookmarks accessible in the "Follow me Online" section of my Web site, *http://www.SusanSweeney.com*, or through my diigo account, *http://www.diigo.com/user/susansweeney*.

Other management resources include software that automatically updates your other social media accounts when you update your Twitter. We talk more about this in Chapter 19.

URL Shorteners

Newcomers to Twitter often have a difficult time trying to find the right words to say within only 140 characters, especially when trying to include a link. In order to help with the limited amount of space, there are a number of URL shorteners available online. These applications allow you to copy and paste a long link that will be shortened down to a tiny URL—one that can fit in

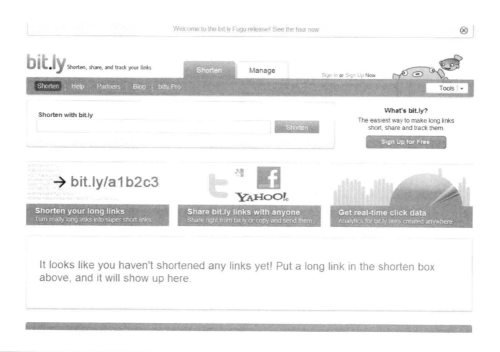

Figure 22.2. Bit.ly is a popular URL shortener, often used by Twitter users.

your tweet. Bit.ly is a very popular tool for shortening URLs (Figure 22.2). The ability to track your shortened URLs is also available with bit.ly, which allows users to see how many people have clicked on their specific link. This can help you to determine how many people actually read and were interested in your tweet—which sometimes can be hard to measure when you have a lot of followers who may or may not be reading your updates. One thing to keep in mind about these URL shorteners is that, at the time of writing this book, they do not provide any search engine optimization benefit. These links don't show the site name information or any clues to the content that is behind the link, and the inbound links don't count for link popularity in terms of search engine result rankings.

Building Your List of Followers

Once your Twitter account is up and running, be sure to include a link from your Web site for visitors to find you on Twitter. This can be done with a simple link or by the use of various online widgets. A widget is several special lines of HTML code that your webmaster inserts on one of your Web pages; just about every social media site provides them. Widgets can allow your tweets to be automatically updated and shown from your Web site. There are widgets to place Twitter content onto your Web site or within Facebook or MySpace. Just go to the bottom of any Twitter page and click on "Goodies." There should be a link on that page for Twitter's widgets. This is where your programmer can get those lines of HTML code.

You may also want to consider providing links to your Twitter page in your email signature and on your business cards. Product packaging and press releases are other great places to include your Twitter account.

Aside from links, you can grow your list of followers by growing the list of people that you follow. Often, if you follow relevant people on Twitter, most of them will follow you back. One great way to find Twitter users who might be interested in your products, services, or industry is to use a source like Twellow (*http://www.twellow.com*)—an online yellow pages for Twitter (Figure 22.3). This way, you can search for users who mention a particular industry (for example, dog grooming) in a particular geographic area. Twellow will provide

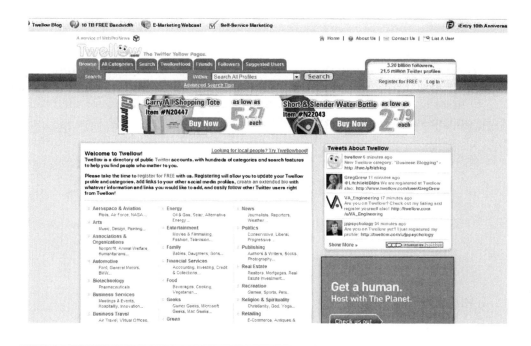

Figure 22.3. Twellow is like an online yellow pages of Twitter accounts.

you with a list of results, from which you can then select users to follow. Using an online source such as Twellow can help you find and build a more-targeted follower base.

Be sure that your involvement with Twitter is relevant to your business and your social media objectives. Read the tweets of the people you're following and re-tweet whenever you find good information related to your industry. People appreciate being re-tweeted. If you see that the people you're following are asking questions and looking for feedback, provide them with an answer and keep the conversation going among your own followers. Stimulating conversation can help to demonstrate to your followers that your Twitter account is not only for the purpose of selling and self-promotion. It's important to provide your followers with valuable information so they don't decide to stop following you.

Internet Resources for Chapter 22

I have developed a great library of online resources for you to check out regarding Twitter. This library is available on my Web site, *http://www. SusanSweeney.com,* in the Resources section, where you can find additional tips, tools, techniques, and resources.

I have also developed courses on many of the topics covered in this book. These courses are available on two of my Web sites, *http://www.SusanSweeney. com* and *http://www.eLearningU.com* (which contains other instructors' courses as well). These courses are delivered immediately over the Internet, so you can start whenever is convenient for you.

23

YouTube, Video-Sharing Sites, and Video Syndication

Video sharing on the Internet has become one of the most popular online activities. Popular sites like YouTube and Vimeo have millions of uploaded videos that are watched by millions of visitors everyday. Video sharing within these online communities includes all sorts of content, ranging from how-to videos, news clips, politics, animation, movie previews, music videos, and sports clips, to personal video-blogs. There are many people who have created a name for themselves through online videos. In this chapter, we cover:

- Publicity through video-sharing Web sites

- Channels and features

- YouTube channel set-up

- Video syndication.

Publicity through Video-Sharing Web sites

Everyone is developing video these days. It is so easy; everyone has a device that records video—webcams, mobile phones, and iPods all provide individuals with easy access to record a video anywhere, anytime. With the Flip video recorder, which has a USB connection, I can record and upload a video to YouTube in a matter of minutes. There are also many video-sharing sites that make it easy to share your videos.

Not only are the videos on these Web sites being used for personally entertaining purposes, but more and more businesses are seeing the value in using online video sharing as a means of promoting their products or services and connecting with their target customers.

What we are seeing on these sites is:

- Personal videos with nothing to do with business

- Businesses providing their own videos

- Customers and third parties providing videos about your products and services—some in a positive light, others in a negative light

- Third-party videos that, although not identifying your products or services directly, might be good for your business.

Amusement parks and other tourist destinations often receive great free publicity as visitors post their personal video clips of their trip. Families often post quick tour-videos of their resorts and of their children having fun at the Kids Club so that grandparents and other family members back home can see how much fun the vacation was. Keep an eye out for some great publicity opportunities and take advantage of the chance to communicate with the customer, or other potential customers who may be viewing the video, by commenting with a nice message letting them know that you're happy they enjoyed their stay.

When Dave Carroll, band member of Sons of Maxwell, had his guitar broken through mishandling when flying with United Airlines, he decided to write a song and video to post to YouTube when he felt he wasn't being treated properly by the airline. His first video earned over 7 millions views. As a result, it was aired on CNN and other television stations throughout North America. He sings about the baggage handlers throwing around his Taylor guitar in full view of passengers. Upon arrival at his destination, his guitar was broken and United Airlines refused to pay for the damage. Due to the popularity of the first song, Dave provided updates to the situation through a second song and video posted to YouTube, which has also received close to a million views. Talk about bad publicity for United! I bet Dave Carroll has seen a spike in requests for the band to play, though!

It is important to watch what is being said about your brand online through social networking sites such as Twitter and Facebook, and also scanning for videos and clips relating to your brand, your products and services, and your business.

Video Details

Your business-related videos can be used for many purposes:

- Providing customer service

- Providing "how-to" instructions

- Promoting your products and services

- Branding.

When developing your videos for business, think things through. Today's online customer does not like the hard sell. How should you present your product or service to provide potential customers with the information they need without driving them away?

How long should the video be? As long as it takes to get your message across. As long as you think your potential customer will pay attention. Generally, shorter is better. YouTube sets a maximum length of 10 minutes and 2 GB in file size.

Think about how you will send traffic to your Web site through the video if it is watched on one of the video-sharing sites rather than your Web site or blog. Can you send them to the site for a coupon related to your product or service? Can you send them there for an e-book or white paper on the subject of the video? Can you do an overlay with your Web address so that if the video goes viral everyone will know who you are and how to get in touch? Do you end the video with your contact information?

There are many great (and often free) video editing software programs that enable you to slice, dice, and edit your videos, add audio overlay, etc.

Using YouTube Videos on Your Site or in Your Blog

One of the great features of YouTube is the functionality to embed your YouTube videos on your site or in your blog. This enables you to quickly, easily, and cost-effectively add video content that will be engaging to your target market.

YouTube enables you to upload videos through a very easy-to-use wizard. Once your videos are uploaded, YouTube provides you with the programming code to provide a link to the video from your Web site, blog, or social media accounts as well as the programming code to actually embed the video into your Web site or blog.

You can have your own channel on YouTube to keep all your videos in one place and accessible to your followers.

YouTube Channels and Features

It's a great idea to set up your own YouTube Channel for your business so that all of your promotional videos, as well as any other videos related to your business posted by other users, can be found in one place. Some of the great features of YouTube Channels include the ability to customize your channel to match your brand and logo, the ability for others to subscribe to your channel so they're notified of new postings, and also the option to provide detailed company contact information to your viewers.

Channels provide a profile section that includes information such as your total channel views, total upload views, last sign-in date, number of subscribers, location, friends, and comments. Businesses should set up a channel to take advantage of all of these opportunities to increase brand recognition and drive more traffic to their Web site.

YouTube Channel Set-Up

In order to set up a YouTube channel for your business, visit the YouTube homepage, *http://www.youtube.com*, and click "Create Account." Here you will be asked for your username, location, postal code, date of birth, and gender, as well as a couple of privacy settings. At this point, you can sign in with an existing Google account or you can sign up for a new YouTube/Google account. Next, you will need to confirm your address through a confirmation email that will be sent to the email address you've provided. You've now set up your own YouTube account.

In order to set up the channel, click on your username at the top right-hand corner of the page. Here you will see how your channel currently looks—

the generic black and gray colors provided for new accounts. In order to edit your settings, click through the areas at the top of the page titled "Settings," "Themes and Colors," "Modules," and "Videos and Playlists" to customize your channel.

Use colors and themes that are consistent with your brand, so there is a good flow if someone were to click through to your company homepage from your YouTube channel. Adjust the privacy settings to choose who has access to your videos. Once your channel is customized to the way that you want it, you can begin to upload videos and send links out to your channel through emails and other social networking sites that you may be a part of.

Additional YouTube Features

YouTube provides many useful features and capabilities. TestTube provides a list of many unique YouTube applications as well as YouTube Advertising, YouTube RSS Feeds, and YouTube on your Site. TestTube allows you to test new features and applications that are being developed by YouTube. Some of these items include:

- Comment searching, where you can search for videos based on the comments that have been made

- CaptionTube, which allows you to add captions and subtitles to your videos

- Video Annotations, which allow for interactive commentary on your videos

- Warp, which allows for browsing videos in the full-screen player

- YouTube Music Discovery, which helps you to discover new artists

- Streams, which allow you to chat with others who are watching the same video that you are.

To visit TestTube, simply go to the YouTube homepage and scroll to the bottom, where you can click on "TestTube" under the "Discover" column (Figure 23.1).

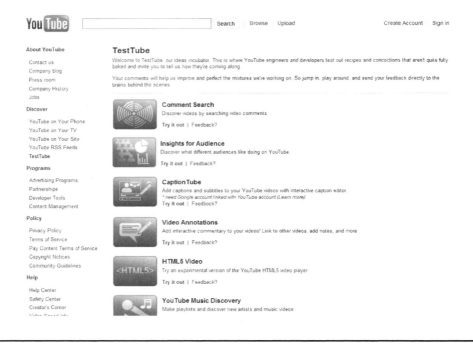

Figure 23.1.   TestTube provides neat applications to use with your YouTube videos.

Video Syndication

For businesses with a strong focus on increasing their online presence and improving search engine results, it may be a good idea to consider video syndication. Video syndication Web sites provide you with the opportunity to upload a video which is then sent out to many video-sharing online communities through one simple process. It saves a lot of time and provides a much greater reach for your video. This is usually a very attractive opportunity for those who have invested in a high-quality promotional video and would like to get the best return on investment possible by making the video available all over the Internet.

One of the most popular video syndication Web sites is TubeMogul (*http:// www.tubemogul.com*). TubeMogul allows you to set up an account and distribute videos to the top video-sharing Web sites. You also have access to detailed analytics about your video and its views. Initial set-up may be somewhat time-consuming as you will be required to set up accounts with any of the major video-sharing Web sites that you wish to post your videos on. However,

Figure 23.2. TubeMogul is a great video syndication site.

once you've entered your account information into your TubeMogul account, it is very simple to upload a video and have it distributed to all of your video-sharing sites in only a few clicks.

Another great feature offered by TubeMogul is the ability to tag your video with search engine optimized keywords in one central place. You can choose the best keywords and description for your video and make sure that your posting is search engine optimized (Figure 23.2). The keyword and description tags then are sent with your video and are used in all your video-sharing sites.

Promoting Your Videos

Once you have developed your video, you usually want to get as wide a distribution as you can. It's a good idea to include viral marketing—"Tell a friend about this video"—to enable your Web site visitors to spread the word.

Other ways to promote your videos include:

- Promote your video on all your social media channels.

- Promote your video in your email signature file.

- Promote your video on partner sites.

- Promote your video through your e-zine or newsletter.

- Invite your friends, fans, and followers from your social media accounts to subscribe.

- Use the "Share" option in YouTube.

- Use the "Find your Friends on YouTube" feature.

- If you do a series, you can promote your video podcast on popular podcast directories. There are many great podcast directories online, like Podcast.com (*http://www.podcast.com*) and Podcast Alley (*http://www.podcastalley.com*).

Internet Resources for Chapter 23

I have developed a great library of online resources for you to check out regarding video-sharing sites. This library is available on my Web site, *http://www.SusanSweeney.com*, in the Resources section, where you can find additional tips, tools, techniques, and resources.

I have also developed courses on many of the topics covered in this book. These courses are available on two of my Web sites, *http://www.SusanSweeney.com* and *http://www.eLearningU.com* (which contains other instructors' courses as well). These courses are delivered immediately over the Internet, so you can start whenever is convenient for you.

24

Flickr

Flickr is an online photo-sharing community that allows users to upload, organize, crop, edit, and share photos. The company has also recently added video-sharing capabilities to the site. There are millions of photos on the site that can be browsed by category, location, or most recent uploads.

Depending on your products and services, Flickr may provide an opportunity for you to promote your business. If you are a destination-marketing organization, pictures of your town that are accessible to the public may promote your area to vacationers. If you are a photographer, your pictures will show your expertise. There are many businesses that benefit by using Flickr. Flickr's terms of use state that "Flickr is for personal use only. If we find you selling products, services, or yourself through photostream, we will terminate your account." You have to determine if you can stay within Flickr's terms of use and still benefit from using Flickr.

Flickr is owned by Yahoo!, and Flickr images will be displayed when someone searches for images on Yahoo!. Flickr photos and videos are also indexed by Google and Technorati.

In this chapter, we discuss how to use Flickr:

- Account set-up

- Uploading and organizing photos

- Photo tagging

- Flickr apps.

Account Set-up

In order to set up an account with Flickr, you will need to either use your existing Yahoo! account or sign up for a new Yahoo! account. Either can be done by visiting the Flickr homepage at *http://www.flickr.com* and clicking on "Create Your Account" (Figure 24.1). Once you've set up an account and logged in, you will be taken to your own Flickr account homepage. Here you can add your profile, your photos, and your contacts.

To set up your profile, click on "Personalize your profile," the first step on your homepage under "How to get started." You will then be taken through four easy steps to get your profile up and running.

First, create your buddy icon. Here's your chance to upload either a personal photo, your company logo, or some other graphic that may be appropriate.

Next, you set your screen name. Many people set this to be their Web address as it is attached to every photo you upload and also to every message you post when you participate in Flickr groups.

Next, you will choose a custom URL for your Flickr page. This can't be changed, so make sure to choose your URL carefully. Your Flickr address will be *http://www.flickr.com/photos/yourname.*

Finally, you'll fill in some profile information including your first and last names, time zone, gender, and a short description. Use this space wisely; be sure to include search engine optimized keywords in your description and use this opportunity to promote your products and services. You may want to include your Web site URL or links to your social media networks in this space.

Figure 24.1. Creating an account on Flickr is easy.

Uploading and Organizing Photos

Once your account and profile are set up, you're ready to start uploading and organizing your photos. To do this, simply click on step 2 on your home page under "How to get started," or click on "You" and choose "Upload photos and videos" from the drop-down menu.

With the basic free account, you will be limited to 100 MB of photos and two 90-second video uploads per month. A Pro account will provide you with unlimited photo and video uploads, unlimited storage and bandwidth, ad-free sharing and browsing, as well as statistics. The Pro account costs $24.95 per year.

Once you've arrived at the upload screen, you will follow three steps. First, you will choose your photos from your computer. You have the option here to set privacy settings if you would like your photos visible to family and friends only or if you'd like them visible to the public. Choose your photos and click on the "Upload" button at the bottom of the screen.

Next, you will be asked to add a description to your photos. Here's your chance to adjust the title, description, and tags of your photos, so be sure to have search engine optimized keywords on hand that will help boost your search engine results. You also have the opportunity to add your photos to a set. A set is like an album, which will help to keep your photos more organized. Add a new set by choosing a name and description. When you've filled in all of this information, click "Save" at the bottom of the page. You will then be taken to "Your Photostream" where you can see your sets, galleries, tags, favorites, and profile.

Flickr also has a great tool called Organizr that allows you to drag and drop photos in order to batch-edit and organize your content. In order to access this, click on the "Organize & Create" tab at the top of your page (Figure 24.2). Here you can add people who are in the photos, add tags, add photos or videos to a set, edit dates, edit permissions, rotate or delete photos, and send your photos to a group. You can also geotag your photos—you can drag and drop your photos to a map using the map tool on the top tabs (Figure 24.3).

Photo Tagging

Tagging can be an important resource for your Flickr account. You should always tag your photos with relevant search engine optimized keywords so that your photos will appear in search engine results. Tags are labels or keywords that you apply to your photos to allow viewers to find your images through the search feature in Flickr and also in Yahoo!, Google, and Technorati.

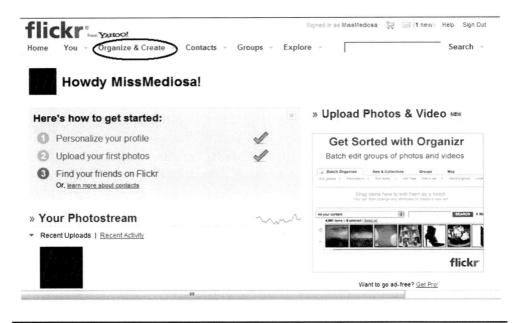

Figure 24.2.   Flickr makes it easy for you to organize your photos.

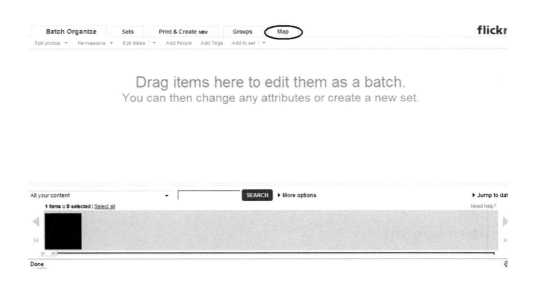

Figure 24.3.   Flick enables you to geotag your photos.

Think about the keywords that you want to use with each photo. What words would your target market use when doing a search? Again, if you're a destination-marketing organization in Hilton Head, for example, you could add keywords like the location of your image so that people searching for images of "Hilton Head Island, South Carolina" might be able to find your photos. Organizations can use tags to get their brand, product information, key individuals, or profession included for search purposes. You can apply up to 75 tags per photo.

You must have at least five photos uploaded in order to appear in search engine results. You may also be interested in learning about machine tags so that other Web sites can perform specific actions when reading your tags, such as automatically appearing on an "Upcoming Events" page. For more information on machine tags, visit *http://www.code.flickr.com* and search for "machine tags."

Promoting Your Photos

Once you have your photos in Flickr, you will want to promote them to the world. As discussed, Flickr photos are indexed by Yahoo!, Google, and Technorati, so if you tag them properly, they may be found high enough in the search results to generate some traffic.

You can also join groups within Flickr that may have members that include your target markets. Once you join a specific group you can submit your photos. If you used your Web address or your brand as your screen name, it is attached to every one of your photos as well as your posts to these groups. In these groups you can also comment on others' photos, thus providing another opportunity for exposure.

You can also provide a link to your photos in Flickr from your Twitter, Facebook, or other social media accounts.

Promote and approve the reuse of your photos if they promote your business or your products or services.

One of the major benefits of Flickr is the ability to embed a Flickr photostream into your Web site or blog, providing it a very professional and impressive look and feel. There are many third-party applications that provide a variety of formats for your photostream for your Web site or blog.

Flickr Apps

By visiting the Flickr App Garden, you can view a collection of applications that have been designed for Flickr users. To get to The App Garden, click on "Explore" at the top of your page and then click on "The App Garden" from the drop-down menu. Here you will see a listing of the latest applications that have been developed. This includes resources like Flickr 2 Twitter, an application that allows you to tweet photos from Flickr; Flickr Machine Tag Browser, which allows you to implement a browser for machine tags in use across Flickr; and Flickaway, an easy way to display your Flickr stream on your Web site. There are many applications listed in The App Garden, and they can easily be searched by entering a keyword into the search bar at the top of the page.

Internet Resources for Chapter 24

I have developed a great library of online resources for you to check out regarding Flickr. This library is available on my Web site, *http://www.SusanSweeney.com,* in the Resources section, where you can find additional tips, tools, techniques, and resources.

I have also developed courses on many of the topics covered in this book. These courses are available on two of my Web sites, *http://www.SusanSweeney. com* and *http://www.eLearningU.com* (which contains other instructors' courses as well). These courses are delivered immediately over the Internet, so you can start whenever is convenient for you.

25

Mobile Marketing

With mobile devices, we can do all kinds of things, like check a flight schedule, transfer money from one account to another, pay bills, make hotel reservations, check the local MLS, and on and on. Today's consumers are very demanding—they want what they want, when they want it. There are billions of people with mobile devices capable of voice, text, image, and Internet communication. The market is huge already, and one that will escalate in the coming years as we see less-developed countries go directly to wireless for their telephones. We are beginning to see location-based services (or LBS) really take hold. Every new advancement in Internet-based technology provides new marketing opportunities.

Mobile devices certainly have had a major impact on social media and social networking as many marketers use their mobile devices to take video and upload to YouTube, tweet, view, and update their Facebook accounts, add photos to their Flickr accounts, read and bookmark the latest news, post to logs, etc. Those applications are covered in the individual social media and social networking chapters.

In this chapter, we cover:

- What is mobile marketing?

- Benefits of mobile marketing.

What Is Mobile Marketing?

Mobile marketing is using a mobile or a wireless device for marketing purposes. Mobile marketing is an organization's dream come true—it enables the organization to communicate directly, one-on-one, to the target market with the opportunity for a direct response in real time.

There are a number of mobile marketing opportunities that are becoming commonplace:

- SMS (short messaging service)

- MMS (multimedia messaging service)

- Mobile search

- Instant messaging

- LBS (location-based services)

- Profile-specific advertising

- Mobile blogging

- Subscribed content.

SMS—Short Messaging Service

SMS is a service that allows text messages to be sent and received on your mobile phone. The messages can also be sent to a mobile device from the Internet using an SMS gateway Web site. With SMS, if your phone is turned off or is out of range, the message is stored on the network and is delivered the next time you power on.

An example of an SMS campaign would be a "text to win free tickets to see the New York Jets" contest. There are many SMS services springing up. Upside Wireless has a text-messaging service that enables advertisers to communicate directly with subscribing visitors. Clickatell (*http://www.clickatell.com*) provides you with a simple, high-speed messaging service (Figure 25.1). Their "any message, anywhere" solutions allow businesses to talk to their customers in an immediate and personal way, no matter which communication device they use.

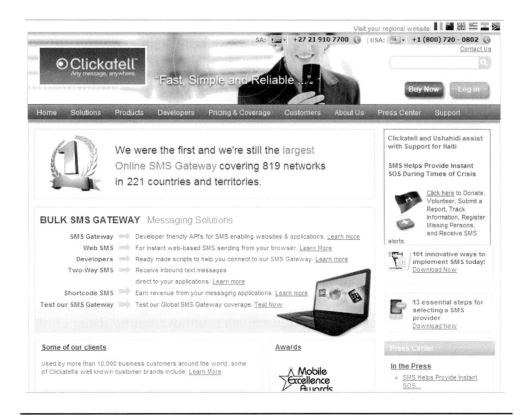

Figure 25.1. Clickatell is the world's leading SMS messaging provider offering connectivity to 819 networks in 222 countries.

For example, if you were the owner of a financial institution, Clickatell allows you and your business to alert customers of identity theft through actionable fraud alerts and real-time transaction alerts, increase customer retention and satisfaction through account notifications, and access and even address new payment methods.

An example closer to home was my shopping experience at Armani in South Beach. When I was checking out, the person at the cash register asked if I had a code for a discount. In a matter of 30 seconds I had sent a text to the address in the poster and got a text back with the code I needed to show the person at the cash register so that I could receive my instant discount. I have been receiving offers on a regular basis ever since. Smart marketing!

MMS—Multimedia Messaging Service

MMS brings a whole new dimension to mobile marketing with its enhanced transmission service that enables video clips, color pictures, text, and audio files to be sent and received by mobile phones. The marketing opportunities are endless using this technology, and the benefits are plentiful—immediate contact, immediate response, and multimedia capacity. With MMS, virtual tours of your products can be provided to potential customers.

Combine MMS with the ability to know where your subscriber is physically located through GPS, as well as having a profile of the subscriber—the possibilities are endless!

LBS—Location-Based Services

Location-based services use location as a key element in providing relevant information to users, and there are many mobile marketing applications for this type of service:

- Finding the nearest hotel because your flight has been canceled

- Finding the closest Thai restaurant in a strange city, including directions on how to get there from where you are.

Location-based services will change the way we do lots of things. With technology available that integrates the GPS capability with your mobile device, marketers are now able to identify your specific geographic location within five to ten yards of the device. The opportunities to send highly targeted location-based advertising is amazing. You can receive coupons for the stores that you are standing outside of.

You can do comparison shopping. RedLaser is an iPhone bar code scanner. With this technology you can scan the bar code of an item you are interested in purchasing and do comparison shopping online. Scan a product bar code and check online reviews for that product.

The real estate industry is one of the leaders in this technology, where your mobile device can feed you real estate listings as you drive through a geographic area.

We have just begun in this exciting world of mobile marketing.

Profile-Specific Advertising

Each mobile phone has a unique identifier in the telephone number, making it possible to build a profile of the owner. Once you have permission and a profile, you can send very targeted advertising messages to that profile. You must be careful when using this type of advertising that messages are permission-based and are not considered spam or are unsolicited.

Mobile Blogging

In a matter of seconds, color pictures, video, and audio files can instantly be added to a blog through a mobile device.

Subscribed Content

Organizations should always be looking for permission-based opportunities where they can send weekly package discounts, upcoming contests, Web site updates, and news announcements along with targeted advertisements and promotions to subscribers. Mobile devices are another avenue for such permission-based marketing. You can provide targeted content to subscribers through RSS from your site to a mobile device. You can also send road conditions, product coupons, or e-specials to subscribers.

Benefits of Mobile Marketing

The different mobile marketing applications provide a variety of benefits:

- Mobile marketing allows direct, personal communication in real time with the opportunity for immediate, direct response.

- By building a customer profile, you can be very targeted with your product packages, promotional campaigns, or offerings.

- Brand awareness can be increased.

- Messages can be sent through this medium very cost-effectively.

- Traffic to Web sites can be increased.

- Customer loyalty can be enhanced.

- Sales can be increased when you provide the right product package at the right time to the right customer.

- Interactivity—the target customer is engaged using this technology.

- The number of potential customers you can reach with this medium is staggering. There are over 4 billion consumers with access to this technology.

- Two-way dialogue between marketer and target market allows one-on-one marketing.

- Impact is immediate.

- Personalized messages get a much higher response rate than generic messages.

- Sponsored messages can be provided.

- Messages are delivered instantaneously.

- This medium makes it easy for people to spread the word quickly and easily.

With the increase in the number of smart devices that are becoming more mainstream and the number of marketers becoming more savvy, the mobile marketplace is significant. We have seen a quick uptake on most mobile marketing opportunities, like voting for your favorite American Idol. We're already seeing a number of businesses implement mobile marketing applications, such as MapQuest (Figure 25.2) and Empire Theatres (Figure 25.3). With Empire Theatres you can subscribe to Empire Mobile and get the most up-to-date information on movies and show times. You also can browse current films and can even buy tickets, all on your mobile phone.

Figure 25.2. MapQuest Navigator provides GPS voice-guided navigation.

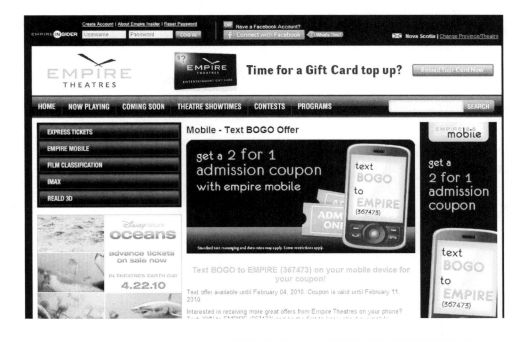

Figure 25.3. Empire Theatres uses mobile marketing to update visitors on the latest movies playing, show times, and even allows users to purchase tickets.

Internet Resources for Chapter 25

I have developed a great library of online resources for you to check out regarding mobile marketing. This library is available on my Web site, *http://www.SusanSweeney.com,* in the Resources section, where you can find additional tips, tools, techniques, and resources.

I have also developed courses on many of the topics covered in this book. These courses are available on two of my Web sites, *http://www.SusanSweeney.com* and *http://www.eLearningU.com* (which contains other instructors' courses as well). These courses are delivered immediately over the Internet, so you can start whenever is convenient for you.

26

Interactive Mapping

Studies show that the more interactive your Web site is, the longer your Web site visitors will stick around. Interactive maps are a great element to feature on your Web site if they allow you to showcase your products and services in a way that makes sense to your target market. Interactive maps are great for those in the travel and tourism industry or the real estate industry, for example.

In this chapter, we cover:

- What is interactive mapping?

- Why is it important?

- How do you do it?

- How do you leverage interactive maps?

What Is Interactive Mapping?

An interactive map is a map your Web site visitors can interact with. It is a map of a specified region, city, town, or neighborhood, or even a building like a shopping center or convention center that has interactive multimedia functionality integrated into it. These interactive multimedia capabilities give users the ability to explore the map in much more depth and give the map, and the location of your business, much more meaning.

Interactive maps give users a visual of where your business, your destination, or your house listing is located. Interactive maps give your Web site visitors the ability to view surrounding neighborhoods and all of the available amenities therein on one map. They can also provide layers of information about a particular area. Along with your hotel listing information, for example, interactive maps can show visitors where the shopping centers, restaurants, and golf courses are located in relation to your hotel. Or, along with the listing information of a particular property, interactive maps can show visitors where the schools are in relation to that property, the parks, or even the grocery store.

Interactive maps can link to visual images, a voice-guided tour, or videos. Add text, slide shows, animations, and panoramas to give your consumers a full view of the surrounding area and the most information they will need for their purchasing decision.

Interactive maps visually and geographically organize visual content. They allow your Web site visitors to get a feel for the layout of a particular area. More-advanced maps provide users with a legend and categories and subcategories of information. Check out the map Down South Publishers, Inc. developed for its Web site, HiltonHead360.com, in Figure 26.1. This map offers users the

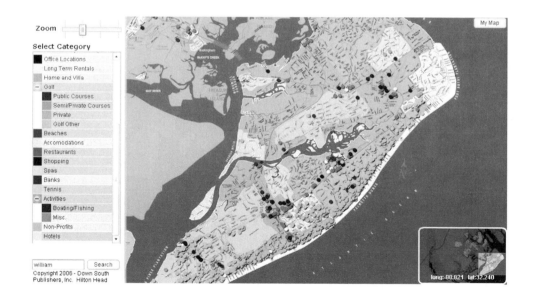

Figure 26.1. HiltonHead360.com's interactive map.

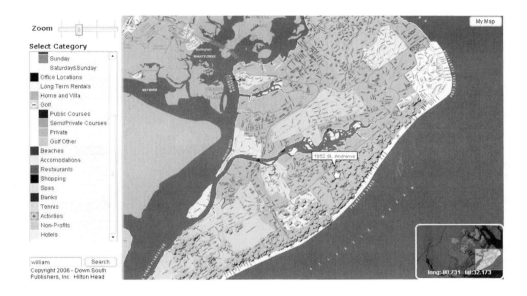

Figure 26.2. The dots on the map for HiltonHead360.com represent all of the vacation rentals and as users drag their mouse over those dots they are given the street address.

ability to see many different color-coded categories and subcategories, including private or open golf courses, restaurants, beaches, shopping centers, and spas. Users can select a category of their choice—for example, spas—to see where on the map all of the available spas are located. The dots on the map represent all of the vacation rental properties, and as the user drags the mouse over those dots, the street address shows up (Figure 26.2); and if he or she clicks on a dot, a picture of the vacation rental is shown, along with other links such as a virtual tour like the one shown in Figure 26.3.

Why Is Interactive Mapping Important?

The first thing people do when they decide to take a trip or a vacation is begin their search online. It is for this reason that interactive mapping is very important to the travel and tourism industry. As well, 85 percent of people interested in purchasing a new home, a piece of land, a vacation property, etc., begin their search online. It is for this reason that interactive mapping is very important to the real estate industry. Interactive maps make it easy for prospective customers to see the physical location of an interesting vacation destination or property in conjunction with the surrounding area.

Figure 26.3. If users click on a dot they are given a picture of the vacation rental along with other links such as a virtual tour.

Interactive maps are still quite new, and by providing an interactive map you are providing leading-edge information and tools to your customers and potential customers. This will help set you apart from other organizations and help reinforce the fact that you are a leader in your field—the industry expert.

Interactive maps are just that—they are interactive. The more interactive your Web site is, the more likely your site visitors are going to stay longer and the more likely they are going to return again and again. The longer your Web site visitors stay, and the more often they visit your site, the more your brand is reinforced, the more your target market feels a part of your community, and the more they feel like they know and trust you; and as I've said before, people do business with people they know and trust.

Once you have established the trust of your Web site visitors, they will be more likely to give you permission to stay in touch through your e-club, newsletter, or new package updates and will be more likely to tell others about your packages and your services. You can also get them to become a friend or fan on Facebook, follow you on Twitter, and participate in any of your other social media efforts. By offering your Web site visitors leading-edge tools and content, the more likely you will be first in mind when they go to research or purchase. When visitors see how you go above and beyond to help them, either in their purchasing decision or in researching all of their options, they will come to you again and again.

The majority of people focus their attention on visual components of a Web site first, such as images, maps, or charts, before they process any text. Interactive maps serve as a visual trigger. They create interest in nonvisual information—"A picture is worth a thousand words," as the saying goes.

How Do You Do It?

Although interactive maps are still in the early stages, there are a number of options available to you for providing this service to your Web site visitors. Each option has its own unique bells and whistles and functionality. Each option has its own technology, ease of development, and varying costs. Therefore, it is important to research each option carefully and decide which, if any, will be the right choice for you, for your Web site, and for your target market.

Depending on the model and the technical capabilities you want your interactive map to have and if you have the right expertise, you can build your interactive map in-house or can use Google Maps. Either way, you must be sure that it will provide the type of information your target market is looking for. Google Maps is a product, offered by Google, that allows you to view maps in your Web browser and offers user-friendly mapping technology.

Google Maps will show you where you want to go and how to get there (with driving instructions) and will also show you what you'll find when you get there, with local business information, including location, contact information, and driving directions. Google Maps allows you to do local searches. If you want to find coffee shops in a particular neighborhood, simply navigate to that area and type in "coffee" and coffee shops will appear at the various locations on your map. It also gives you phone numbers and a link for each location on the left side of the page (Figure 26.4). If you click on the link for one of the listed coffee shops, Google Maps gives you the shop's name, address, and phone number, as well as links for driving directions, reviews, and much more.

With Google Maps you can view an aerial perspective of any location on Earth with its satellite view (Figure 26.5), and in certain locations you can view and navigate street-level imagery (Figure 26.6). You can even create your own personalized, customized maps complete with explanations, footnotes, place markers, photos, and videos.

Another option available to those businesses that want to offer their visitors interactive maps on their Web sites is to use an application service provider,

Figure 26.4. Google Maps provide phone numbers and a link for each location on the left side of the page.

Figure 26.5. With Google Maps you can view an aerial perspective of any location on Earth with its satellite view.

Figure 26.6. Google Maps allow users to view and navigate certain locations through street-level imagery.

or **ASP.** The ASP provides you with the basic infrastructure or the software you need to develop your interactive map. In other words, the ASP provides you with the technology you need to upload your map and populate it with all the information you want to provide your Web site visitors—including tourist destinations, property listings, restaurants in the area, beaches, shopping centers, golf courses, schools, and parks.

ASP—Application Service Provider

An organization that hosts software applications on its own servers within its own facilities.

As with many software programs available today, the variety of interactive-mapping software that is available is broad. Some are really simple, while others offer robust options. It is important that the ASP you choose is able to meet your needs, the needs of your Web site objectives, and the needs of your target market. Research each one carefully to be sure it has the ability to offer all of the information you want your Web site visitors to see, such as virtual tours, podcasts, videos, links, and other listing information.

Many users will access this content on their iPhone, Blackberry, or other Web-enabled mobile device, so make sure everything is accessible. (One of my pet peeves is when people put their phone number in a format that isn't clickable on my phone.)

Figure 26.7. Igemoe is an ASP that allows you to add its highly interactive self-managed maps to your site.

It is extremely important that all of your listing details are up-to-date. If something is sold out or is no longer available, it must be removed from your interactive map immediately. You may choose to update your map in-house, or you may choose to outsource that activity to the ASP or to someone else who provides that as a service.

Igemoe (*http://www.maps.igemoe.com*), pictured in Figure 26.7, is an ASP that allows you to add highly interactive self-managed maps to your site. Go to the Resources section of my Web site, *http://www.SusanSweeney.com,* for more interactive mapping solutions.

How Do You Leverage Interactive Maps?

I am a big proponent of leveraging everything you do for maximum marketing results. By offering interactive maps on your Web site, you are opening up many avenues for online marketing success.

You can leverage interactive maps to get reciprocal links and increase your link popularity with the search engines. If you are featuring the shopping centers in the area and the restaurants and fitness centers, provide a link to their Web sites from your map and ask for a link back from their site. The more links you have, the higher your search engine ranking. Links are discussed more in Chapter 13.

Another way to leverage your interactive map is through viral marketing. Provide a "Tell a friend about this map" button (see Chapter 5). Use permission marketing to your advantage here as well by asking Web site visitors if you can send them notifications of new features added, new package listings, or new resources. (See Chapter 4 for more on permission marketing.)

Some real estate and travel and tourism companies are using interactive maps as a source of revenue generation. This can be done several ways depending on the software you are using. For example, for each category of resources you have available on your map (schools, restaurants, or shopping centers), you can offer different types of listings at different fees—a free listing, a basic listing, and a premium listing. Let's take golf courses as an example. You can offer all the golf courses in the area a free listing. This could include simply the name of the golf course. The basic listing would have more-enhanced features like a link to the golf course's Web site, their address and phone number, a picture, and a list of tee times, and it would have an associated cost. The premium listing could incorporate links to their specials and promotions page, a podcast, a video or a virtual tour, and again would have an associated fee that is higher than the basic listing.

Another way to use your interactive map as a source of revenue generation is to offer advertising on the results page. If your interactive map had golf courses listed in the legend, you could sell those golf courses advertising on the results page.

Find others' interactive maps where you can participate to gain more exposure for your business.

Stay tuned. Interactive mapping is very important for many industries, and I expect over the next year a number of new players will be emerging on the market with added features and new bells and whistles, and there will be a few emerging leaders in the field.

Internet Resources for Chapter 26

I have developed a great library of online resources for you to check out regarding interactive mapping. This library is available on my Web site, *http://www. SusanSweeney.com,* in the Resources section, where you can find additional tips, tools, techniques, and resources.

I have also developed courses on many of the topics covered in this book. These courses are available on two of my Web sites, *http://www.SusanSweeney. com* and *http://www.eLearningU.com* (which contains other instructors' courses as well). These courses are delivered immediately over the Internet, so you can start whenever is convenient for you.

27

The Power of Partnering

We have talked about many different online marketing opportunities through the course of this book. Often there are great opportunities that are overlooked because of their simplicity. Partnering is one of those often-overlooked opportunities. There are many other sites that are selling to your target market. Quite often they are selling noncompeting products or services. And quite often they have significant traffic to their sites or significant databases that they communicate with on a regular basis. If you can find a win-win opportunity to partner with these sites, you can have significant results.

In this chapter, we cover:

- Ideal partners

- Partnering opportunities.

Ideal Partner Sites

When you look for partners, you are looking for:

- Partners that have your ideal target market as their site or blog visitors

- Partners that have significant targeted traffic on their Web site or blog

- Partners that have significant fans, followers, or friends who are your target market

- Partners that have a significant permission-based database

- Partners that have noncompeting related products or services.

Once you identify the types of partners or the types of noncompeting products or services of potential partners, it will be easier to find and develop a list of potential partners. For example, if you sell pots and pans, you might identify appliance sites as potential partner sites. If you make rubber stamps, you might identify scrapbooking sites or craft stores as potential partners—you are both selling to the same target market, but you are selling noncompeting products and services. If you have a ski hill, you might identify local hotels, attractions, and restaurants as potential partners. Once you have identified the types of partners you are looking for, you will be able to do research online to find specific potential partners.

Partnering Opportunities

Once you have found potential partners, next you need to look at win-win ways to partner with these sites. There are all kinds of ways to work together to do cross-promotion, leverage the exposure on each other's site, or provide exposure through each other's database.

- Cross-promotion through advertising. You can exchange ads on each other's site. If you have pots and pans and you are partnering with the appliance site, you can have an ad that indicates that any customer of yours can get a 10 percent discount on the appliance site, with a link to their site in the ad. The appliance site can provide the quid pro quo—your advertisement on their site can provide their customers with the same 10 percent discount for purchasing from your site.

- Co-operative advertising. Drop-down ads provide the viewer with the option to click on different parts of the ad and be taken to different sites. You could partner with four others who are all selling to the same target market to develop and place this type of drop-down menu ad. The result is either the same amount of advertising you did previously at 20 percent of the cost, or spending the same amount and getting five times the exposure.

- Partner with others on Facebook, Twitter, and other social media venues. Have your partners recommend and provide a link to your specials, packages, promotions, products, or services through their social media participation. You in turn can agree to do the same for them.

- Partner with others on contests. Find sites that are selling to the same target market and offer your products as part of the prize for their contest as long as the other site provides some details on your products and a link to your site. Leverage the link by getting your most important keywords in the text around the link pointing to your site to increase your link relevancy score and your search engine placement. You can also partner with others on your contests. The greater the prize, the more exposure you'll see through the contest.

- Partner with others' e-specials. Look for sites that provide e-specials to their target market and see if you can provide them with a great e-special. If you have a health food store, providing a great package at a great price to a local fitness facility that has a significant database could result in not only significant new business, but also new visitors to your site and, if you develop the landing page properly, new members to your e-club.

- Partner with directories or meta-indexes that provide links to your type of site. Look for a mutually beneficial opportunity. At the very least, look for an opportunity to have your listing appear at the top of the page and have it stand out in some way, or have your banner ad appear on the most appropriate page of their directory.

- Partner with your industry associations. If you have a listing, make sure that your description is as appealing as it can be. Provide a call to action in your description. Have the link go to the most appropriate page of your site—it's not always the home page! Look for areas on their site where you can gain a little extra exposure. Do they have sections like:

  - Top 10

  - Featured

  - Recommended

  - Site of the day/week

  - Suggested.

These all provide an opportunity for added exposure. Another example is that if you have a community event coming up, look for all the local organizations and popular sites in your geographic area for things like "Upcoming Events" to get your event included—even if you have to write it yourself. There are lots of these opportunities—the local newspaper Web site and the local chamber of commerce sites would be a great start.

Partner with industry associations to get your press releases or story ideas in front of the media. Most industry associations have a media center. If you've got a press release or a story that would be of interest to the media, the industry association's media center would be a great place for exposure. Perhaps they'd be interested in a joint press release to their media list.

Be a contributing journalist to e-zines that have your target market as their subscribers. Make sure you have your contact information in the resource box, with a link back to your Web site.

There are all kinds of partnering opportunities available; you just have to do a little brainstorming. Think about who is selling noncompeting products or services to the same target market you are and figure out a win-win opportunity.

Internet Resources for Chapter 27

I have developed a great library of online resources for you to check out regarding partnering. This library is available on my Web site, *http://www. SusanSweeney.com,* in the Resources section, where you can find additional tips, tools, techniques, and resources.

I have also developed courses on many of the topics covered in this book. These courses are available on two of my Web sites, *http://www.SusanSweeney. com* and *http://www.eLearningU.com* (which contains other instructors' courses as well). These courses are delivered immediately over the Internet, so you can start whenever is convenient for you.

28

Web Traffic Analysis

You had 50,000 unique visitors to your Web site this month? Up from 35,000 last month? Wow! That must have had quite an impact on your bottom line! Oh, you don't know . . . ?

Unfortunately, most companies that monitor their Web site traffic are in this very position, though at least they're doing something. Even more unfortunate is that many more companies don't give any attention to Web site analytics at all.

To make your online presence a valuable part of your business, you need to be paying attention to Web site analytics.

In this chapter, we look at:

- Web analytics defined

- Common measurements of performance

- Monitoring what matters to your business

- Determining what works—A/B testing as a start

- Go deeper—use it or lose it

- Bringing it all together—use what you've learned from other sources

- Segmenting your target market

- Choosing a Web analytics solution

- Closing comments on Web analytics.

It is not our goal in this chapter to tell you step by step how to roll out Web analytics in your organization; it would take far more than a chapter to do that. What we do want you to walk away with is a good understanding that this can help your business, and we want you to question how you can make it work for you. Everyone needs to start somewhere. This is where you should start.

Web Analytics Defined

Any time you're watching over what happens with an online marketing campaign or your Web site, you're technically partaking in Web analytics. Since there was so much controversy over what exactly Web analytics was, the Web Analytics Association (*http://www.webanalyticsassociation.org*) was founded, and it offers this concise definition:

> *Web analytics is the measurement, collection, analysis, and reporting of Internet data for the purpose of understanding and optimizing Web usage.*

Basically, it encompasses all that is involved in measuring the success of your online activities.

When speaking of Web analytics, you will commonly speak of both qualitative and quantitative research. Qualitative research, usually accomplished through interviews, surveys, or focus groups, offers insights into people's motivation—why did they do what they did? Think of it as feedback or opinions. Quantitative research, on the other hand, offers results that you can measure, such as the number of unique click-throughs to a Web page, the number of people in North America with broadband Internet access, and so on.

When speaking of Web analytics, most of the time you're talking in terms of quantitative data—"This happened 2,000 times over 24 hours." Qualitative research is often used with quantitative research to help explain what happened by providing insight into an individual's motivation, attitude, and behavior. Together they provide very useful insight.

Key Performance Indicators

Key performance indicators (KPIs) is a common phrase in the business world, and you will see it come up often when discussing Web analytics. Key performance indicators are also known as key success factors.

A KPI is measurable and reflects the goals of a company. KPIs are used in everything from measuring the average time that customer service representatives spend on the phone with a customer to the graduation rate of a high school. When thinking in terms of Web analytics, your KPIs concern those measurements that make a difference to your business in relation to the Internet. In the next section we cover some of the more common measurements of performance.

Common Measurements of Performance

The first thing you need to do is establish what key performance indicators are important to your business model. What questions about your Web site visitors do you want an answer to? Following are some of the more common measurements for you to evaluate.

Click-Through Rate

Your click-through rate pertains to how many people actually followed your online advertisement to your Web site or landing page out of the total number of advertising impressions delivered. This measurement is very basic and cannot tell you a whole lot except for an approximation of how much overall interest there is in a particular online marketing campaign you are running. Think of this as a general measure of popularity. This measure is general in scope because it could contain hits by search engine spiders, a single potential customer who makes multiple visits, and competitors who decide they want to exhaust your click-through budget.

Unique Visitors

"Unique visitors" pertains to how many individual people came to your Web site or landing page over a specific period of time. This is a very basic measurement as well, but it offers a more accurate look at just who has taken an interest in you by filtering out double data and irrelevant visits. Make sure you remove the search engine spiders and crawlers from your statistics so that they are not mistaken as potential customers.

Bounce Rate

Bounce rate is the percentage of single-page visits or visits in which the person left your site from the entrance (landing) page. This metric is used to measure visit quality—a high bounce rate generally indicates that the landing page was not relevant to your visitors or they didn't like what they saw. It could be the result of your graphics and content not grabbing their attention.

Time Spent

You want people to stay on your Web site for awhile—you want a "sticky" Web site. You can look at time spent per page or spent during an overall visit. If a lot of people are leaving within a matter of seconds of hitting your landing page, they likely are dissatisfied with what they see. On the other hand, if the target market is spending an inordinate amount of time on your landing page, they likely are confused, or are having a good time, or maybe they got up to go to the kitchen to make lunch. Time is only one indicator. You need to monitor the click stream of your visitors.

Click Stream Analysis

What paths does the target market follow when they hit your Web site or landing page? Is the target market hitting a particular page and then leaving your site? Monitoring the behavior of your target market on your Web site enables you to refine the navigation and lay out a simple trail of bread crumbs to lead your customer down the intended path.

Single-Page Access

Look at the number of one-page visits to your Web site or landing page. This is where the visitor comes to your page but takes no action other than to leave. If that is happening on a frequent basis, you undoubtedly have a problem. It could be that your landing page is not effective at converting, that the page the client hits does not show a direct relationship to the ad or link the target clicked on to reach you, or that perhaps a shady competitor is trying to exhaust your ad campaign. Understand what percentage of your visitors are coming to your site and are immediately taking off. If you have a very low percentage of single-page accesses, then you are fine; however, if you see a lot of single-page accesses, that should throw up an immediate red flag that you need to do some further research.

Leads Generated, or Desired Action Taken

Every organization wants to know how many leads a particular advertising campaign generated over a specified period of time. This is also a very basic measurement. How many leads did you get through your Web site during, say, the month of May? When tracking the number of leads generated through your landing page or Web site, you should also look at the number of those leads who become customers down the road. You may also want to measure how many people signed up for your newsletter or e-club or downloaded your coupons.

Customer Conversion Ratio

Of all the potential clients, how many followed through on the action you wanted them to take? Here you are looking at the effectiveness of your ability to convert customers. Make sure you are looking at unique visitors so that you are not counting the person who came back 10 times as 10 different people. The higher your customer conversion ratio, the better—the average conversion rate for a Web site falls between 2 and 5 percent.

Net Dollars per Visitor

This is simply a look at how much each visitor is worth to your business. How much money, on average, is each Web visitor worth to your bottom line?

Cost per Visitor

This information pertains to all visitors to your Web site or landing page, not just to consumers who make a purchase. It is important to understand how much each visitor to your Web site costs you so that you can work toward bringing that cost down to maximize profits. This information is also useful for forecasting and budgeting.

Form Abandonment

The average online form abandonment rate is around 40 percent. How many people gave up somewhere along the line in the process or on the second page of a three-page information request form? You have to know where the process fails in order to improve it. Do everything in your power to understand your market and make the intended objective as easy to accomplish as possible.

Do not just look at the number of people who gave up, but be sure to look at *where* they gave up so that you can pinpoint where the potential issue lies and fix it.

Impact on Offline Sales

Do not neglect the impact your online marketing campaigns have in the offline environment. Your landing page might be converting customers and you do not even know it, unless you are watching for it. How? Your Web site or landing page will likely include other methods of contact the target market can use to do business with your company.

This can be a difficult thing to track; however, you can make it manageable. You might consider setting up a phone number that is available from your Web site only, so that when a call comes through you know it is because of the phone number that rests on your landing page.

Return on Investment (ROI)

ROI is a measure of overall profitability. To figure out the ROI, take your profit from an activity, particular promotion, month, and so on, and then factor in the total capital you invested to accomplish your activity.

It came to my attention recently that nearly 75 percent of online advertisers don't monitor their ROI. They could be spending $60 to make $50. Boy, that seems like a great idea.

Ultimately, the most relevant key performance indicators for your business depend entirely on what you are trying to accomplish with your online marketing initiatives.

Monitor What Matters to Your Business

What do you want people to do? That's a question you should be asking yourself. Businesses have Web sites that are focused on generating sales. Measurements that matter to most of you will:

- Produce accurate and cost-effective information

- Be supported by and for company stakeholders

- Reflect and drive business results through positive change.

As the owner of an e-commerce Web site, you're going to be interested in critical data like the total sales conversions, how easy it is to go through your site's purchase process, and how well a promotion sold during a specific period of time. For example, how many of those 25-percent-off hat-and-mitts packages did we sell during the promotion week of December 3 to December 9? That's good stuff to know.

What you monitor will be unique to your business. For a brand-new company, your efforts might be on getting as many new acquisitions as possible, whereas a more-established company might focus more of its efforts on customer retention. Monitor what matters.

Determine What Works—A/B Testing as a Start

If you're going to make Web analytics work for you, then testing is one thing you cannot live without. Direct marketers obsess over testing to see what changes generate the best responses. Why is it, then, that the typical online marketer does not measure and test its efforts? It is the most measurable medium out there!

A/B testing is a common approach to testing different creatives in order to make incremental improvements. Let's explore this a bit more here. You might want answers to questions like:

- Is short or long copy more effective?

- Is it better to use bulleted lists to emphasize key points as opposed to paragraphs of information?

- Does separating content with tag lines or headers increase the number of responses?

- What happens if I bold or emphasize key points in the copy?

- What impact does changing the writing style, or tone, of my copy have on a page's ability to convert?

- What impact does changing the presentation of the offer itself have on results? Saying "50% off" and "1/2 price," both showing the original $200 price tag with a strikethrough and the new price next to it emphasized in bold red font as $100, are two different ways of presenting the same offer. Which method generates the best response from the target market?

- Does my offer perform better with a lot of pictures, only a few pictures, or no pictures?

- What colors on the page elicit the most favorable responses? Does the contrast between the page copy and the background influence the response rate?

- What font types, styles, and sizes are most effective?

- How many navigation options work best? Am I providing the target market with too many navigation options such that they get distracted, or would the page be effective with more navigation options?

- Where is the best position on the page to place the "contact me" or "request information" button? When the target market completes the request form, the first thing you want them to do is submit their request, not cancel it. This means putting the "submit" button as the obvious next step, before the clear or cancel option. Actually, don't put the clear or cancel option there at all—they're just distractions.

- Does the wording of the "request information" button generate more of a response if I play with the wording? For example, "Request a Free Make-up Application Guide Now!" versus "Submit."

- Have I tested different approaches for completing the action I want the target market to take? Does a short or a long form work best? Does the same request form perform better if it is split across two steps on two different pages?

- Have I tested variations of my offer to see what generates better results? Maybe a free gift will help boost the response rate.

A/B testing helps you address answers to questions like those just mentioned. There is always something you can do a bit better to maximize your results based on your page goals and what you have determined as the basis for measuring success. There are any number of tidbits you can test and tweak to refine your campaigns—some things will work, some things will not, but you obviously want to find out what works the best and do more of it. Even the smallest changes can have a big impact. When running a marketing campaign, employ A/B testing to see which landing page techniques generate the best responses from your target market.

Here is a simplified way to think about A/B testing. Say you have an e-mail promotion you want to send out to your house list of 10,000 subscribers. What you're going to do is send 5,000 of those subscribers to one landing page and the other 5,000 subscribers to another landing page to learn which version is more effective. (Landing pages are discussed more in Chapter 7.)

When running a new campaign for the first time, it is difficult to say what will trigger the best response, so you might test two, three, or even five dramatically different e-mail campaigns, landing pages, PPC ads, or whatever it is you are testing. You would use the one that performs the best as your starting point for future refinements.

Keep It Simple

It is best to test one element at a time during refinements so that you can measure results and determine the effectiveness of the new change. If you change too many items at once, it will be difficult to attribute how much of an impact the items you changed had on the effectiveness of the page. If you made three adjustments to your landing page at once, it might be that two of the three components have increased the response rate, but the third might have dragged it down a bit, so you are not quite reaching your potential. If you change just one element at a time, you can tell what impact your change has on the landing page's ability to convert.

Give It Time

When running a test, you must let it run long enough to enable you to pull accurate results. You need to gather enough responses and give people enough time to respond to your campaigns. If you're curious about the immediate responses, you might look at some preliminary results a couple of hours after your email campaign launch, but a 1 percent sample is not really an accurate representation of the total campaign success. How much time you give a campaign ultimately depends on what you're testing; it could need days or even weeks to paint the complete picture.

Tracking Your Tests

There are many ways to make tracking your test results easier. If you want to get people to sign up for your e-club, test a couple of different offers to entice them to do so. You might issue a different code for each offer that the customer must enter at the time of sign-up. This makes it quite easy to determine the offer that was more appealing. Alternatively, you can use scripts or send people to different servers or different pages. As mentioned earlier, you might test two variations of a landing page to see which one more people respond to.

If A/B testing is something you would sooner not have any part in, there are companies that can help you run tests and conduct performance measurements. Optimost (*http://www.optimost.com*) is a reputable source that can help you with A/B testing and other types of testing such as multivariate testing.

Web analytics will tell you how well you did, but you must conduct tests to cause change. One test alone will not give you all the answers. Using Web analytics and testing together will help you measure and improve your results and is an ongoing process. Capitalizing on any great campaign requires a great closing, so keep at it!

Go Deeper—Use It or Lose It

For lead-generation Web sites, knowing the conversion rate is a big deal. No doubt, knowing your site's conversion rate is hugely important, but here's the kicker. Knowing your conversion rate is like getting a grade on your high school report card. It will tell you how well you're doing, but not what happened between start to finish getting to that score. Did people get freaked out by the length of your contact form? Was the call to action not properly worded? Heck, did you go after the wrong people altogether?

When monitoring your results, analyze what happens at every stage of the process your potential client engages in. If nine out of ten people are dropping out of your "contact me" form or your e-club sign-up form at the same step in the process, you know something is clearly wrong and you can investigate it further.

When measuring your performance online with Web analytics, compare and contrast the information you gather with historical information. By looking at historical information, you can see the results of your current efforts against the past to identify trends and variations in the results. If you notice a new landing page has not performed as well as your previous landing page, then you know that little tweak you made did not benefit you and you can eliminate it from your next online marketing effort. If the little tweak you made to your landing page paid off, then you keep it and try something else to further improve your conversions and return on investment.

It helps to track the differences in behavior between first-time buyers and repeat clients. What motivates a first-time buyer, in comparison to what motivates a return client, is different. With repeat clients, you have less convincing to do in most cases. You can use the knowledge you learn about new clients and repeat clients to tailor the experience to each market segment's needs.

Now, you've gone through all this effort to find out how you're doing, but in order for that knowledge to make a difference, you have to be proactive and encourage positive change. Test different changes to watch their impact on your results. In the previous section we covered the topic of A/B testing and a variety of things you can test on your own. The whole purpose behind monitoring your performance is so that you can use what you've learned to change the future. You know that old adage, "learn from your mistakes"—don't lose sight of the big picture.

Bringing It All Together—Use What You've Learned from Other Sources

When deciding what actions you are going to take to make updates to your online initiatives, the more you know, the better. You can use information from other sources along with your Web analytics to paint a more complete picture of the situation at hand. Let's look at a few examples:

- Industry studies and metrics—Studies by market research companies, such as Forrester Research (*http://www.forrester.com*), JupiterResearch (*http://www.jupiterresearch.com*), nielsen/netratings (*http://www.nielsen-netratings.com*), and eMarketer (*http://www.emarketer.com*), provide great industry benchmarks that you can use to sit back and ask, "Okay, how is my business performing in comparison to the industry as a whole?"

- Usability studies—By conducting usability studies, you can pinpoint a problem and find out what to test to make improvements. Usability studies are labor-intensive and require skills that are highly sought after. For more information on usability studies, we recommend you check out Jakob Nielsen's Web site at *http://www.useit.com*. Jakob is a highly regarded usability expert.

- Eyetracking studies—These studies allow you to look at your Web site through the eyes of your visitors. An eyetracking analysis produces heat maps that show you where a person's eyes are drawn by tracking eye movement on a page. A company like Eye Tools (*http://www.eyetools.com*) can provide you with eyetracking analysis services. The results of the studies then allow you to better position, add, or remove items on your Web site that you want your customers to see and act on.

- Competitive studies—To make sure you do not neglect the online activities of your competitors, perform an online competitive analysis. Look at what they are doing and how you can do it better.

- Clients, partners, and affiliate studies—Simply ask the people you deal with on a daily basis for their input. Interviews or online surveys or feedback forms can be set up as part of your site. Ask a simple question about your Web site visitors' experiences. If they like what you are doing, great; if not, then follow-up to find out what you can do better.

- Mobile—Access your Web site from your iPhone, Blackberry, and other mobile device to see what your target customers see. Is the phone number clickable? Can they get the key information they are looking for?

- Social media metrics—Use your Web site analytics to see how much traffic is coming to your site from social media networks. If Twitter is bringing you lots of traffic, use tools like TweetReach, Twist, TweetEffect, Twitalizer, and Qwitter (which tells you on what tweet a follower stopped following) to determine your strengths and weaknesses and to see what is working and where you can do better. Check out the Resources area of my Web site at *http://susansweeney.com* for tons of tools to help in social media and social networking analysis.

- Site performance studies—Don't neglect the basics. Your Web site might have exactly what the client is looking for, but it takes 20 minutes to load, so he or she simply can't be bothered. Look at everything that could cause problems and potentially tarnish your image, such as errors on the Web site, the speed of the server you're hosting with, the load time of your pages, and cross-browser compatibility.

There is a challenge in getting your offline and online data together, but you're not alone. Everyone struggles with this. Make use of other sources to try to close the gap on some of your unknowns.

Segmenting Your Target Market

Get to know who uses your site and why. The next leap in getting the most out of your online presence is to know how to speak to people and get them to respond—not everyone responds the same way when put in the same situation.

As an example, what we are asking you to do is to think beyond sending everyone on your e-mail list the same newsletter and look beyond sending everyone in your database all the same product packages. You will get more bang for your buck if you can segment your target market to appeal to their specific interests and needs. Someone looking for a weekend hockey game will not be interested in your dinner-and-a-show package.

You will find with your newsletter that certain content is of interest to group A but not to group B, and that group B responds very well to certain words that group A ignores, and so on. Confused? Think of it this way: Client A's name is John and he has been your client for years. John has purchased many product packages from you, from computer virus software to double solitaire. Customer B's name is Jane and she is in the market for her first-ever computer, but she has no idea who you are or how you stack up against the competition. Jane is at a different stage of the cycle and is going to react differently to a call to action than John might. John knows you offer what he wants and he likes dealing with you, so he just wants to make his purchase. Jane, on the other hand, isn't so sure about you and wants information that will persuade her into becoming a first-time client.

How does all this tie into Web analytics? You can monitor the behavior of your visitors and establish segments based on that. Very basic segments might include:

- People who are new or are repeat visitors

- People who are new or are repeat customers

- People from marketing campaign X, Y, or Z

- People who subscribe to your newsletter

- People who are bargain hunters and book at the last minute

- People who are booking online for the first time

- People who arrived at your site from search engines, email, or through partner networks. (You would be surprised at the behavioral differences of people depending on how they find out about you.)

You really could go on and on, but again it depends on what you need to know. For your business, it might be important to segment your target market first by geographic region and then by another qualifier to get more specific.

Segmenting your target market allows you to get into targeted ads and customized content that appeal to the different characteristics of the segments. The more you adapt your message to your target market, the more likely they are to respond favorably.

Choosing a Web Analytics Solution

Forrester has just released the "U.S. Web Analytics Forecast, 2008 to 2014" report. In it they predict the U.S. Web analytics market will reach $1 billion by 2014, with a steady growth of 17 percent per year! It is clear that the value of Web analytics is steadily gaining recognition.

Companies effectively using Web analytics know that marketing plans are just paperweights unless you can measure performance. They know that if they do not measure their performance, they increase their risks; and they know that by measuring performance, it helps them make informed business decisions that result in a better return on investment, more client satisfaction, and in turn more customer loyalty. Another perk of Web analytics is that marketers are able to prove that their efforts actually do something—a great thing when trying to justify one's job or when asking executives for funding.

Look at Yourself

The very first thing you need to do is figure out what you're going to use the Web analytics package for. What are you going to measure and how does it relate to your business objectives? Some available solutions offer far too little and some solutions offer far too much. There is no need to pay for what you will not use until you are ready for it, but be sure to choose a solution that will grow with you as your needs grow.

Beginners and most small companies may decide to take advantage of the free Web site analytics tools available like Google Analytics. Others that are entrenched deeply in Internet marketing may want more robust alternatives.

What reporting capabilities will you need and who will be using the package? If you need to be able to produce real-time reports, add it to your requirements. If different reports are needed for different departments, such as marketing, make a note of that too. If you do a lot of historical comparisons, you will want to make sure you choose a solution that will let you compare data over time.

Perhaps you want to be able to group visitors into specific segments. Assess the reporting needs of your business or organization.

What can you afford? There are open-source solutions that will cost you nothing, to more complex Web analytics packages that will cost tens of thousands of dollars. If you know what you need it for, you will be in a much better position to spend the right amount of money for your needs.

Look at Technology

There are many traffic analysis solutions to choose from, ranging in price from free to thousands of dollars per year. As just noted, one great free solution is Google Analytics. Google purchased the popular Urchin Software Corp. in 2005, renamed it, redesigned it, and improved its functionality. Now Google Analytics offers over 80 distinct reports, each customizable (to some degree). Reports are very comprehensive and include things like mobile tracking, e-commerce tracking, analytics intelligence reports, custom reporting, and advanced segmenting.

Google Analytics now provides more-advanced features, including visitor segmentation and custom fields. It also provides integration with its own Google Adwords (Google's pay-per-click campaign) so that users can see their PPC campaign performance as part of their reports. (See Chapter 8 for more on pay-per-click.) Users can now add up to 50 site profiles—each profile corresponds to one URL.

Other Web analytics packages are typically ASP-based (hosted or on-demand) or stand-alones (software). ASP-based applications will use a snippet of code, such as a Java tag, to label every page of your Web site that must be measured. A stand-alone application is often a program you install on a local system to analyze log files.

WebTrends is a very popular Web analytics vendor that offers an on-demand version as well as a software version of its popular analytics package. Lyris (formerly ClickTracks) provides a very robust Web analytics program.

What are your internal technology capabilities? Do you have the ability to install, run, and maintain an application in-house?

Is the Web analytics solution compatible with your current Web site? Some Web analytics packages have trouble with dynamic content—content generated on the fly and usually with longer addresses that include database query strings. A dynamic address often will look something like: *http://stores.skipjack.com/dells/Search.bok?no.show.inprogress=1&sredir= 1&category=swiss+maid+caramel+apples*. What about pop-up window content or content that spreads across different servers?

Is the Web analytics solution compatible with your Web server? A package that can be installed on a UNIX box will not work on a Windows box.

Do you require integration with third-party software? For example, you might want to link the Web analytics package with your customer relationship management package. Think about the uniqueness of your business and its infrastructure to determine how you want a Web analytics package to fit into the picture.

Is the Web analytics package easy for you . . .

- To set up—will they install it for you?

- To maintain—are upgrades easy to handle?

- To customize for a unique situation—a flexible solution is good to have.

- To use—are the reports easy to generate and do they make sense?

If a solution is going to cause more headaches than benefits, you don't want it. There is something available for every business, and it is just a matter of taking the time to find the solution that works best for you.

Many Web analytics packages offer evaluation copies for you to try out. Take advantage of it!

Look at the Vendor

Look beyond the technology and the functionality of the Web analytics package and look at the vendor.

Does the vendor keep on top of changes in Web analytics and how often are offerings upgraded or improved? This will give an indication of how current the vendor is and what is invested in research and development. You want to deal with a company whose focus is Web analytics, not 20 other things with Web analytics as a side dish.

What is the vendor's track record like?

- Does it have a history of happy, loyal customers?

- What are some of the results the vendor has helped companies achieve?

- How long has the vendor been in operation, and has there been a recent merger or acquisition?

Look at the stability of the company and customer satisfaction. You want to deal with a company that is well respected.

- Are newer features such as social media and mobile analytics available?

- What is the vendor's training and support like?

- Do you have to pay for support? If so, what does it cost?

- What are the support hours?

- What support options are available? Examples include an online knowledge base, e-mail, and toll-free phone support.

- What training does the vendor provider (online courses, manuals, etc.)? Does the training cost anything?

- Does the vendor have community support? Packages that are widely adopted often will have a community of users that support each other to work out solutions. Odds are, if you're having an issue, someone else has already encountered and solved it. Take a look around for support groups and online communities.

Closing Comments on Web Analytics

To measure the key performance indicators for your Web initiatives, you are going to rely on a number of assistive tools and old-fashioned analysis. Many e-mail marketing solution providers, pay-to-play search engine sites, and companies offering ad placement services offer detailed reports and self-service tools for monitoring your campaigns that can be used along with your Web analytics package to give you more information about your efforts than any other marketing medium.

There are statistics packages available that can track everything from click-throughs, your ROI, the lifetime value of a customer, the pay-off between organic and paid search engine marketing campaigns, whether your static ad or flash ad is performing better, and even the effectiveness of a link positioned at the top of a page versus one near the bottom. If you are running an online marketing campaign, then it is important to know if your efforts are justified.

At the end of the day, remember that no marketing measurement is exact, but they provide you with insight on how well your Web site is doing and offer guidance so that you can make positive changes in the future. Strive to make your clients' lives better and you will reap the benefits.

Internet Resources for Chapter 28

I have developed a great library of online resources for you to check out regarding Web traffic analysis. This library is available on my Web site, *http://www. SusanSweeney.com,* in the Resources section, where you can find additional tips, tools, techniques, and resources.

I have also developed courses on many of the topics covered in this book. These courses are available on two of my Web sites, *http://www.SusanSweeney. com* and *http://www.eLearningU.com* (which contains other instructors' courses as well). These courses are delivered immediately over the Internet, so you can start whenever is convenient for you.

About the Author

Susan Sweeney, CA, CSP, HoF

Renowned Internet marketing expert, consultant, best-selling author, and speaker Susan Sweeney, CA, CSP, HoF, tailors lively keynote speeches and full- and half-day seminars and workshops for companies, industries, and associations interested in improving their Internet presence and increasing their Internet traffic and sales.

Susan has developed many Internet projects over the years—her latest is eLearningU (*www.eLearningU.com*), a comprehensive online learning site. Susan is a partner of Verb Interactive (*http://www.verbinteractive.com*), an international Web development, Internet marketing, and consulting firm. She holds both the Chartered Accountant and Certified Speaking Professional designations. Susan has been inducted into the Canadian Speakers Hall of Fame.

Susan is the author of many books on Internet marketing and e-business: *101 Ways to Promote Your Web Site* (a best seller with over 77,000 copies sold, now in its eighth edition; it has been translated into German and Spanish), *Social Media for Business, 101 Internet Businesses You Can Start from Home, Internet Marketing for Your Tourism Business, 3G Marketing on the Internet, The e-Business Formula for Success*, and *Going for Gold*. She is also the developer of a two-day intensive Internet Marketing Boot Camp. Susan offers many Web-based teleseminars, seminars on CD, and e-books related to Internet marketing.

Susan is a member of the Canadian Association of Professional Speakers, the National Speakers Association, and the Global Speakers Federation.

Verb Interactive is a marketing firm that provides Web development, Internet marketing consulting, and training services to industry and government. Their primary services include Web site design and development, Internet marketing strategies and campaigns, SEO, Web site report cards, Internet marketing consulting, and competitive analysis.

Susan has been sharing her vast Internet marketing expertise with corporate and conference audiences around the globe for over 10 years. Susan's passion for the subject, her depth of knowledge, and her enthusiasm fuel her dynamic presentations. To discuss hiring Susan to speak for your next event or having her do a private Internet Marketing Bootcamp for your organization, contact her speaking office at 1-888-274-0537; or to find out about Susan's upcoming Webinars, her Internet Marketing Bootcamps, her latest e-books and podcasts, or to sign up for her newsletter, visit her Web site at *http://www.SusanSweeney.com.*

Contact information
Susan Sweeney, CA, CSP, HoF
www.susansweeney.com
www.verbinteractive.com
susan@susansweeney.com
Phone: 888-274-0537
www.LinkedIn.com/in/SusanSweeneycsp
http://twitter.com/susansweeney
http://www.diigo.com/user/susansweeney
http://www.facebook.com/susan.sweeney01
http://youtube.com/SusanSweeneyInternet

Index

Reader Feedback Sheet

Your comments and suggestions are very important in shaping future publications. Please email us at *info@maxpress.com* or photocopy this page, jot down your thoughts, and mail it to:

Maximum Press

Attn: Jim Hoskins

605 Silverthorn Road

Gulf Breeze, FL 32561

_____

_____

_____

_____

_____

_____

_____

_____

_____

_____

_____

_____

_____

_____

_____

_____

_____

_____

_____

Social Media for Business
by Susan Sweeney, CA
and
Randall Craig, CFA
185 pages
$24.95
ISBN: 978-1-931644-90-7

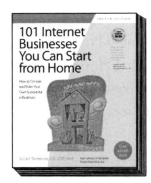

***101 Internet Businesses
You Can Start from Home
Fourth Edition***
by Susan Sweeney, CA
345 pages
$29.95
ISBN: 978-1931644-79-2

***3G Marketing on the
Internet,
Seventh Edition***
by Susan Sweeney, CA,
Andy MacLellen, and
Ed Dorey
216 pages
$34.95
ISBN: 978-1-931644-37-2

Podcasting for Profit
by Leesa Barnes
376 pages
$34.95
ISBN: 978-1-931644-57-0

To purchase a Maximum Press book, visit your local bookstore,
call (850) 934-4583, or visit *maxpress.com* for online ordering.